IMAGES
*of America*

# SOUTHPORT

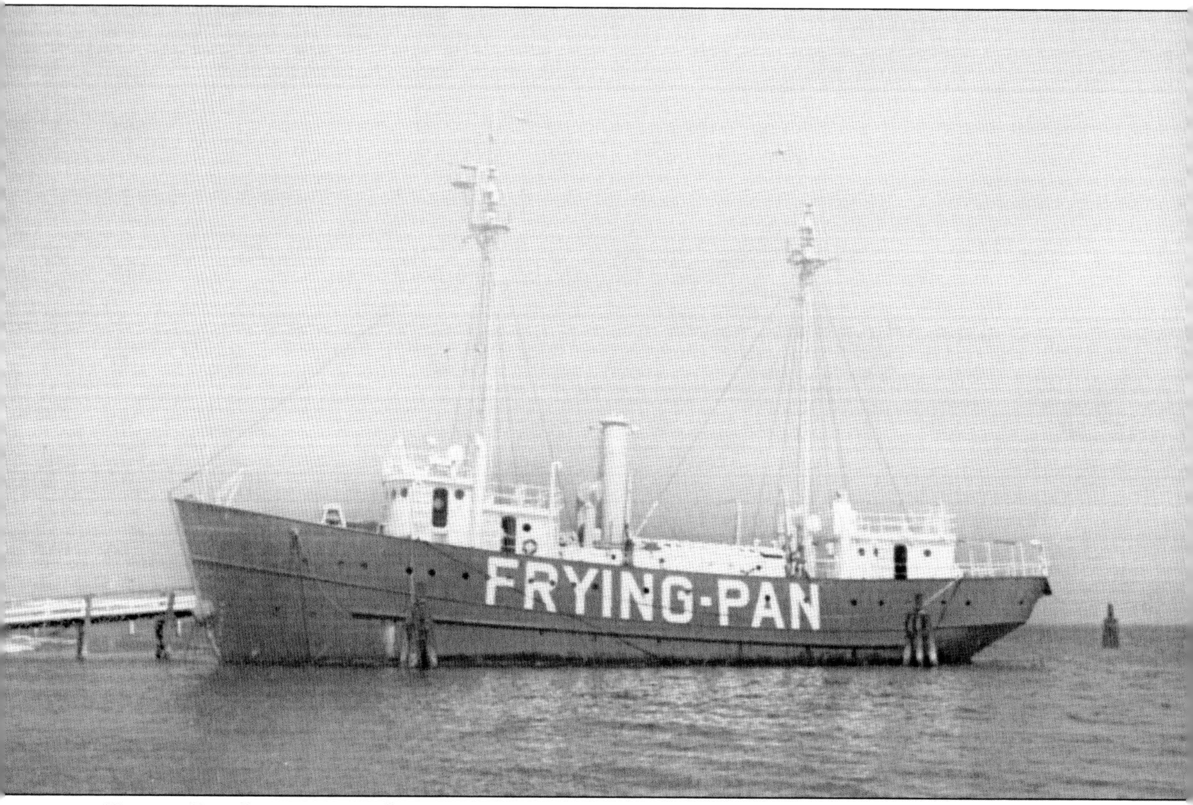


**FRYING PAN LIGHTSHIP.** The *Frying Pan* arrived at the Southport waterfront in October 1967 and was to be converted into a nautical museum. The lightship was stationed at the foot of Howe Street and was later replaced by a light tower. It was placed in the National Register of Historic Places in 1999 and is now moored in the Hudson River in New York City. (Courtesy of Norfrette Bellamy.)

**ON THE COVER:** Shrimp boats are docked at the Southport Yacht Basin in the 1940s. (Courtesy of Lewis J. Hardee Jr.)

IMAGES
*of America*

# SOUTHPORT

Sharon Claudette Smith and Sherry Monahan
Foreword by Thomas Harrelson

ARCADIA
PUBLISHING

ISBN 978-0-7385-9233-6

Published by Arcadia Publishing
Charleston, South Carolina

Printed in the United States of America

Library of Congress Control Number: 2011941052

For all general information, please contact Arcadia Publishing:
Telephone 843-853-2070
Fax 843-853-0044
E-mail sales@arcadiapublishing.com
For customer service and orders:
Toll-Free 1-888-313-2665

Visit us on the Internet at www.arcadiapublishing.com

*This book is dedicated to my father, James "Bubba" Smith, who harbored a profound affection for the Southport community and its residents. His life is the inspiration for this collection of images and stories. He left a legacy of memories and lessons that will inspire generations to follow.*

# Contents

# FOREWORD

Southport holds a special fascination for those who grew up here and for many of those who have moved into the area. When I grew up here, most people from other parts of the state did not know much about it unless they had visited area beaches or the Baptist Assembly at Fort Caswell or had come here to fish on our charter boats.

It was historically a fishing village, but it once was the county seat and has had a respected community hospital for years. The addition of the Military Ocean Terminal at Sunny Point, the Carolina Power & Light Company (now Progress Energy) nuclear plant, Cogentrix, and Pfizer (now Archer Daniels Midland) brought much-needed, well-paying jobs to the area. Now Southport is a tourist destination with fine dining, ethnic cuisine, antiques, gift shops, and bed-and-breakfast establishments. We have had a lot of change over the years. However, what has always distinguished Southport is our diverse and congenial population, as well as the great beauty of the river and many of the buildings.

This book captures in pictures and words some of Southport's rich history. Author Sharon Claudette Smith comes from one of our most respected families. Her parents, James "Bubba" and Rebecca "Becky" Smith, set a wonderful example of community service as well as hard work and encouraged all their children to do the same and to pursue educational opportunities. Sharon was able to persuade local families to open up their treasured albums to bring images and stories to light that had not previously been known. I welcome Sharon and her coauthor Sherry Monahan to the list of people who love Southport and who have contributed to telling our story.

—Thomas Harrelson

# ACKNOWLEDGMENTS

A project like this cannot be completed alone. Working on this book required me to reach out to family, friends, and strangers who allowed me access to their lives—both past and present. This writing journey has shown me how generous, kind, and friendly Southport natives truly are.

I have so many people to thank and a short space to do it in. These people shared their family stories and photographs, their knowledge of Southport's history, and their time. I cannot thank them enough. This an alphabetical list so I do not leave anyone out: Yvonne McKenzie Adams, Norfrette Bellamy, Michael and Andrea Clemmons, Marjorie Clemmons, Kim Cumber of the North Carolina State Archives, Tom L. Frink, Col. Willie L. Gore (Ret.), Caroline Gore Hankins, Lois Gore Thompson, Lewis J. Hardee Jr., Thomas J. Harrelson, Churchill Hornstein, Leda Hornstein Sloat, Katherine Hufham, Donnie Joyner, Sarah P. Joyner, Joann Kimball, Jimmy and Mae Moore, Charlie Perry, Joy Smith, Ennis Tobler, and Trudy M. and Jobie Young.

A special thank-you to my coauthor and friend, Sherry Monahan, who provided perfect guidance in this process, and to Niki Cutter for the tremendous amount of time spent providing information and searching for photographs. These friends provided great support and encouragement: Tonya Dixon and Thierry Guiralou, who sought out people who had old photographs and checked out reference books from Southport Library; Viviane Jones McKeithan, who provided information on photographs; James Sanders, who provided help in the last hours as the deadline was closing in; and Shelley Warnett, who made calls seeking photographs.

A special thank-you to my siblings and my mother who always provide great support no matter the endeavor: Maurice R. Smith, Julie P. Webb, Gina R. Smith, and Rebecca B. Smith.

—Sharon Claudette Smith

As coauthor, I would like to thank Sharon for asking me to collaborate with her on this wonderful piece of history. Through her love of Southport, I have come to appreciate this friendly, humble fishing community. I'd also like to thank all those who contributed to this wonderful book.

—Sherry Monahan

Last, we want to thank our editor, Lindsay Carter, at Arcadia Publishing, who went out of her way to provide support during the entire process.

# INTRODUCTION

Southport's history began long before the establishment of a town. Situated where the mighty Cape Fear River meets the Atlantic Ocean, it made an excellent location for a new fort. On April 20, 1745, a legislative act was passed by the Colonial Assembly in New Bern, North Carolina, providing for the construction of Fort Johnston on the lower Cape Fear River. Three years later, the legislature appropriated funds for construction costs, and work on Fort Johnston began.

Southport has not always been called so. The town's rich history began in 1792, when an Act to "lay off" and establish a town near Fort Johnston, on the west side of the Cape Fear River, was ratified. Benjamin Smith, William Lord, Joshua Potts, Robert Howe, and Charles Gause were appointed the commissioners to lay out a town to be named Smithville. It became a busy fishing village and military town, and in 1808 Smithville became the county seat of Brunswick County. In 1887, Smithville's name was changed to Southport in hopes of attracting a port. Much to the disappointment of her citizens, the port was located in Wilmington.

In the early 1900s, the menhaden fishing industry was very lucrative and was the main source of income for the small fishing village. The fish's oil was Southport's commodity, and it was extracted and sold to produce paint and used in pharmaceuticals; the leftover scraps were sold for fertilizer.

Shrimping joined the menhaden industry in Southport in the mid-1900s, and the waterfront was lined with numerous shrimp houses. The industry grew, and the shrimp trawlers could not keep up with the demand, which meant employment for local residents.

Seaside living offers benefits and hazards. While residents enjoy ocean breezes, fresh seafood, and boating, nature can wreak havoc on seaside towns. Hurricane Hazel made landfall on October 15, 1954, during the highest full-moon high tide of the year and delivered the greatest storm surge in North Carolina's recorded history. But, like most seaside villages, Southport recovered.

Southport is listed in the National Register of Historic Places and has been observing Independence Day since 1795. Every Fourth of July, Southport hosts the official North Carolina 4th of July celebration, but the town now uses fireworks instead of the 1795 tradition of ships shooting their cannons in the harbor. Thousands of people from all around the country travel to Southport for four days of fun and excitement downtown.

*One*

# The Early Years

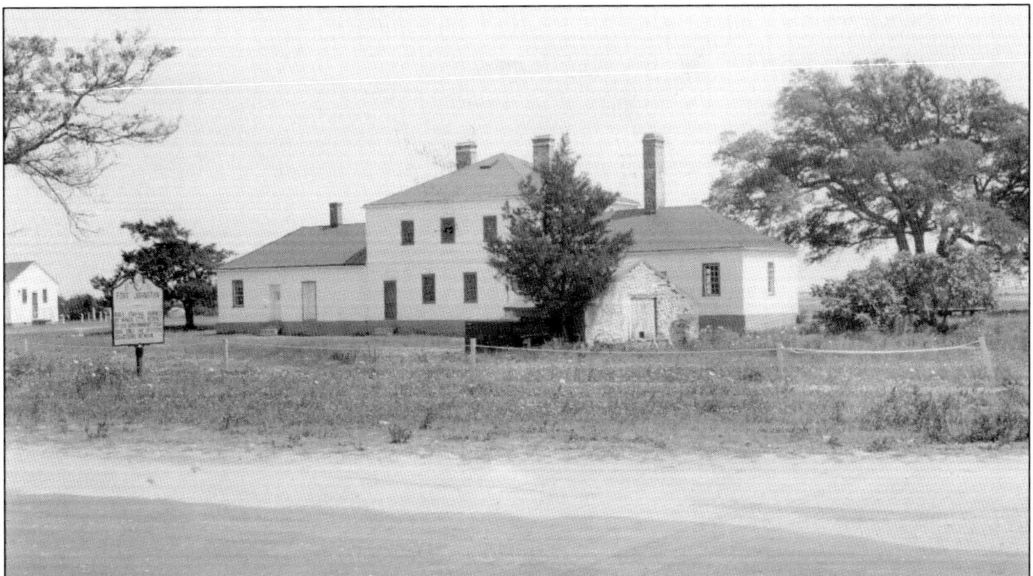

**Fort Johnston.** In 1745, a legislative act was passed by the colonial assembly in New Bern, "providing for the construction of Johnston's Fort on lower Cape Fear River." In 1749, Gov. Gabriel Johnston announced the completion of the new fort, named in his honor. An officer and two men were stationed there with four old cannons. In 1751, it became a quarantine station for inspection of incoming ships. (Courtesy of Andrea P. Clemmons.)

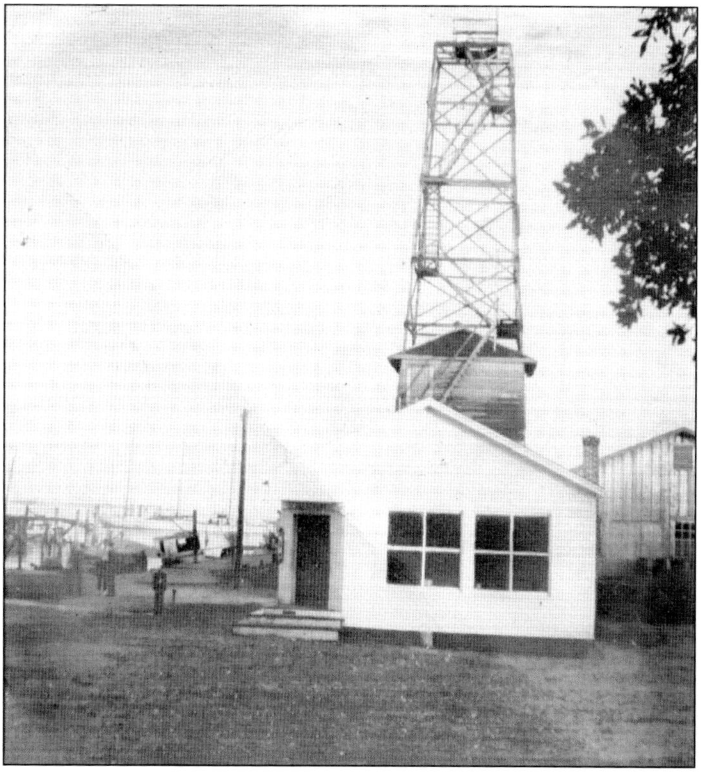

**SUTTON SHIPS CHANDLERY, C. 1915.** Sutton's Ships Chandlery was owned by Charles E. Gause and was located at the end of Howe Street in front of the pilot observation tower. Years later, it became Mack's Café. (Courtesy of Trudy M. Young.)

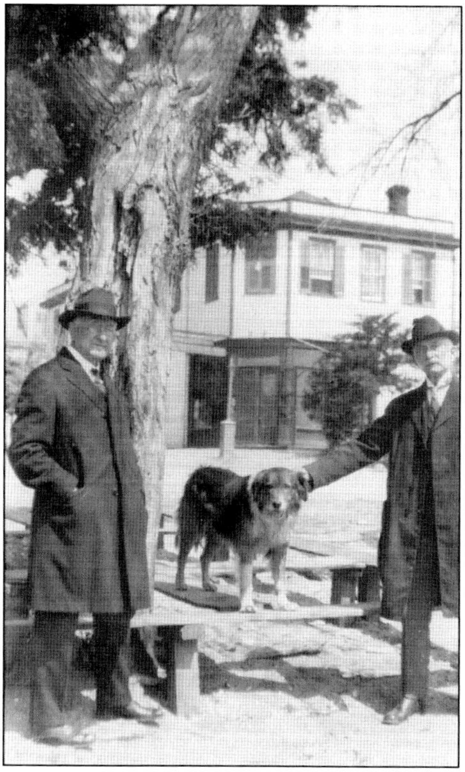

**WHITTLER'S BENCH, 1920S.** Whittler's Bench is located at the foot of Howe Street and was a favorite gathering place for men to debate politics and talk about current events. R. Johnson (left) is pictured here along with J.W. Dey, who established the Southport Fish Scrap and Oil Company with his brother in 1914. In the background is the Miller Hotel, built by Leonhard Miller in the early 1900s. It was a thriving business on the Southport waterfront until it was destroyed by fire in the early 1960s. (Courtesy of Trudy M. Young.)

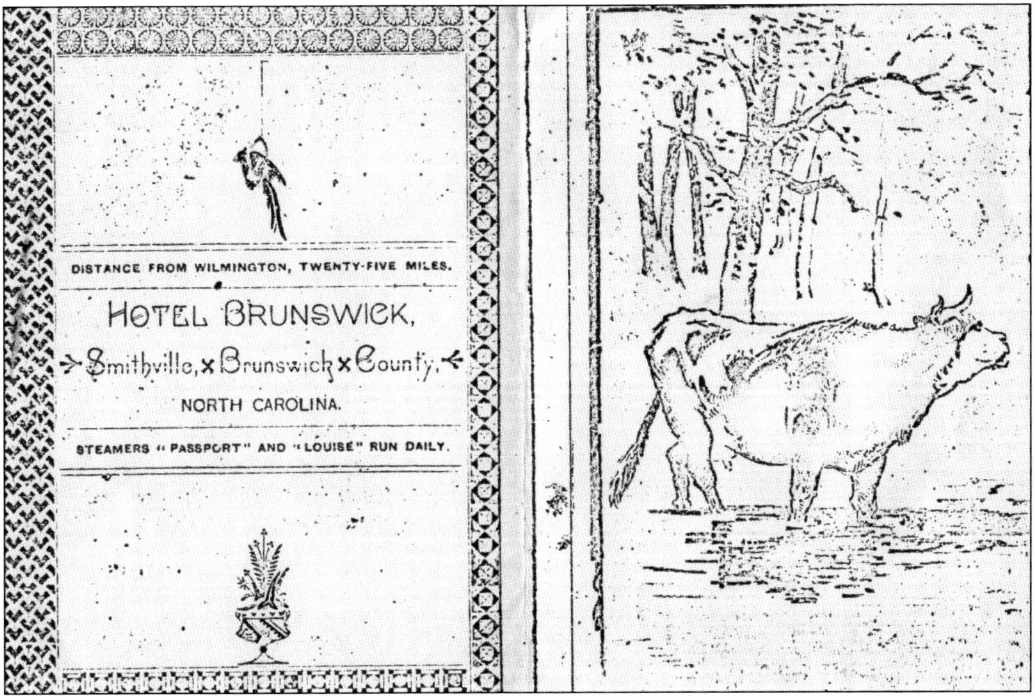


**Hotel Brunswick.** The hotel was built in Smithville in the early 1800s as a summer home for Benjamin Smith. Around 1859, Thomas Meares, owner of Orton Plantation, tore it down and on the same site, at the corner of Bay and Potts Street, rebuilt the structure now known as the Brunswick Inn. (Courtesy of Andrea P. Clemmons.)

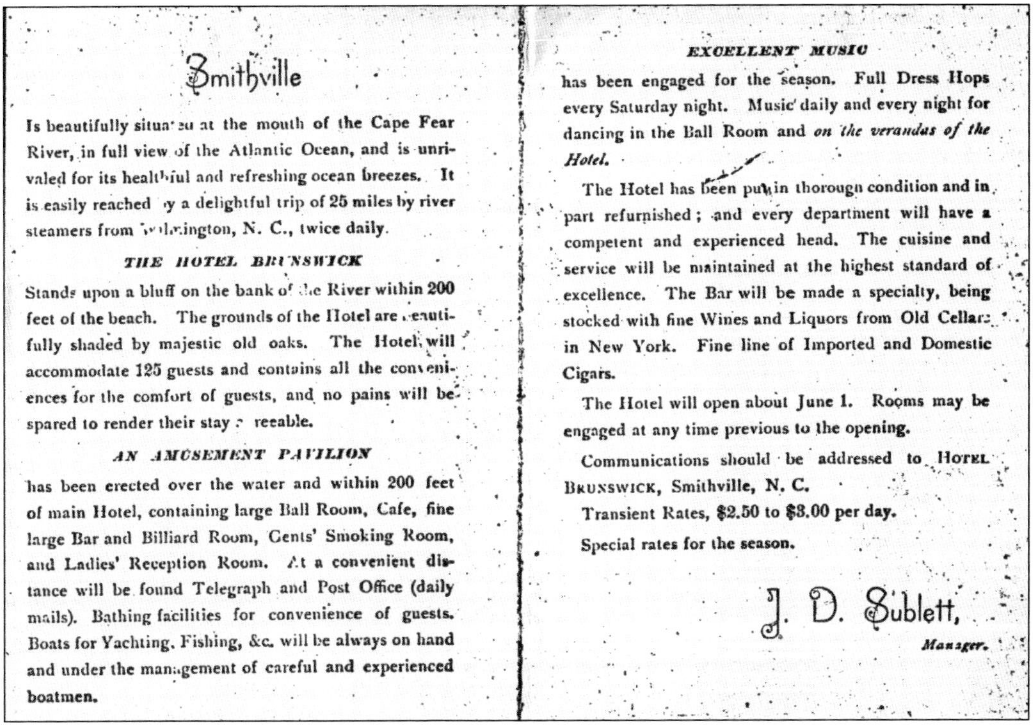

Smithville

Is beautifully situated at the mouth of the Cape Fear River, in full view of the Atlantic Ocean, and is unrivaled for its healthful and refreshing ocean breezes. It is easily reached by a delightful trip of 25 miles by river steamers from Wilmington, N. C., twice daily.

*THE HOTEL BRUNSWICK*

Stands upon a bluff on the bank of the River within 200 feet of the beach. The grounds of the Hotel are beautifully shaded by majestic old oaks. The Hotel will accommodate 125 guests and contains all the conveniences for the comfort of guests, and no pains will be spared to render their stay agreeable.

*AN AMUSEMENT PAVILION*

has been erected over the water and within 200 feet of main Hotel, containing large Ball Room, Cafe, fine large Bar and Billiard Room, Gents' Smoking Room, and Ladies' Reception Room. At a convenient distance will be found Telegraph and Post Office (daily mails). Bathing facilities for convenience of guests. Boats for Yachting, Fishing, &c. will be always on hand and under the management of careful and experienced boatmen.

*EXCELLENT MUSIC*

has been engaged for the season. Full Dress Hops every Saturday night. Music daily and every night for dancing in the Ball Room and *on the verandas of the Hotel.*

The Hotel has been put in thorough condition and in part refurnished; and every department will have a competent and experienced head. The cuisine and service will be maintained at the highest standard of excellence. The Bar will be made a specialty, being stocked with fine Wines and Liquors from Old Cellars in New York. Fine line of Imported and Domestic Cigars.

The Hotel will open about June 1. Rooms may be engaged at any time previous to the opening.

Communications should be addressed to Hotel Brunswick, Smithville, N. C.

Transient Rates, $2.50 to $3.00 per day.

Special rates for the season.

J. D. Sublett,
*Manager.*

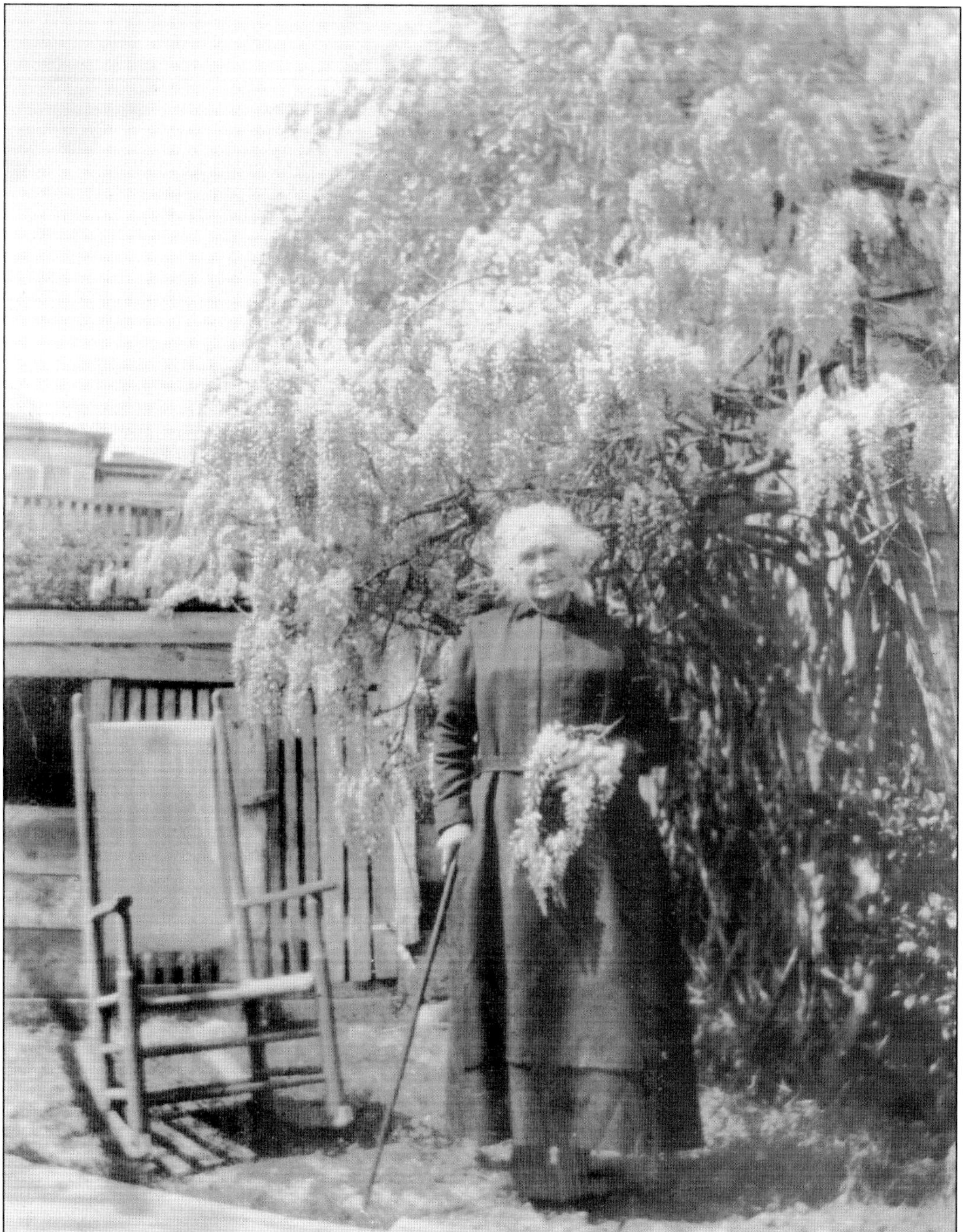

**KATE STUART, C. 1929.** "Miss Kate" was born in Smithville on August 17, 1844, in the Stuart House, which operated as a hotel and was known for its hospitality and excellent cuisine. Besides managing the Stuart House, Miss Kate taught school at the Smithville Academy. Later, she became the principal of Smithville Academy as well as the Peabody School. She was involved in the affairs of the community and was an active member of the Methodist church. Of her many accomplishments, she was the first president of the Southport Civic Club and was responsible for getting a rail line from Wilmington to Southport. (Courtesy of Andrea P. Clemmons.)

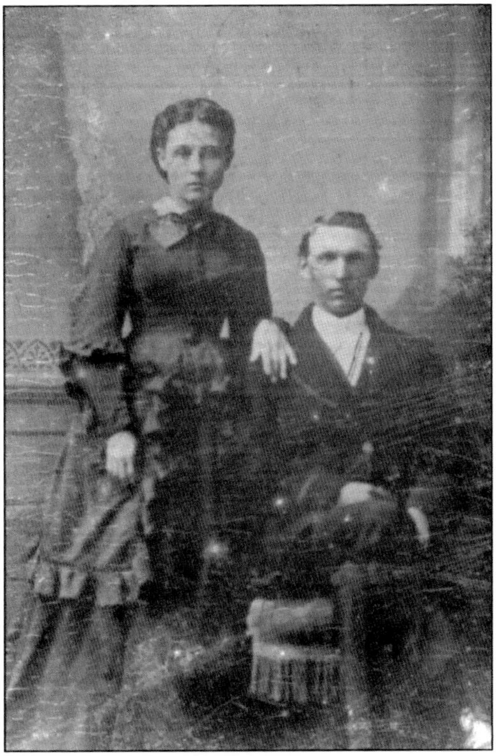

**John and Sarah Rebecca Drew Wescott, 1867.** John Wescott was born in 1845 and fought for the Confederacy as a foot soldier during the Civil War. He married Sarah Rebecca Drew and farmed in the old Bethel community. In later years, they moved to a house on Atlantic Avenue in Southport. As the oldest surviving member of the Brunswick Confederate Veterans, John inherited the minutes of its annual meetings, which have been placed in the Hardee Special Collection at Randall Library at UNC-Wilmington. He suffered a stroke in his last years, leaving him helplessly on his back in bed. He was nursed by relatives and survived on a semi-annual pension check of $132.50. He passed away on March 17, 1936, and is buried at Old Bethel Cemetery. John and Sarah are the parents of Alta Wescott Dosher and the great-grandparents of Lewis J. Hardee Jr. (Courtesy of Lewis J. Hardee Jr.)

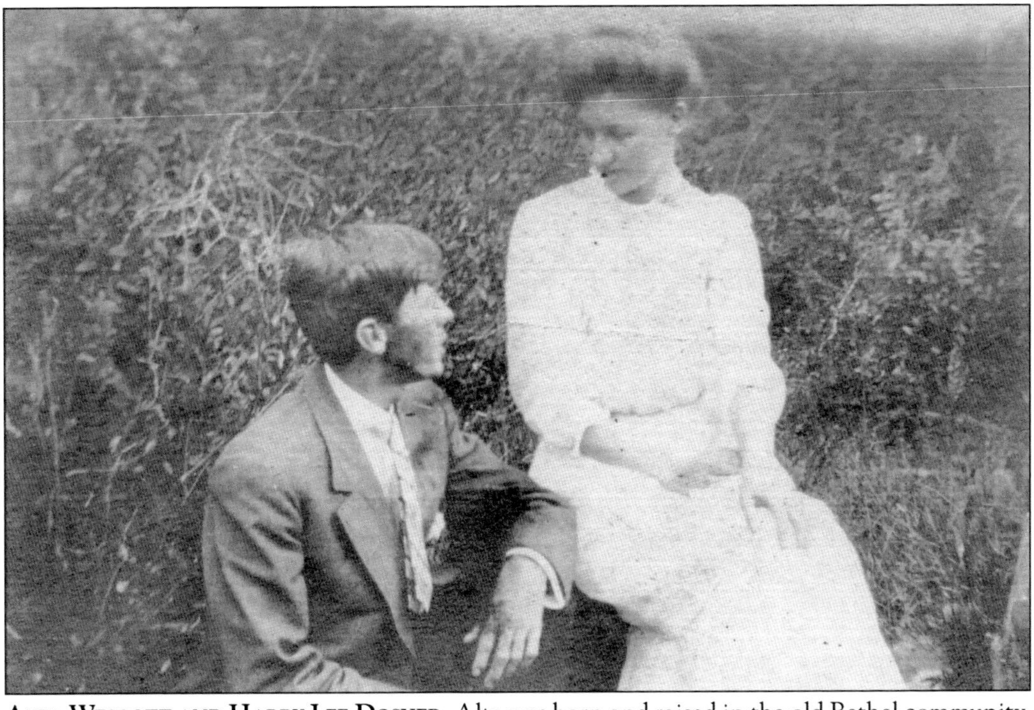

**Alta Wescott and Harry Lee Dosher.** Alta was born and raised in the old Bethel community. She married mechanic Harry Lee Dosher and they had three children: Dorothy, Leighton, and Paul. (Courtesy of Lewis J. Hardee Jr.)

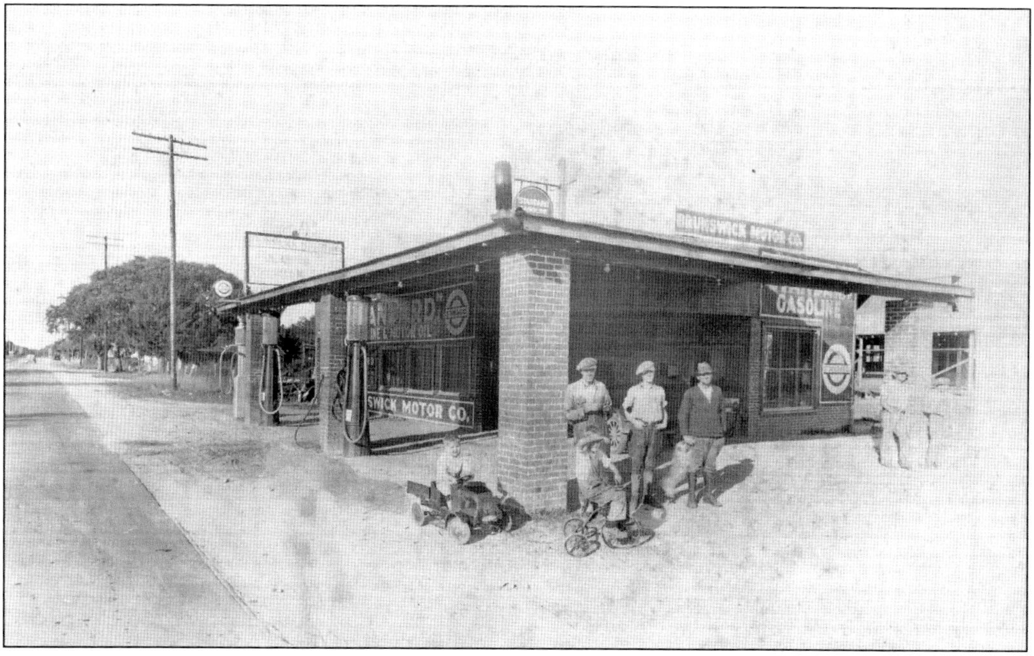


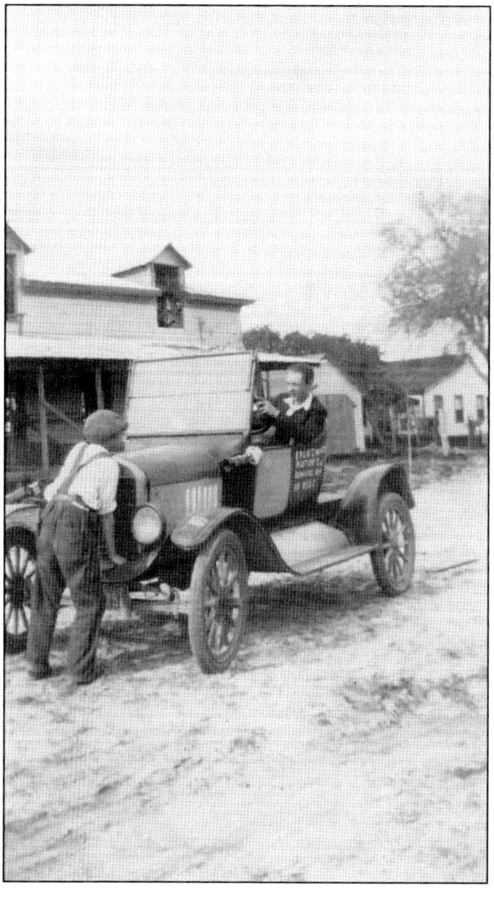

**Brunswick Motor Company, c. 1928.** In 1927, Harry Lee Dosher bought two lots at the northeast corner of Howe and Leonard Streets and opened the Brunswick Motor Company. The men standing in front are, from left to right, Harry Lee Dosher, Leighton Dosher, and Calvin Wescott. (Courtesy of Lewis J. Hardee Jr.)

**Brunswick Motor Company Truck.** This photograph was taken in the 1920s. (Courtesy of Lewis J. Hardee Jr.)

**SCANDINAVIAN BLACKSMITH.** Charles Almaghren was a mechanic at Harry Lee Dosher's garage across the street from Gus McNeil's filling station on North Howe Street. (Courtesy of Lewis J. Hardee Jr.)

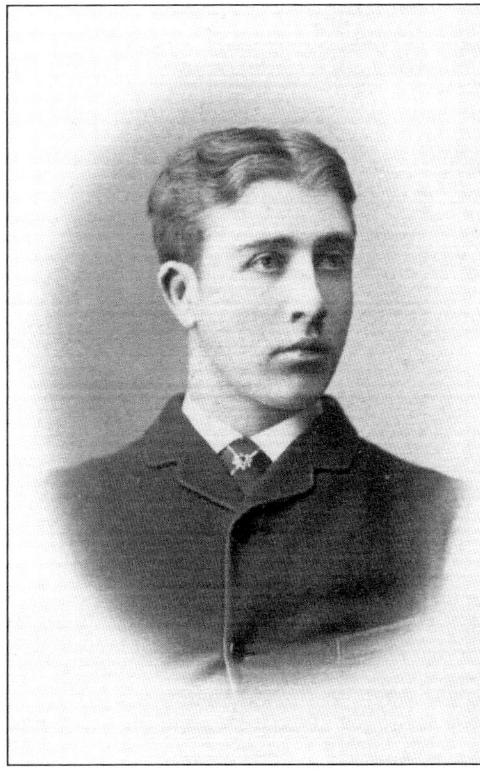

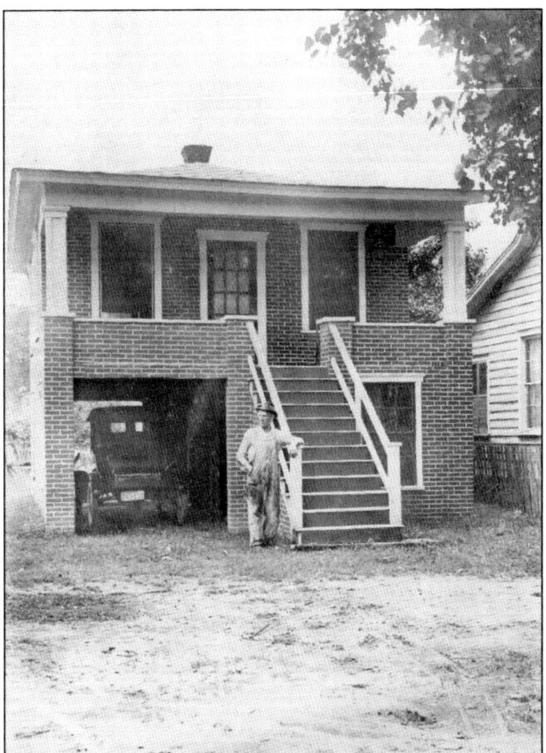

**GARAGE APARTMENT, 1920S.** Almaghren lived in this apartment over the garage where he worked. (Courtesy of Lewis J. Hardee Jr.)

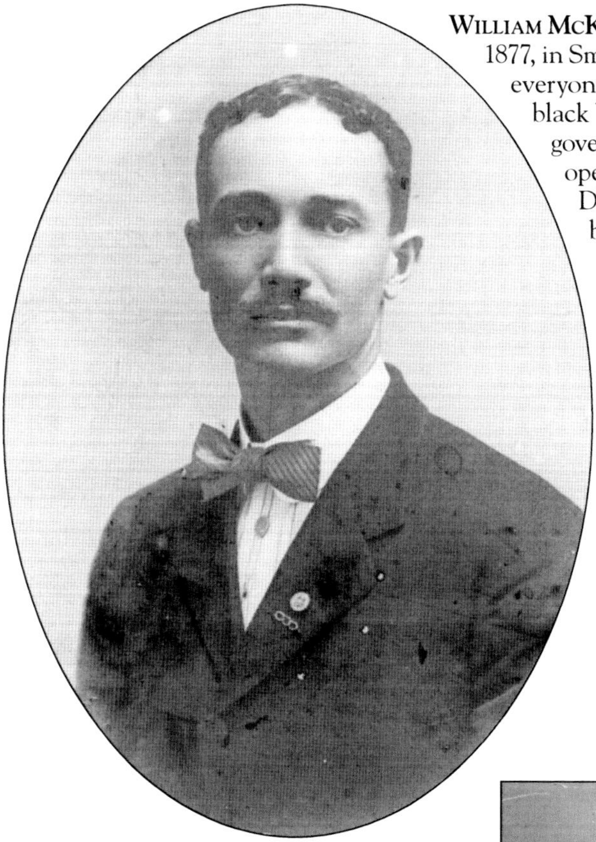

**WILLIAM MCKENZIE, EARLY 1900S.** Born on August 28, 1877, in Smithville, "Mr. Willie," as he was known by everyone in the community, was one of the first black business owners in town. He worked on a government boat, saved his money, and in 1910 opened an ice cream shop. He married Anna Deborah Lee, and the couple operated the business together for 58 years. (Courtesy of Yvonne McKenzie Adams.)

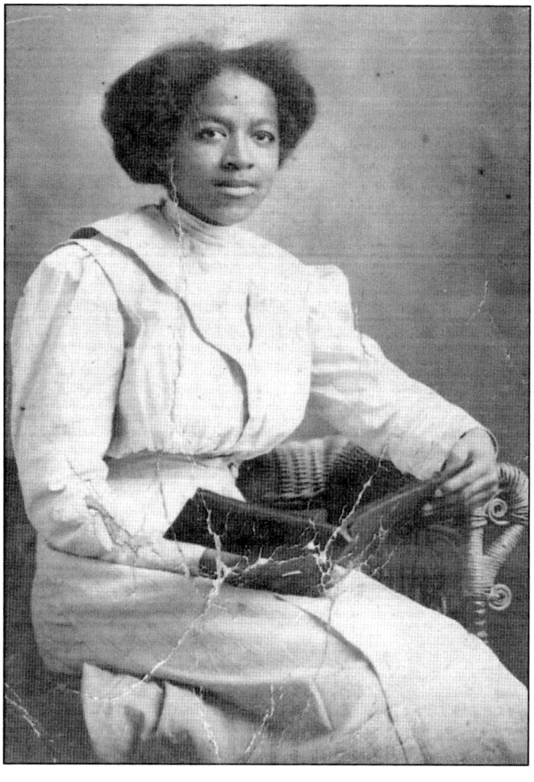

**ANNA DEBORAH LEE-MCKENZIE, EARLY 1900S.** Anna Deborah Lee was born in Smithville and married William McKenzie. Together they had four children. She worked alongside Mr. Willie in the ice cream shop. (Courtesy of Yvonne McKenzie Adams.)

**KATHERINE MAY MCKENZIE, EARLY 1900S.** Katherine May was one of four McKenzie children; here sister was Annie and her brothers were William and James. (Courtesy of Yvonne McKenzie Adams.)

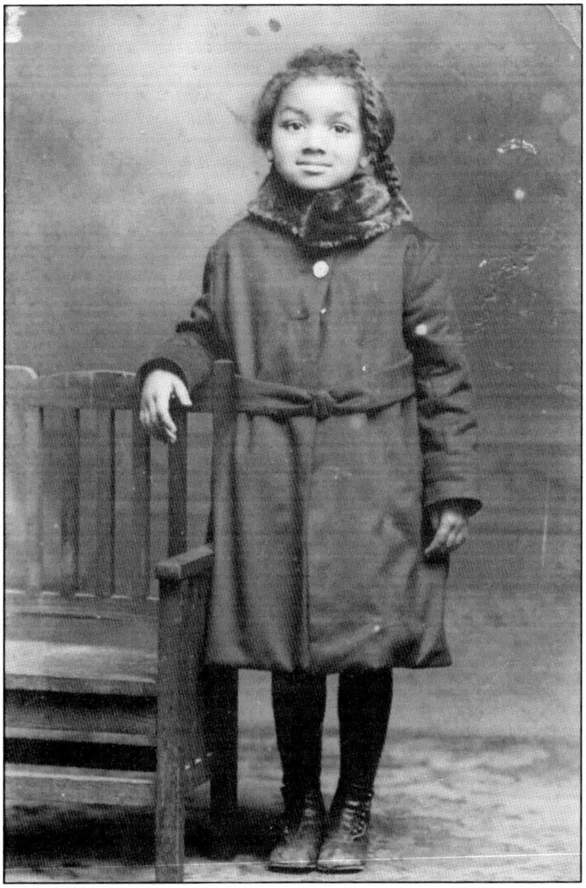

**1877 SMITHVILLE MARRIAGE CERTIFICATE.** Robert McKenzie and Sallie Davis were married on January 30, 1877, at the African Methodist Episcopal Zion Church in Smithville. They were the parents of Mr. Willie and the great-grandparents of Yvonne McKenzie Adams. (Courtesy of Yvonne McKenzie Adams.)

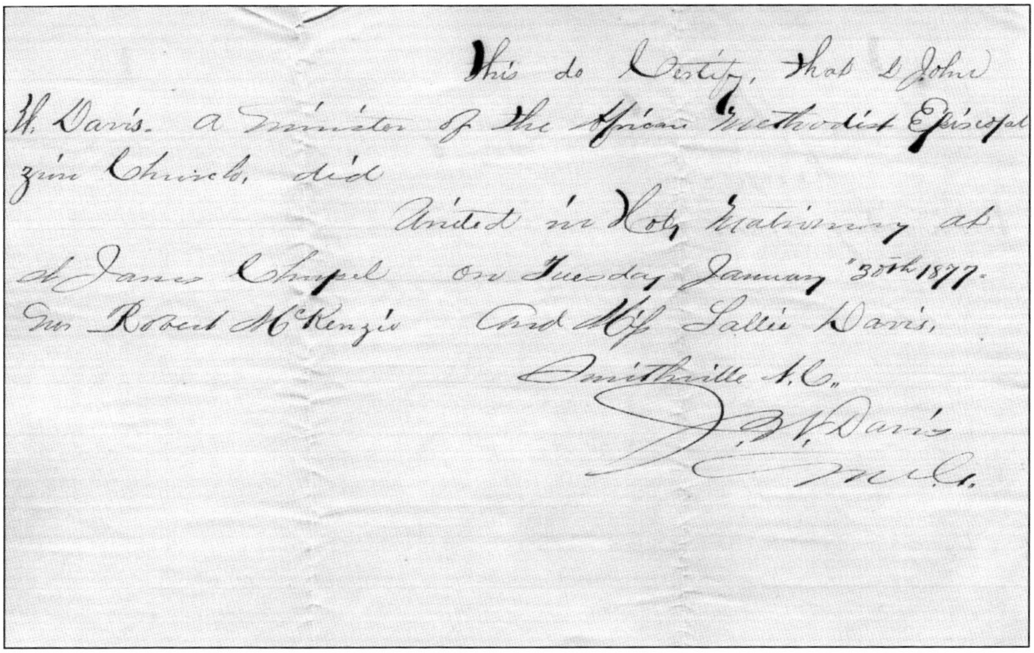

This do Certify, that I John W. Davis a Minister of the African Methodist Episcopal Zion Church, did
United in Holy Matrimony at
St James Chapel on Tuesday January "30th 1877.
Mr Robert McKenzie And Miss Sallie Davis,
Smithville N.C.
J. W. Davis
M.C.

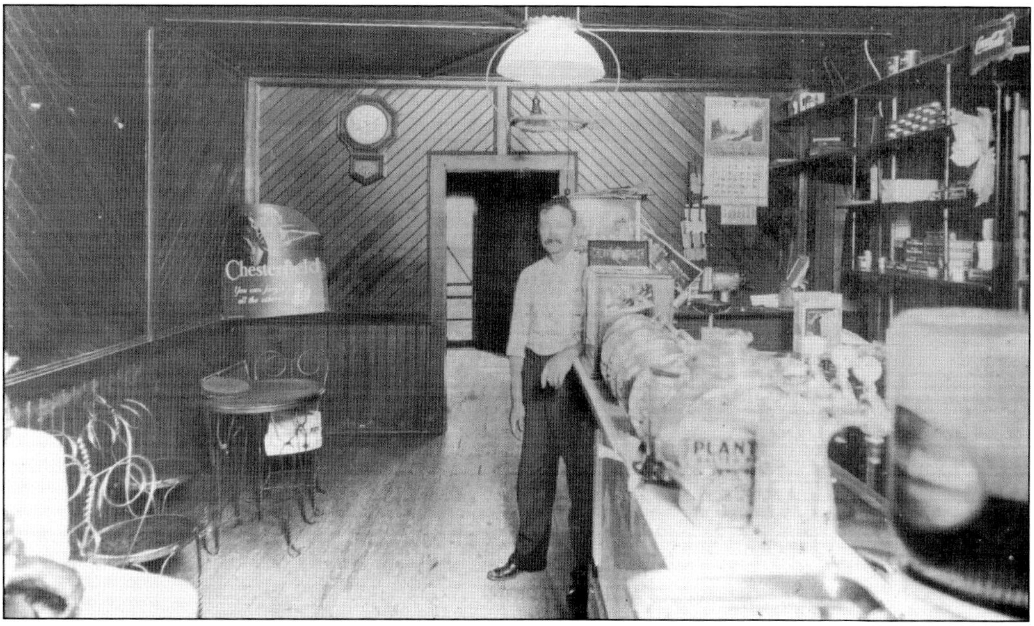

**Mr. Willie's Ice Cream Parlor, 1929.** Mr. Willie and his wife, Anna, made their own ice cream, and Anna made other goodies like small sweet potato pies and brown dogs. Made with sugar and peanuts, brown dogs were an old Southport candy recipe passed down in the black community. (Courtesy of Yvonne McKenzie Adams.)

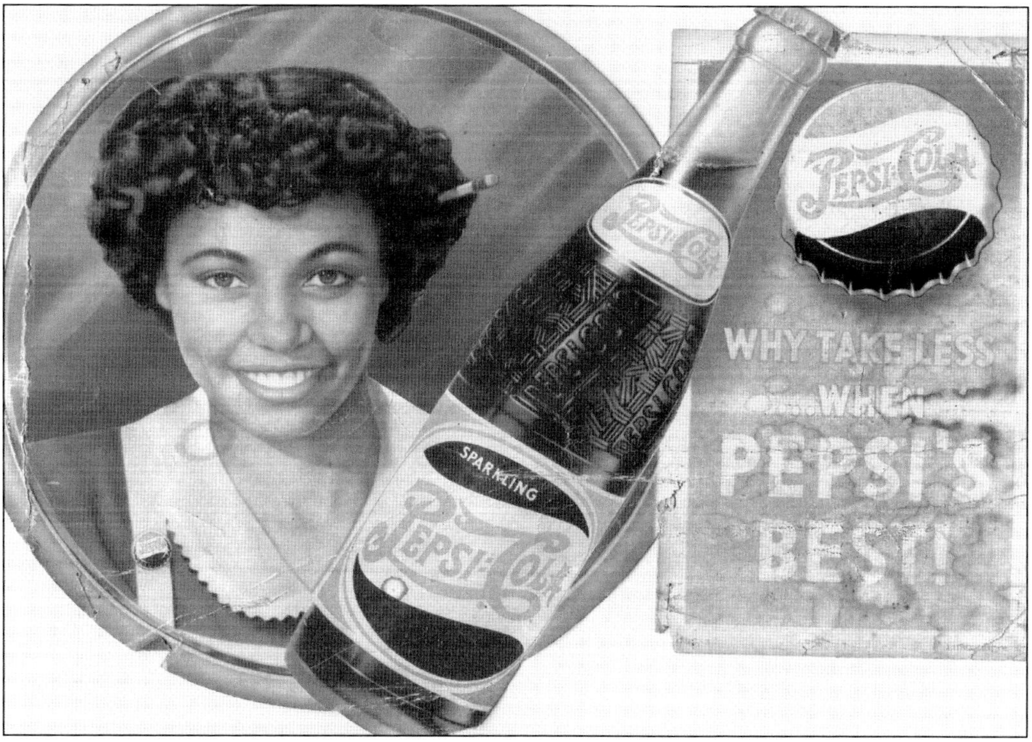


**Pepsi Advertisement, 1950s.** This was one of the first Pepsi advertisements targeting blacks, displayed at Mr. Willie's Ice Cream Parlor. (Courtesy of Yvonne McKenzie Adams.)

THE EVENING STAR.
Southport,N.C.,Sat.2I, 'I4.

The only colored paper in Brumswick Co.

LOCAL & PERSONAL

Mr.P.S.Berny was in town Thursday.

Mr.Daniel Reaves was in town Court week.

Mr.J.R.Evans left Southport,N.C. for Wilmington,N.C. on bisiness.

There will be A Summer school in Southport,Sept.

Mr.J.J.Loughlin is carring A line groceries in his dry goods department.

IN MEMORIAM.

Mar.2I,'I4.--
please allow me space in your paper to memorlize our departed one gone but not forgotton in loving rememberance Mr. Paris Frink,departe Mar.I5,'I4.

Call not back, the dea departed.

Anchored safe where storms are o'ver.

In the borderland he has left,to meet and part no more.

His be loved widow,
HARRIET FRINK.

---

J.WILSON
Dealer in general merchandise.

J.R.EVANS
Dealer in fancy & staple groceries.

NO.666
This isA prescription prepared especially for MALARIA orCHILLS & FEVOR. Five or six doses will break any case , and if taken then as a tonic the Fevor will not return. It acts on the liver better than Calomel and does not gripe or siken.Price 25c.

PRICE OF THIS PAPER IS 2CTS.

***Evening Star.*** The *Evening Star* was the only black newspaper in Brunswick County. This document has been preserved since 1914. (Courtesy of Yvonne McKenzie Adams.)

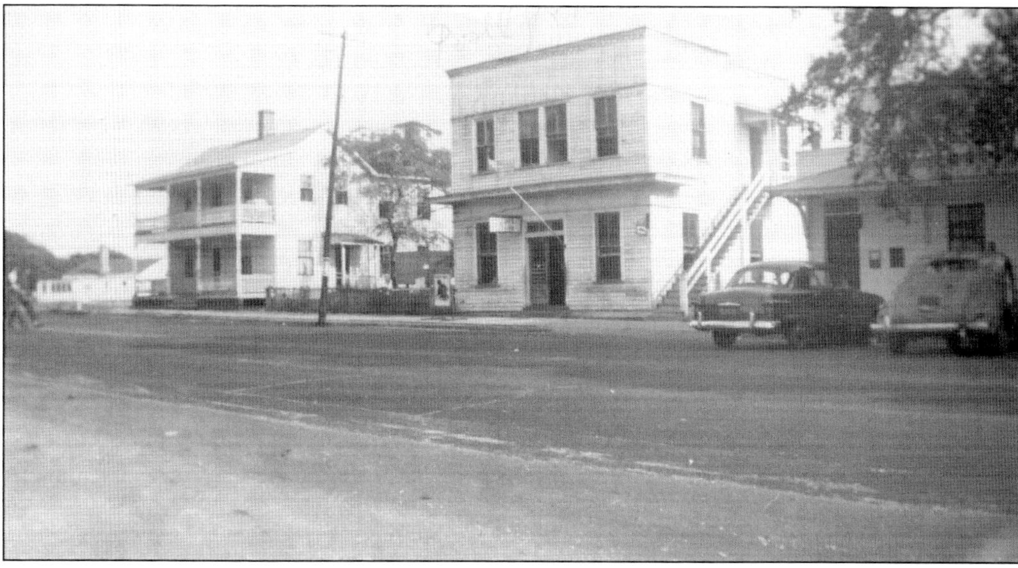

**Post Office.** The post office was located on Moore Street in the 1950s. The first Smithville postmaster, John Conyers, was appointed on July 1, 1811. (Courtesy of Lewis J. Hardee Jr.)

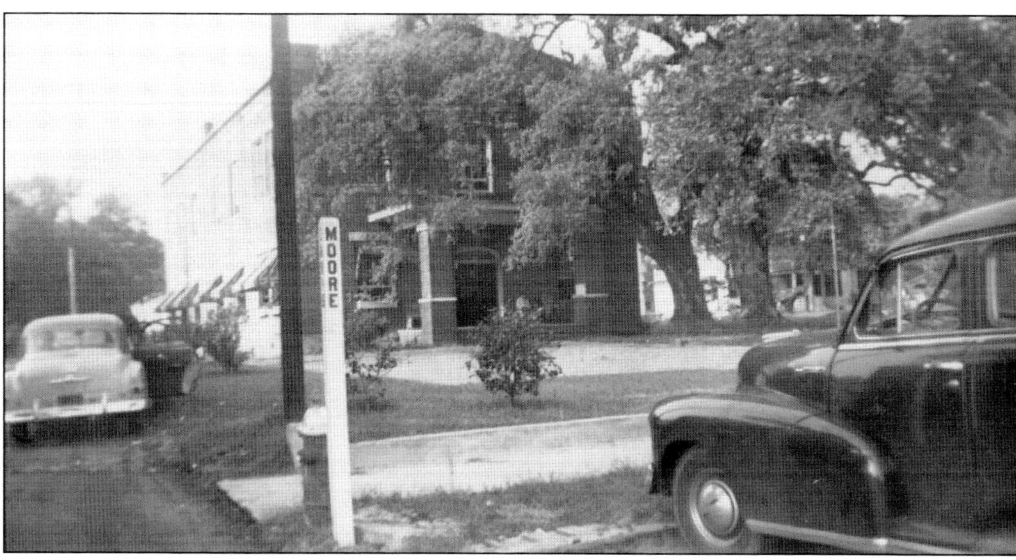


**Brunswick County Courthouse.** The courthouse, seen here in the 1950s, now houses Southport City Hall. (Courtesy of Lewis J. Hardee Jr.)

# *Two*

# THE BOATS AND THE NETS

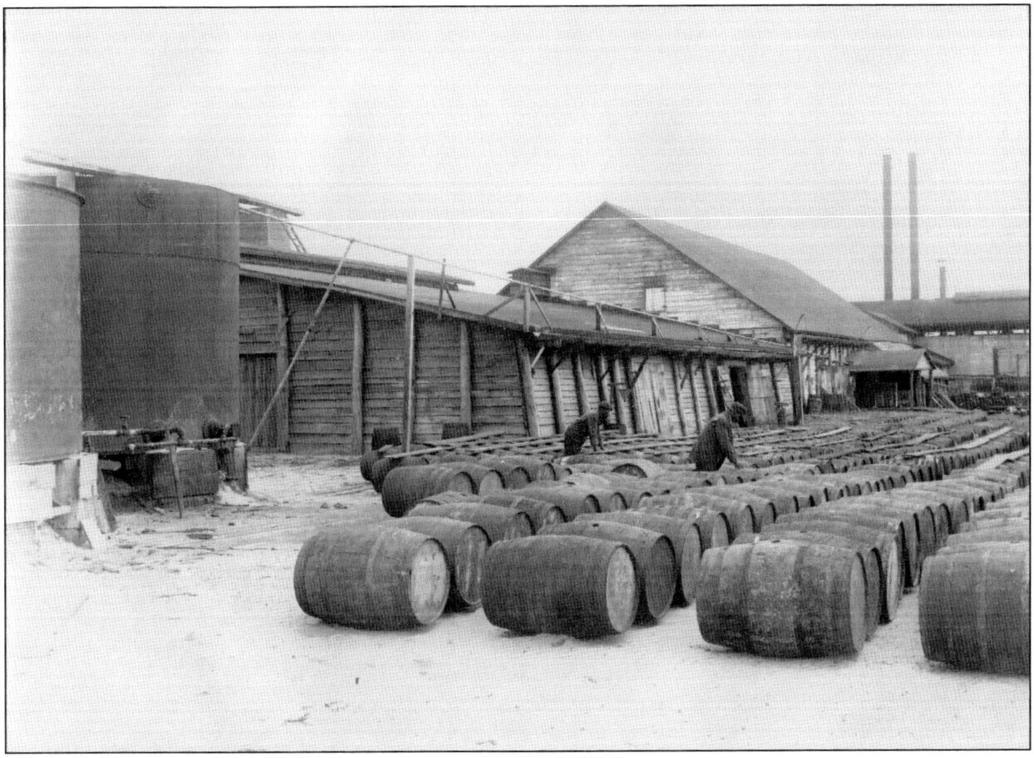

**BARRELS OF FISH OIL.** The menhaden fishing industry was very lucrative and a large source of income for Southport. Menhaden are small, boney fish and not good for eating, but their oils were extracted and used in products such as paint, soaps, linoleum, tanning solutions, and pharmaceuticals. These barrels of fish oil are ready to be shipped from the Southport Fish Scrap and Oil Company. (Courtesy of Trudy M. Young.)

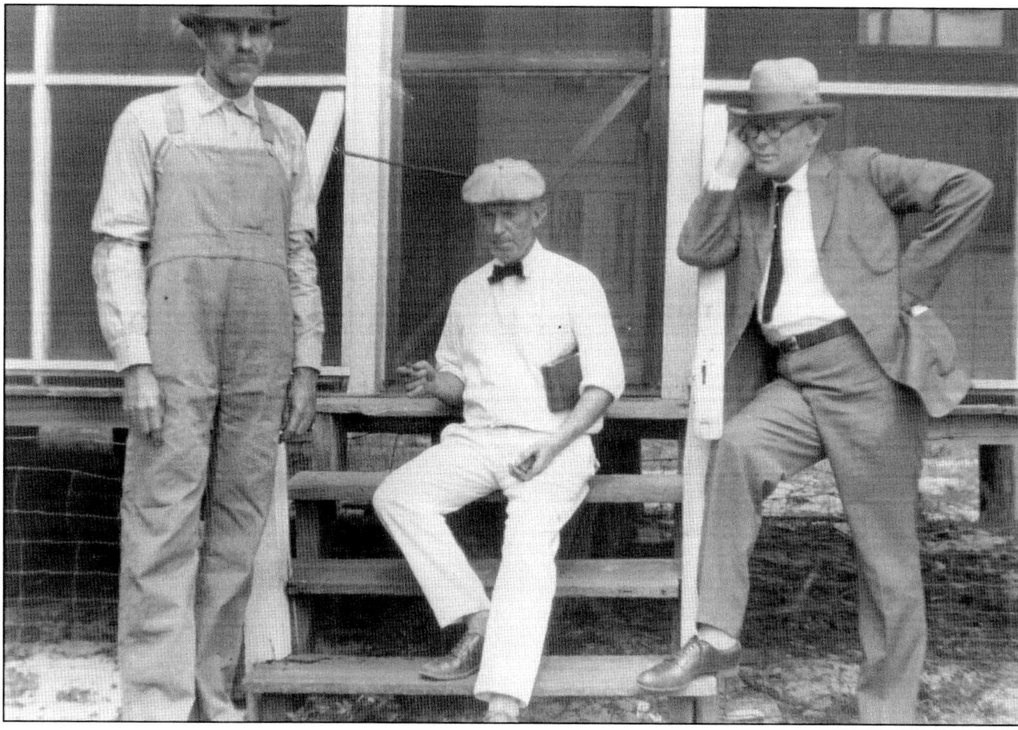

**CHARLES E. GAUSE.** The Southport Fish Scrap and Oil Company flourished under the management of Southport native Charles E. Gause. The company reincorporated in the early 1920s, but the old name was retained and most of the old stockholders remained. It became Southport's largest and most successful industry. Pictured here are, from left to right, Hiram McKeithan, Jimmy Sutton, and Charles E. Gause. (Courtesy of Trudy M. Young.)

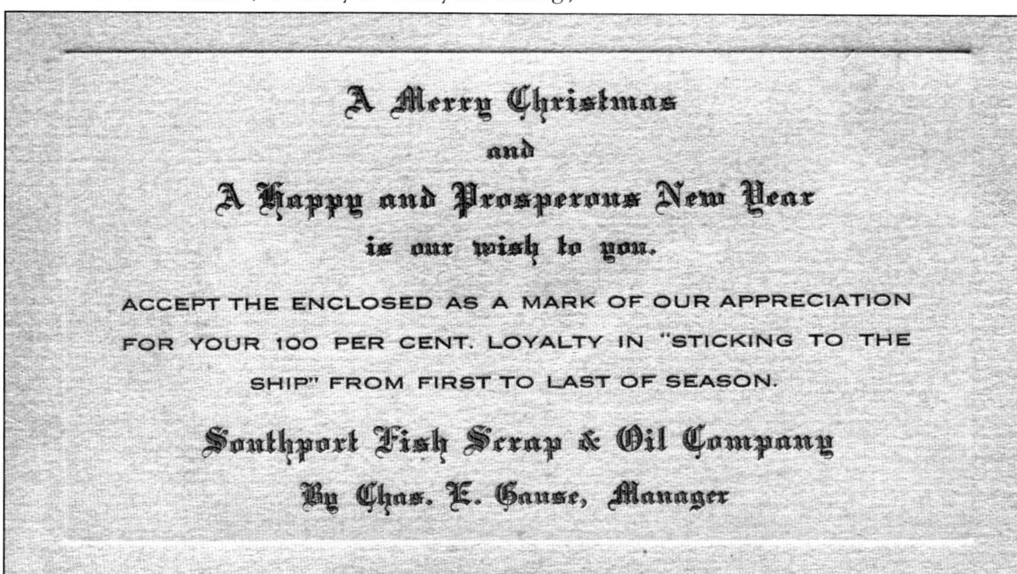

A Merry Christmas
and
A Happy and Prosperous New Year
is our wish to you.

ACCEPT THE ENCLOSED AS A MARK OF OUR APPRECIATION FOR YOUR 100 PER CENT. LOYALTY IN "STICKING TO THE SHIP" FROM FIRST TO LAST OF SEASON.

Southport Fish Scrap & Oil Company
By Chas. E. Gause, Manager

**CHRISTMAS CARD, 1920s.** Charles Gause gave each employee a Christmas card like the one seen here. (Courtesy of Trudy M. Young.)

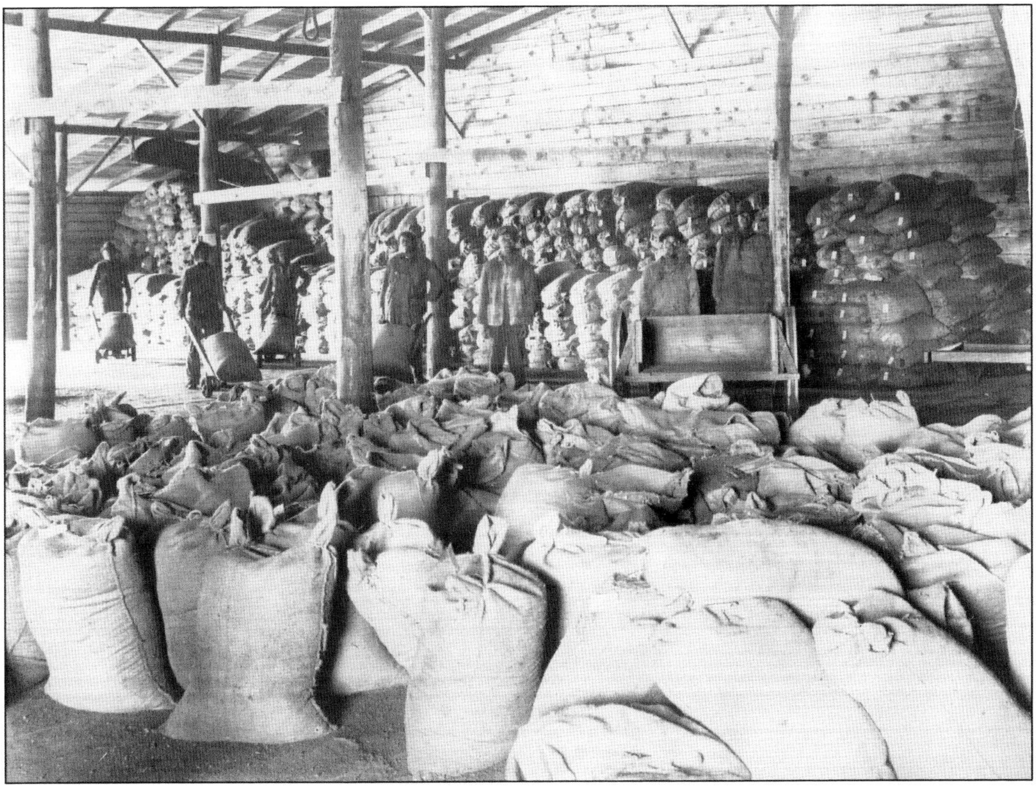

**Fish Scraps, 1920s.** These bags stored dried menhaden scraps that would be turned into fertilizer and feed for cattle, poultry, and swine. (Courtesy of Trudy M. Young.)

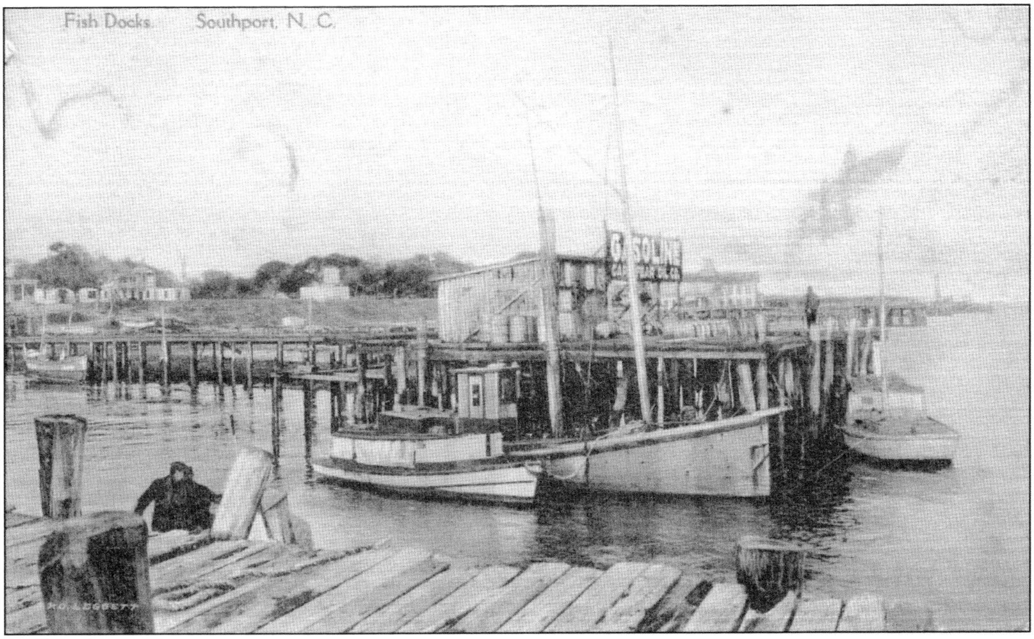


**Southport Fish Docks.** This postcard from the early 1900s shows a dance hall to the right of the gasoline station in the distance. (Courtesy of Trudy M. Young.)

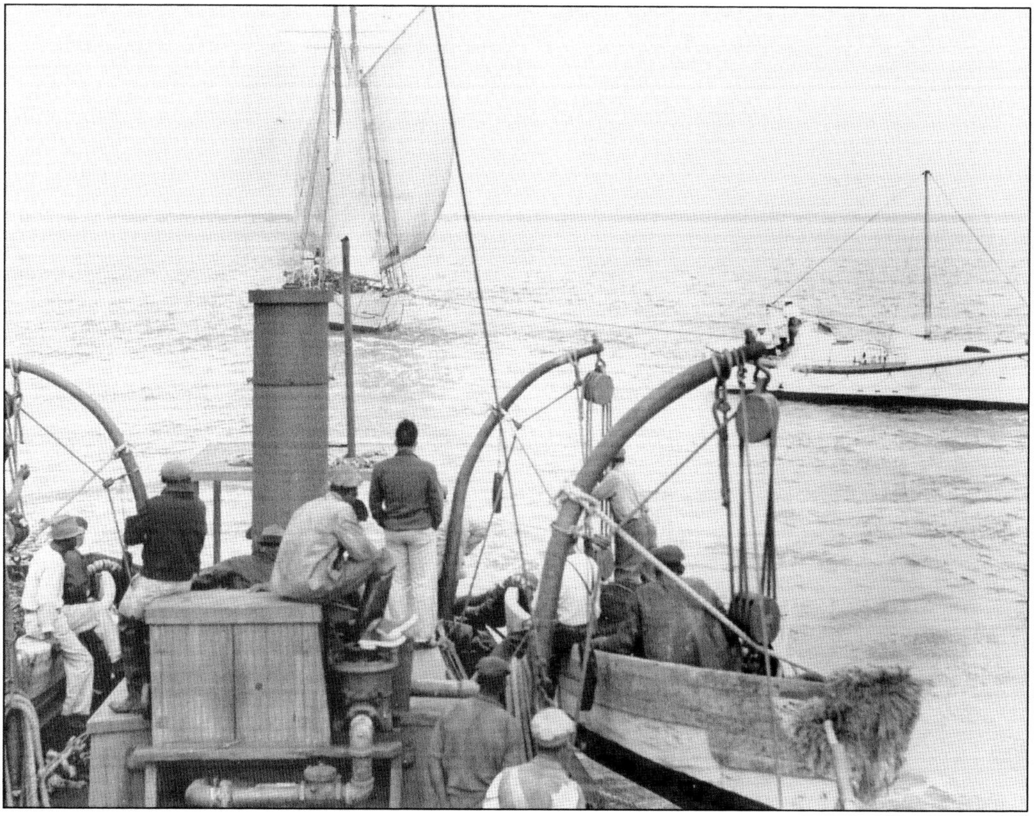

**Menhaden Fishing Crew.** Southport Fish Scrap and Oil Company employees wait for the big catch on menhaden boats. (Courtesy of Trudy M. Young.)

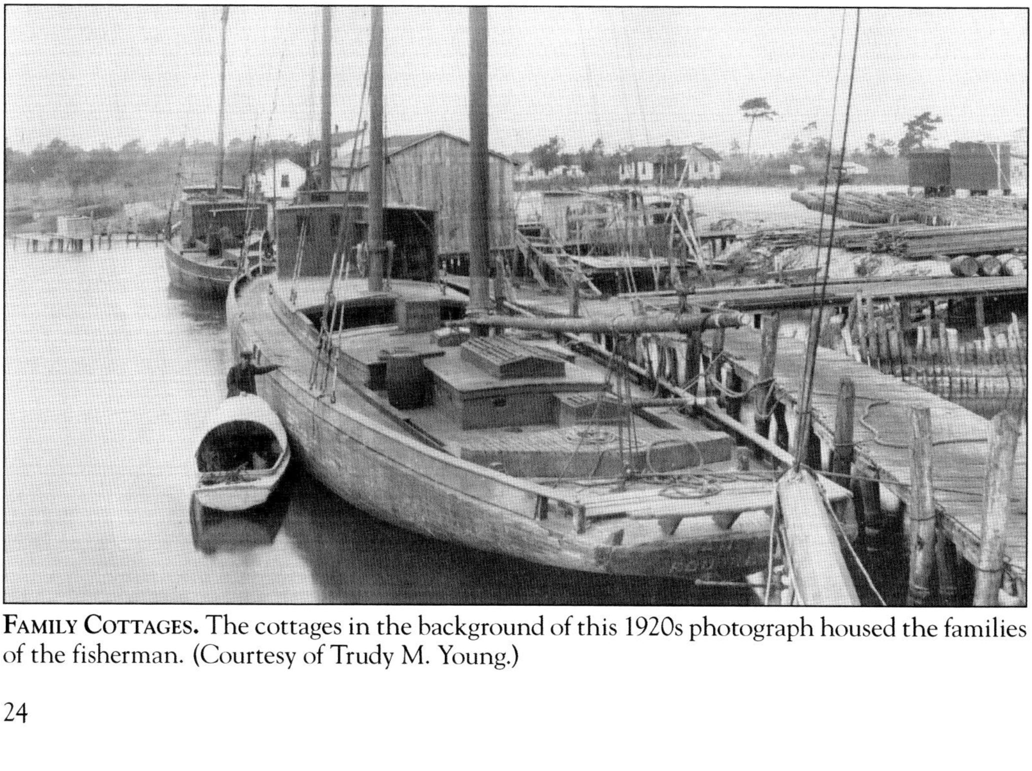

**Family Cottages.** The cottages in the background of this 1920s photograph housed the families of the fisherman. (Courtesy of Trudy M. Young.)

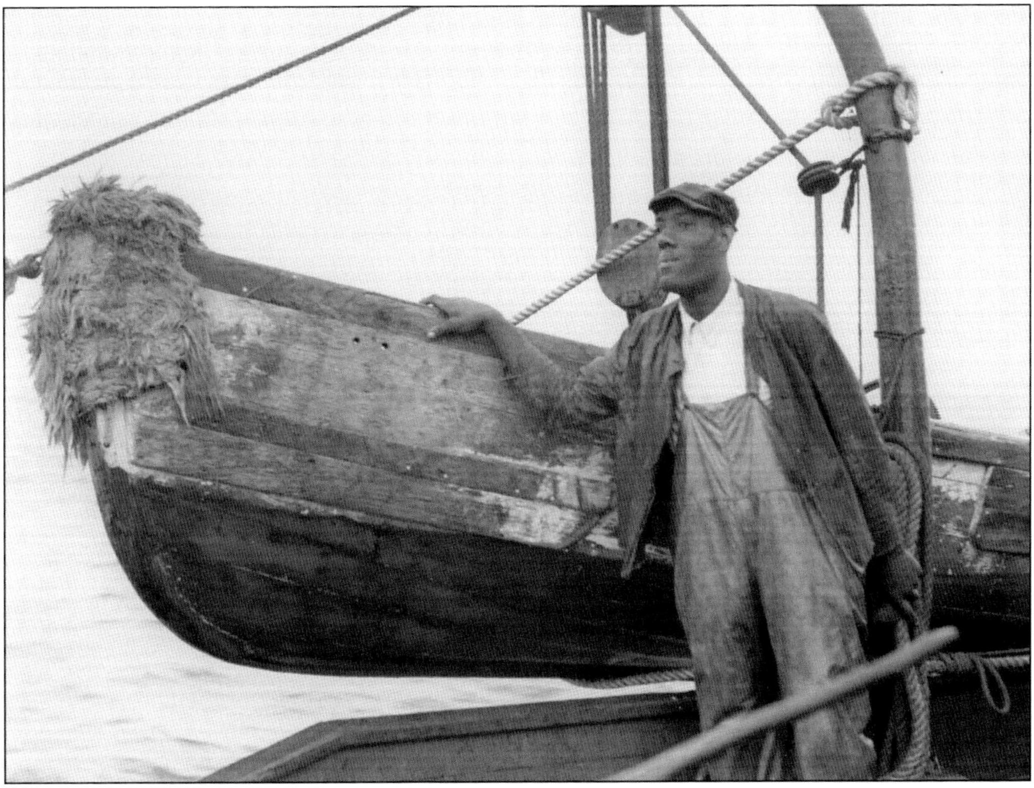

**Gentle Giant.** Elias Gore was born in 1906 and was said to be around seven feet, eight inches tall. During the Depression years, he and his brother Alex Jr. dropped out of school to work so their siblings could get an education. He was known as "Nehi" to everyone who knew him. Gore was dedicated to his family, his church, and the community. He worked as a menhaden fisherman in the mid-1920s and was known for his strength as well as his gentle and kind manner. He died in January 1944. (Courtesy of the North Carolina State Archives.)

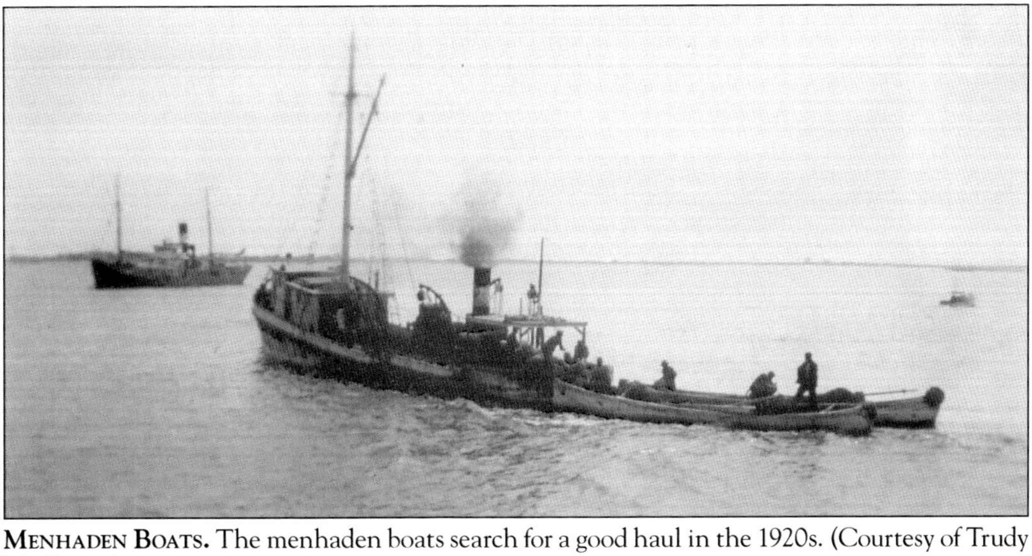

**Menhaden Boats.** The menhaden boats search for a good haul in the 1920s. (Courtesy of Trudy M. Young.)

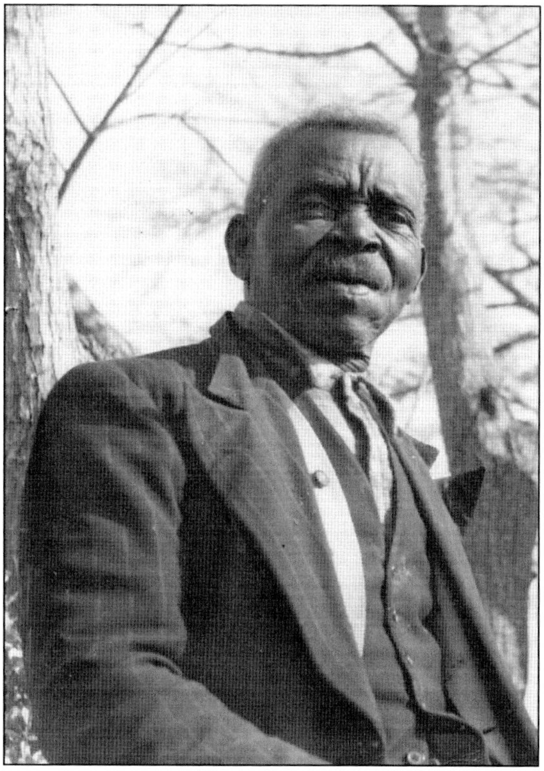

**River Legend, 1960s.** George Wortham, born in 1873, was a well-known fishing guide for over 50 years and knew the secrets of the sea and fishing. He served as an oarsman for Cape Fear pilots on their 15-mile trip to sea before powered vessels were used. He married Mary Eliza, who was a midwife, and they had three children: Sylvester, Marie, and Mattie. Wortham was the grandfather of Ennis Tobler and the great-grandfather of author Sharon Claudette Smith. (Courtesy of Ennis Tobler.)

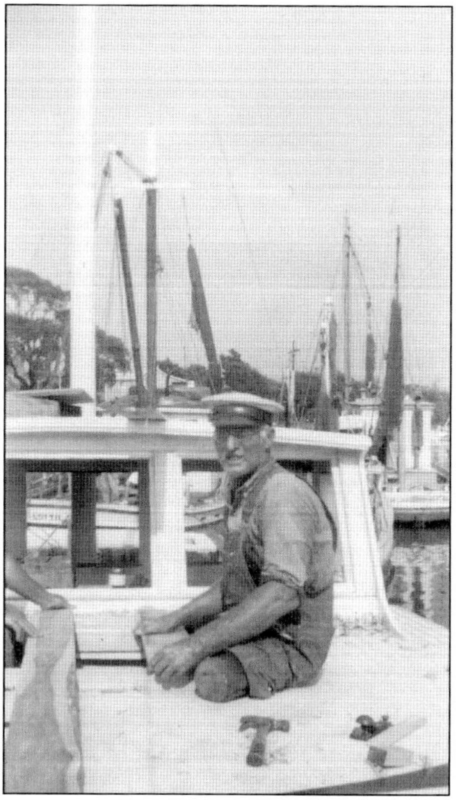

**Boat Builder.** When Cratie Arnold was 15 years old, he developed an illness that caused the amputation of both legs—but it did not hold him back from having a productive life. Pictured here in the 1940s, Arnold started a boat-building business and was known for his superior craftsmanship. He married and had three daughters. (Courtesy of Andrea P. Clemmons.)

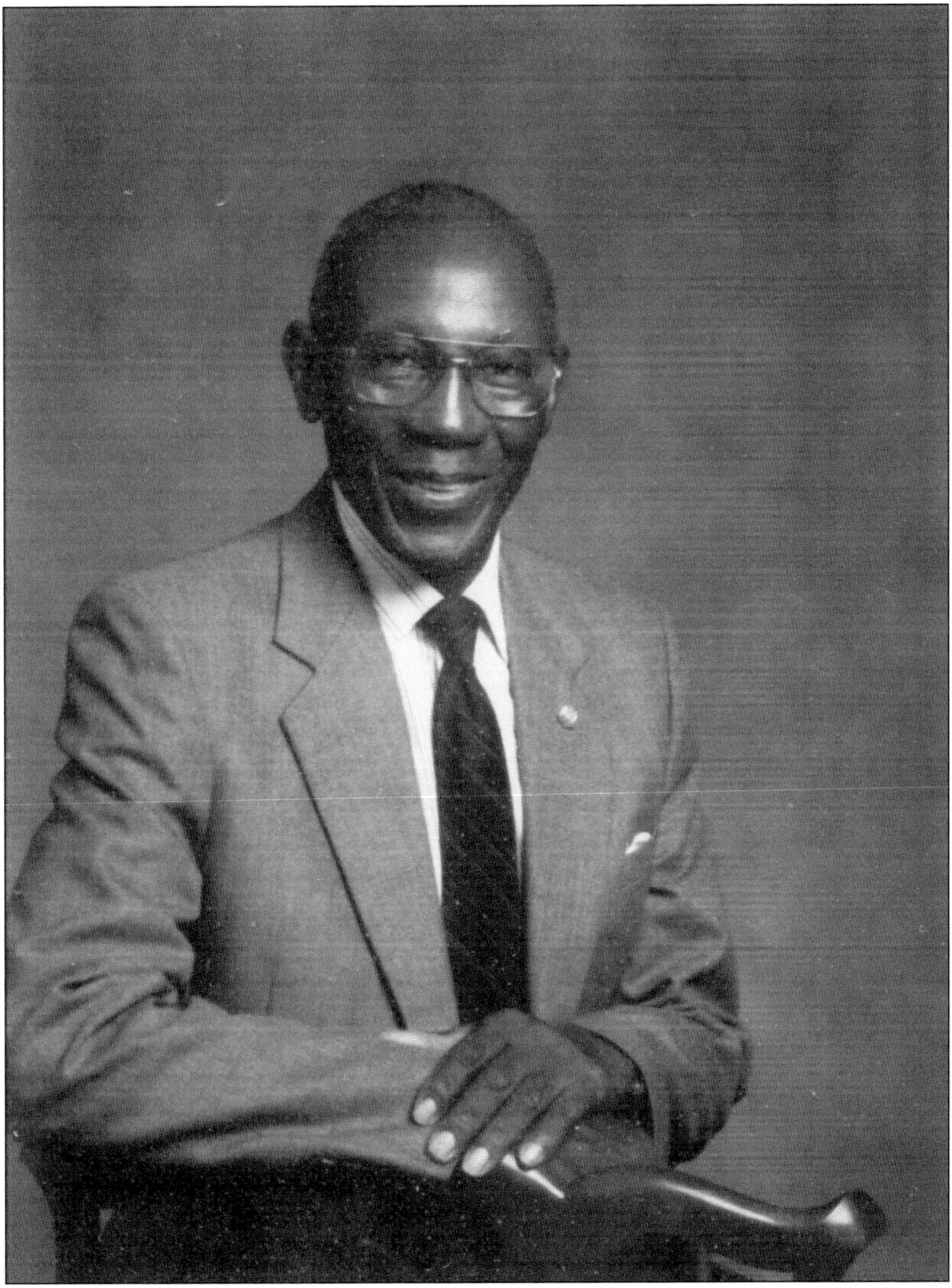

**CAPT. EUGENE W. GORE.** As a young boy in the early 1900s, Captain Gore went out on the menhaden vessels with his grandfather, who was a cook. He worked his way up from a kitchen boy to become one of the first black captains in the menhaden fishing fleet of North Carolina. He later became the pilot of the Southport Fort Fisher Ferry. (Courtesy of Lois Gore Thompson.)

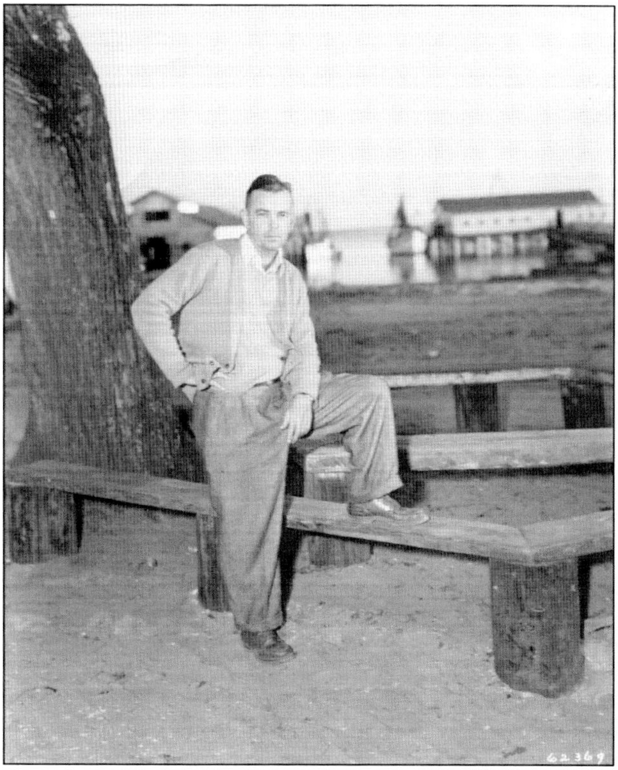

**Lewis Hardee Sr. at the Old Whittler's Bench, 1948.** Lewis Hardee Sr. was born in 1910 and came to Southport in 1934 from Fernandina, Florida. His father was a pioneer in the shrimp-canning business in the Fernandina area, so he grew up grown up knowing the industry. Hardee built one of the most successful shrimping businesses in Southport, Colonial Shrimp Company, and had a series of shrimp boat fleets. (Courtesy of Lewis J. Hardee Jr.)

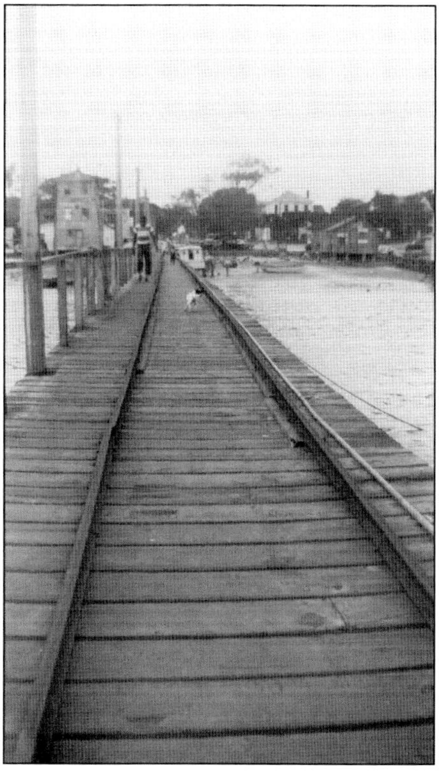

**Southport Docks, 1950s.** Note the old pilot observation tower in the background. (Courtesy of Lewis J. Hardee Jr.)

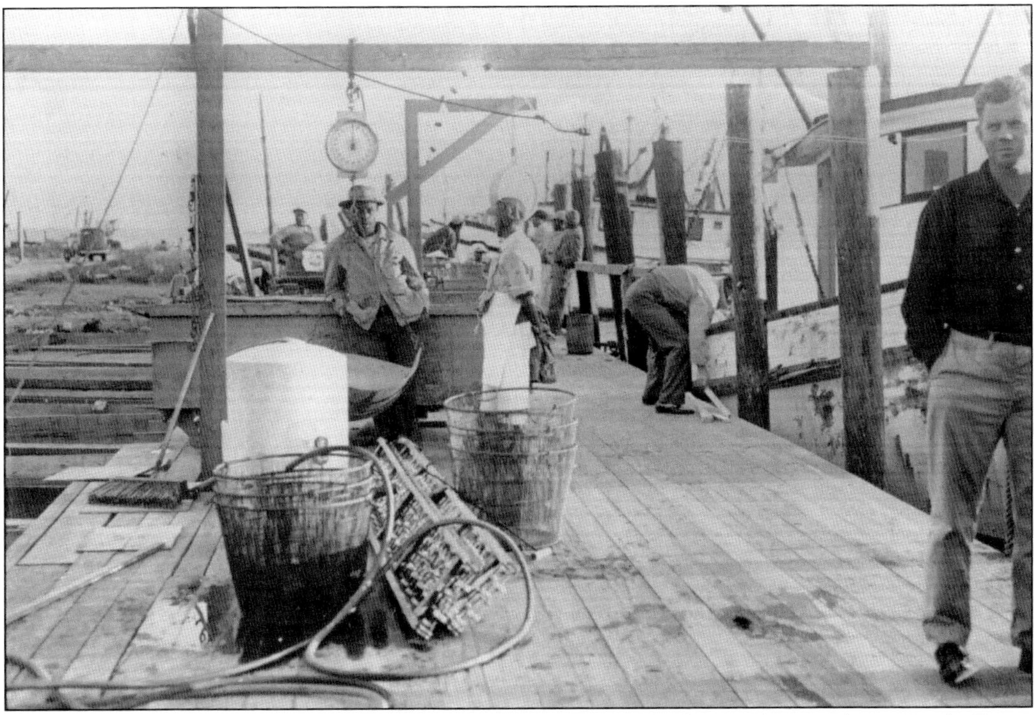

**SHRIMP-PACKING FACILITY.** This temporary shrimp-packing facility in the Southport Yacht Basin is pictured shortly after Hurricane Hazel destroyed the piers. Prim Ray, Hardee's right-hand man for many years, is behind the scales. (Courtesy of Lewis J. Hardee Jr.)

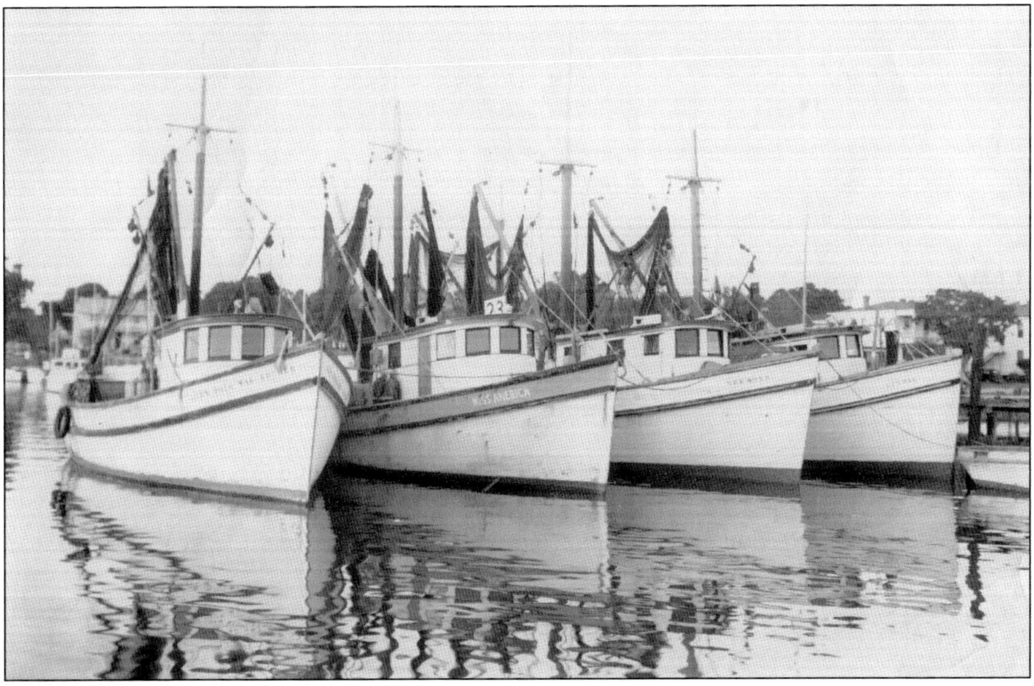

**HARDEE FLEET.** This 1948 photograph shows several boats from the Hardee fleet. (Courtesy of Lewis J. Hardee Jr.)

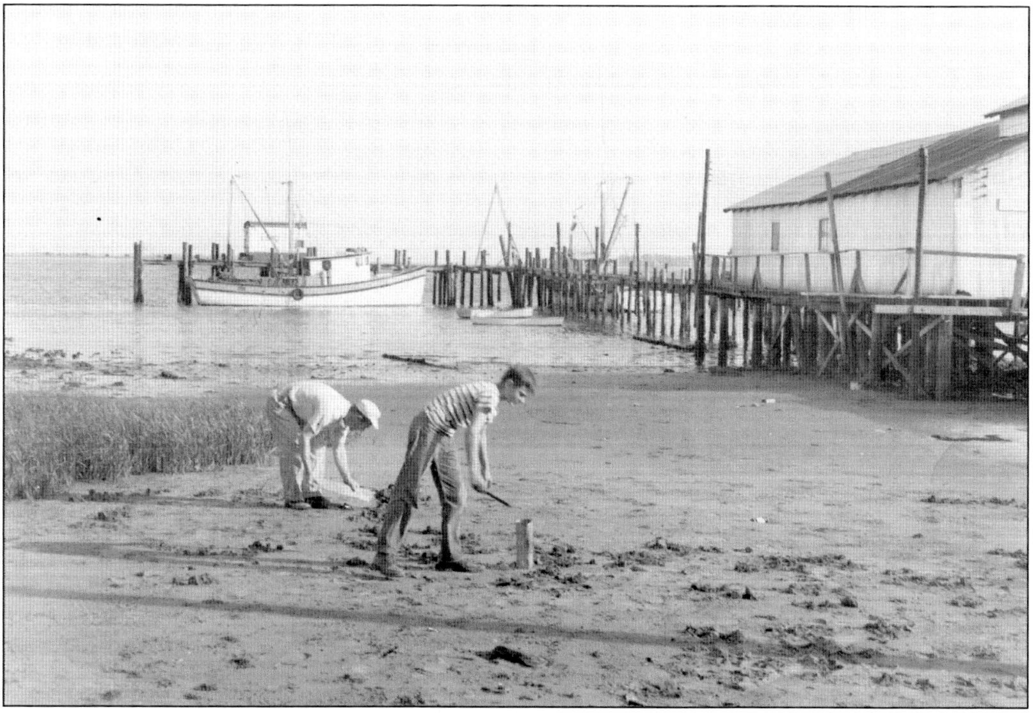

**The Docks, 1950s.** A man and a boy search for clams near the docks. (Courtesy of Lewis J. Hardee Jr.)

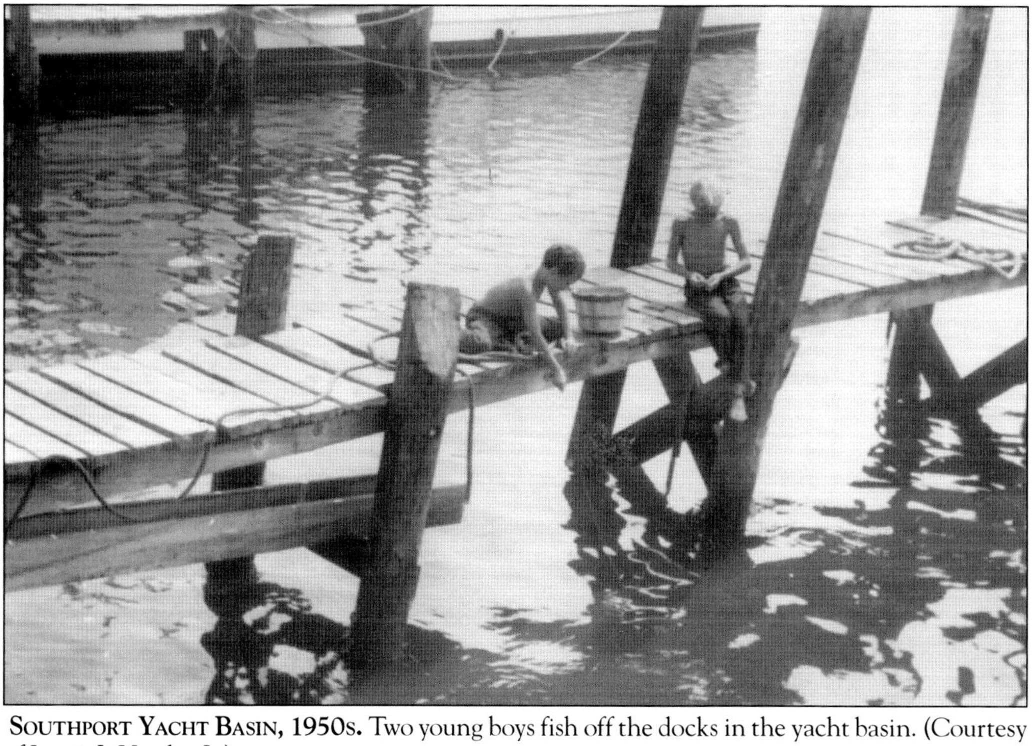

**Southport Yacht Basin, 1950s.** Two young boys fish off the docks in the yacht basin. (Courtesy of Lewis J. Hardee Jr.)

**Mending Nets, 1950s.** Capt. Merritt Moore (left), an unidentified man (middle), and John Carr Davis get the nets ready for the next big catch. (Courtesy of Jimmy Moore.)

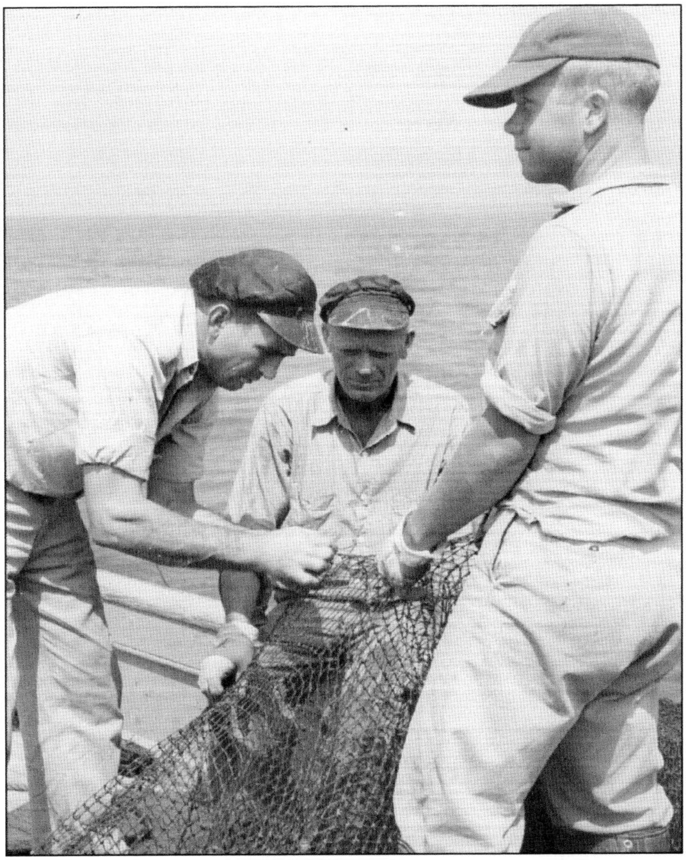

**Watching Dad.** Young Jimmy Moore carefully watches his dad, Capt. Merritt Moore (center), and John Carr Davis as they untangle the nets in the 1950s. Jimmy worked in the shrimping industry like his father and has three children with his wife, Mae Moore. (Courtesy of Jimmy Moore.)

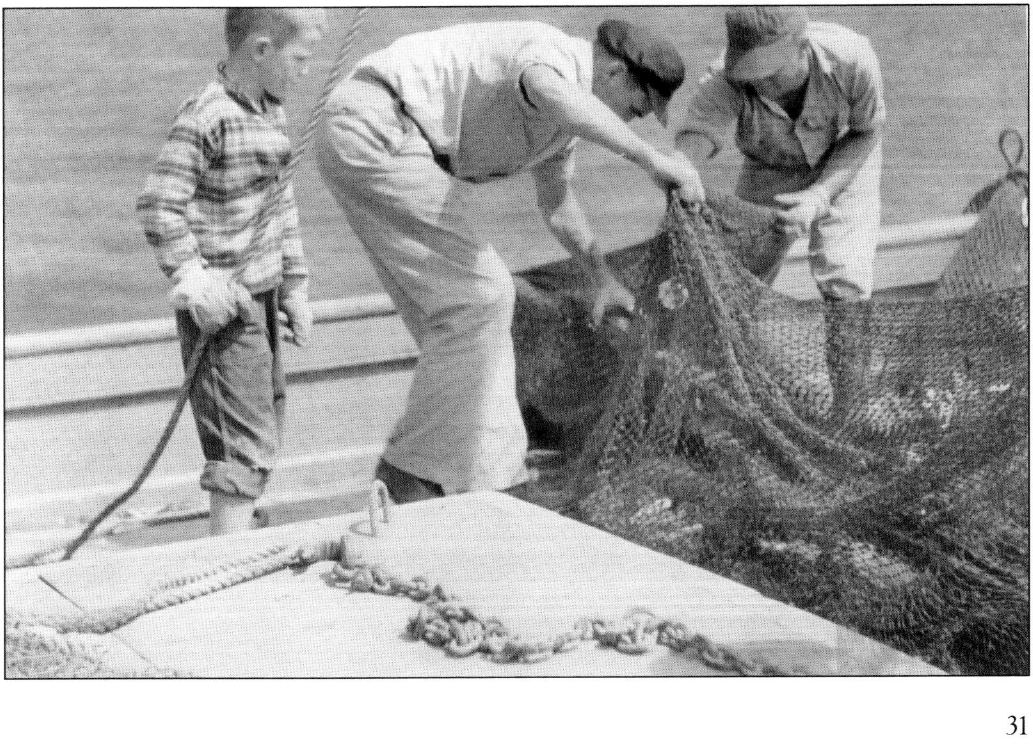

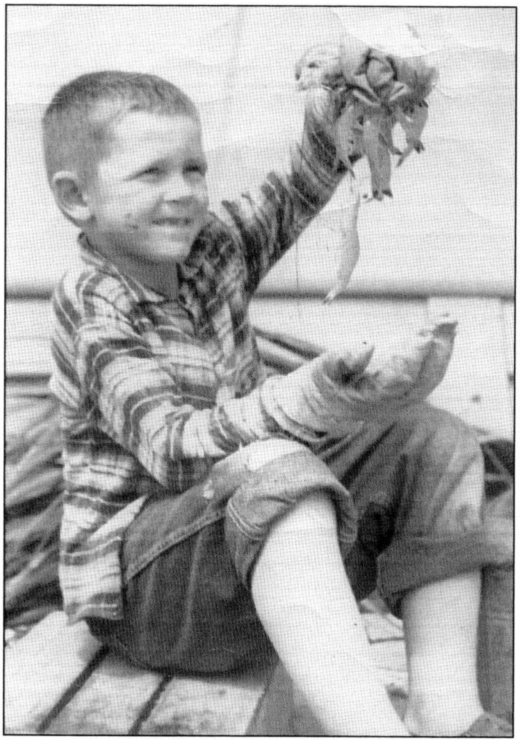

**Shrimp in the 1950s.** Young Jimmy Moore shows off some freshly caught shrimp on the *Penny* shrimp trawler. He wears gloves because of the sharp shells. (Courtesy of Jimmy Moore.)

**Hardee Shrimp House.** In the 1950s, shrimp were plentiful, and the Southport Harbor was crowded with shrimping fleets. Lewis Hardee Sr. was appointed to the Fisheries Committee of the North Carolina Department of Conservation and warned that trouble would come to the shrimping industry because of the pollution in breeding grounds, rampant development, and overfishing. They dismissed his warning, but he began to sell his boats; today, the fleets no longer exist. (Courtesy of Lewis J. Hardee Jr.)

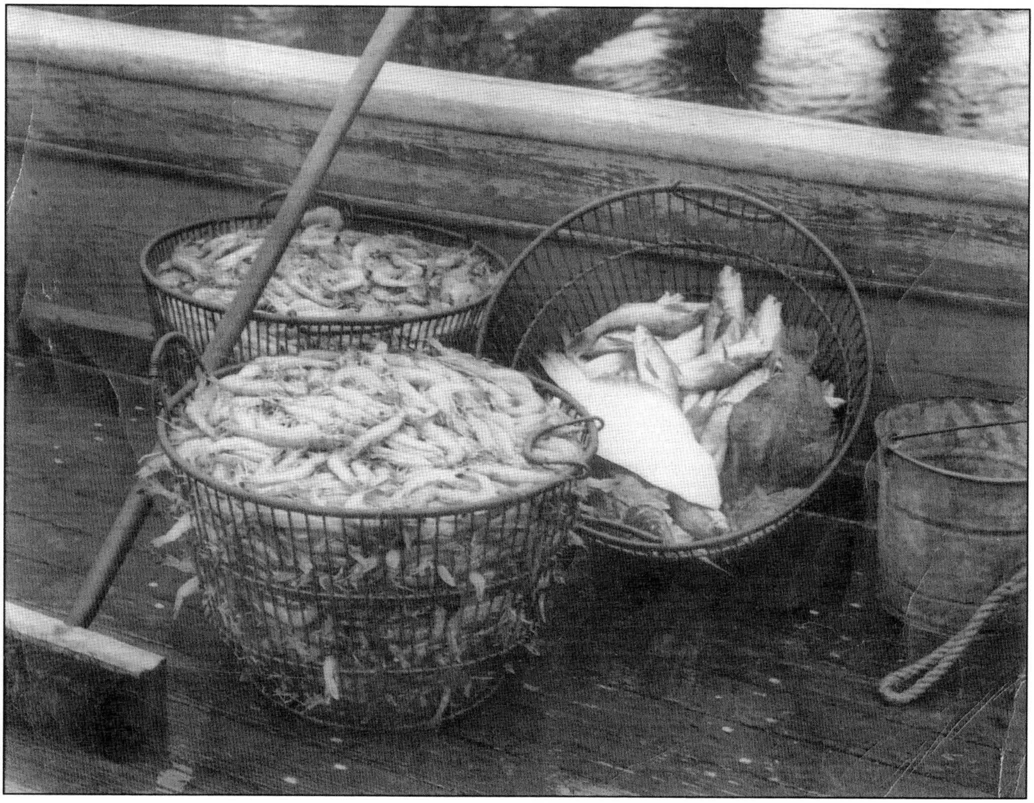

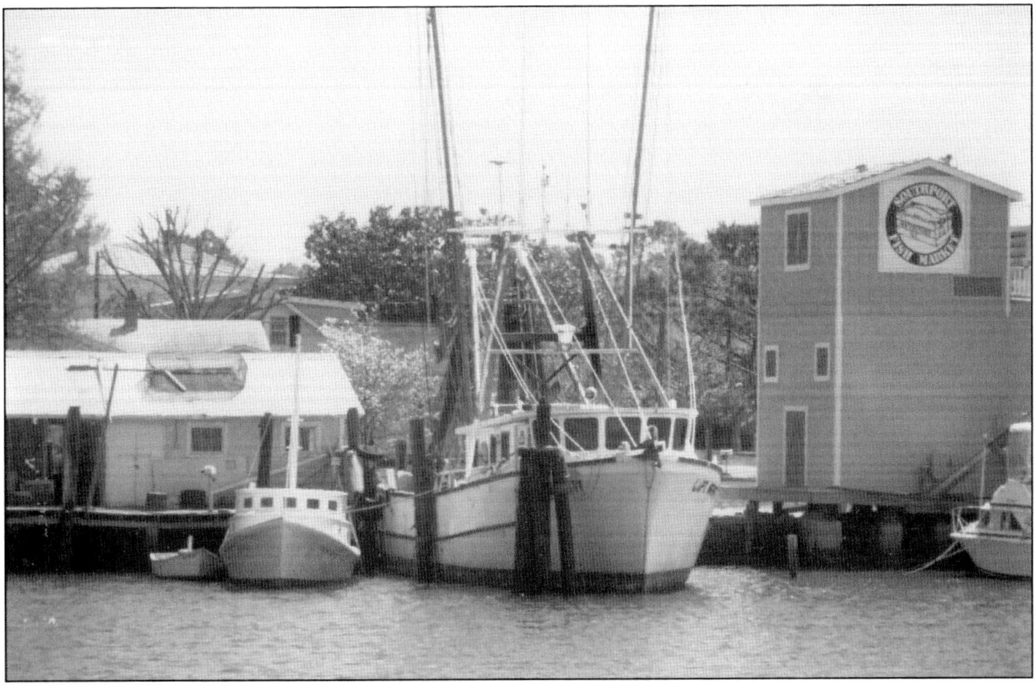

**Moore's Boats.** Boats rest at the docks in this tranquil scene. (Courtesy of Jimmy Moore.)

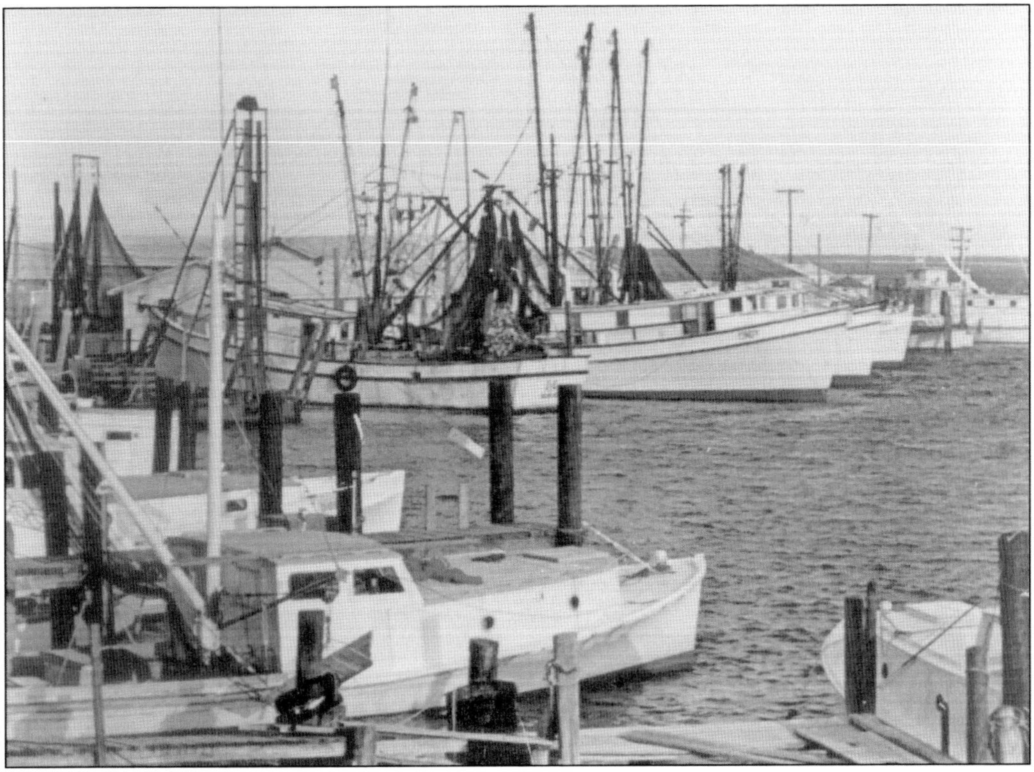

**The Old Southport Yacht Basin.** Merritt Moore's shrimp boat fleet, seen here in the 1970s, featured boats named after his grandchildren Cindy, Lindy, and Cathy. (Courtesy of Jimmy Moore.)

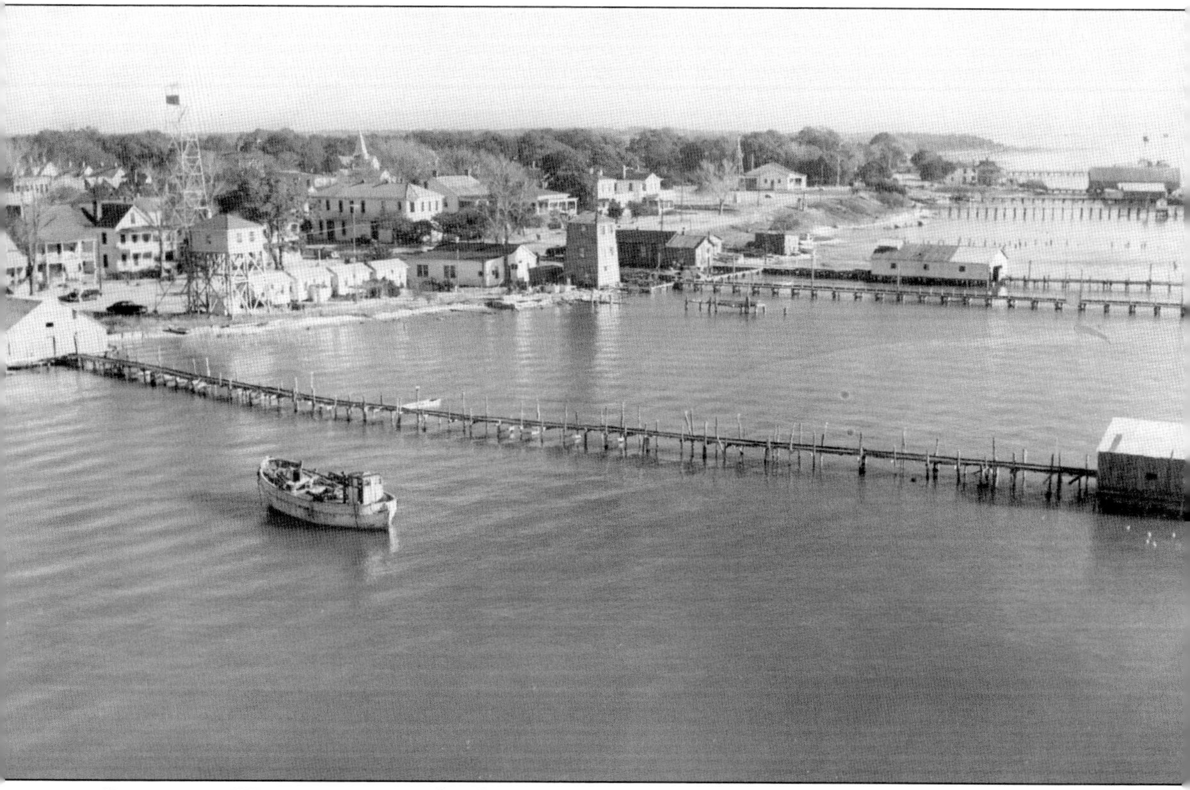

**Southport Waterfront.** On the shore in this 1950s photograph are, from left to right, the pilot tower of the Cape Fear Pilots Association, four tourist cabins, Mack's Café, and the old pilot observation tower. (Courtesy of the North Carolina State Archives.)

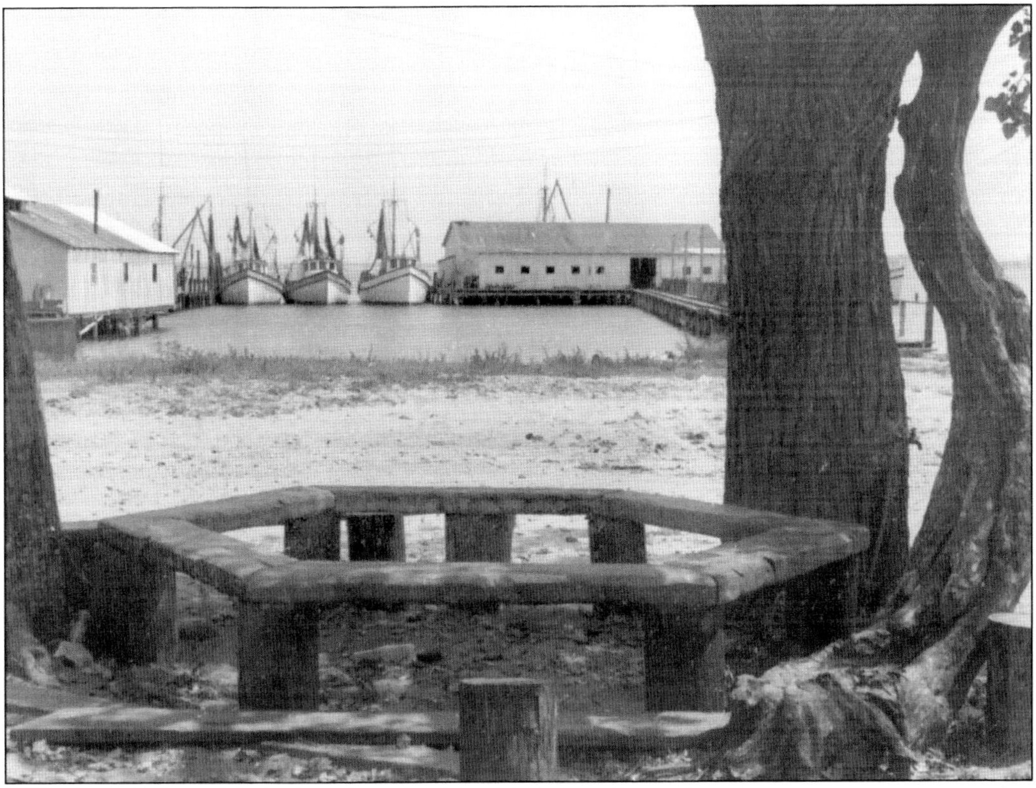

**WHITTLER'S BENCH, C. 1951.** The Hardee Shrimp House is in the distance on the right in this scene. (Courtesy of Lewis J. Hardee Jr.)

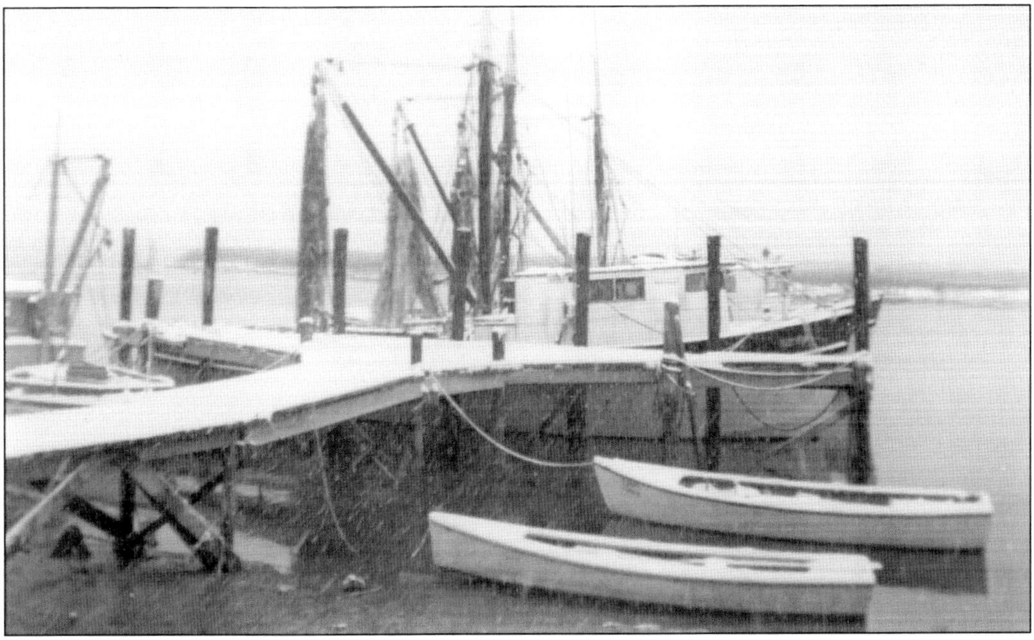

**SNOW ON THE DOCKS, 1951.** During a snowstorm in 1951, the docks were covered in a coating of snow. (Courtesy of Lewis J. Hardee Jr.)

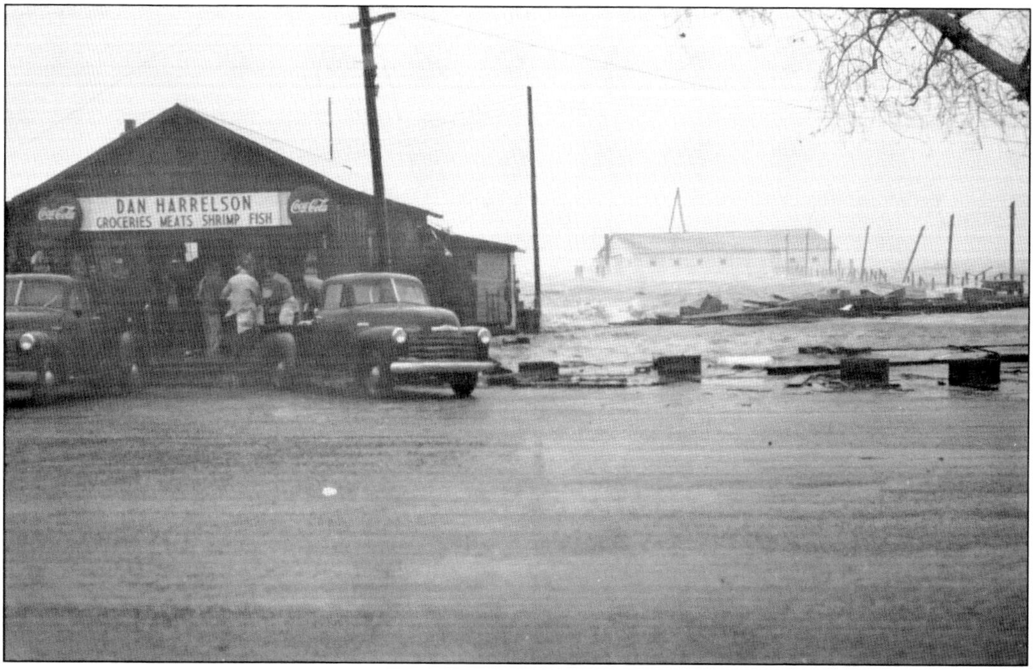


**HURRICANE HAZEL.** Hurricane Hazel came ashore near the South Carolina-North Carolina border on the morning of October 15, 1954, during a full-moon high tide. It was a deadly, costly, and powerful hurricane. Early that morning, volunteers helped to evacuate Dan Harrelson's grocery store (above) at the foot of Howe Street. After the storm passed, residents came out (below) to survey the damage. (Courtesy of Lewis J. Hardee Jr.)

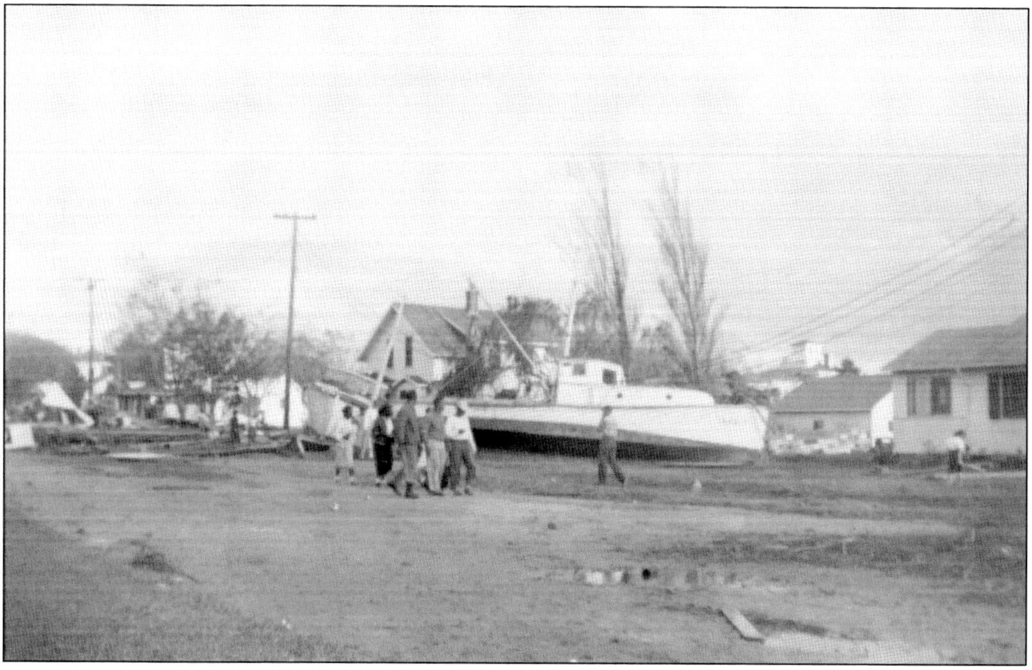

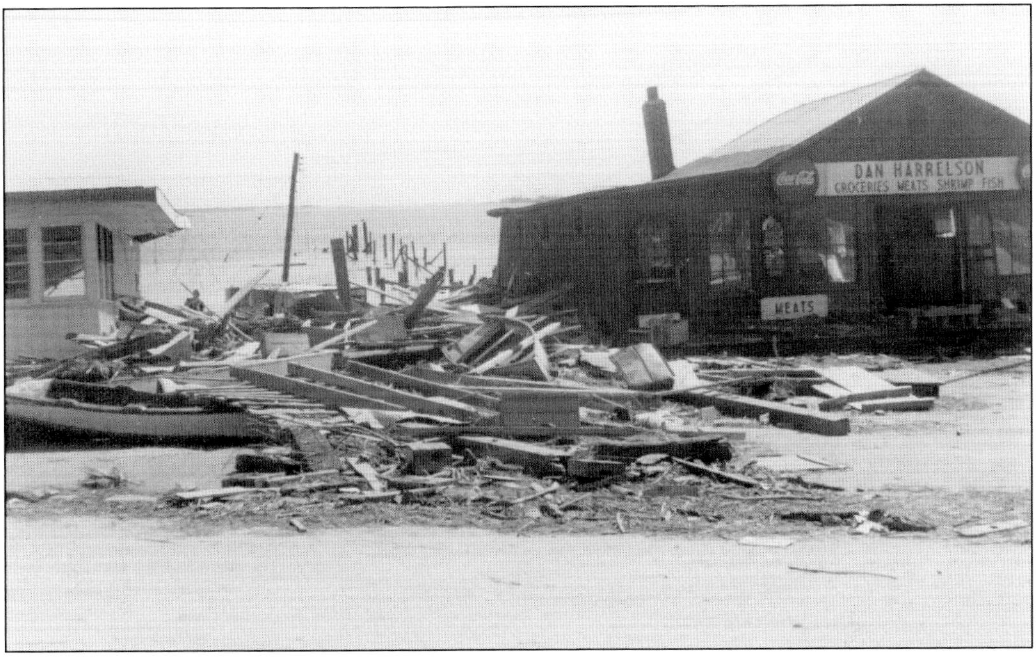


**The Morning after Hurricane Hazel.** These photographs of the docks and Dan Harrelson's grocery store after Hazel hit show the destruction of the hurricane. (Courtesy of Lewis J. Hardee Jr.)

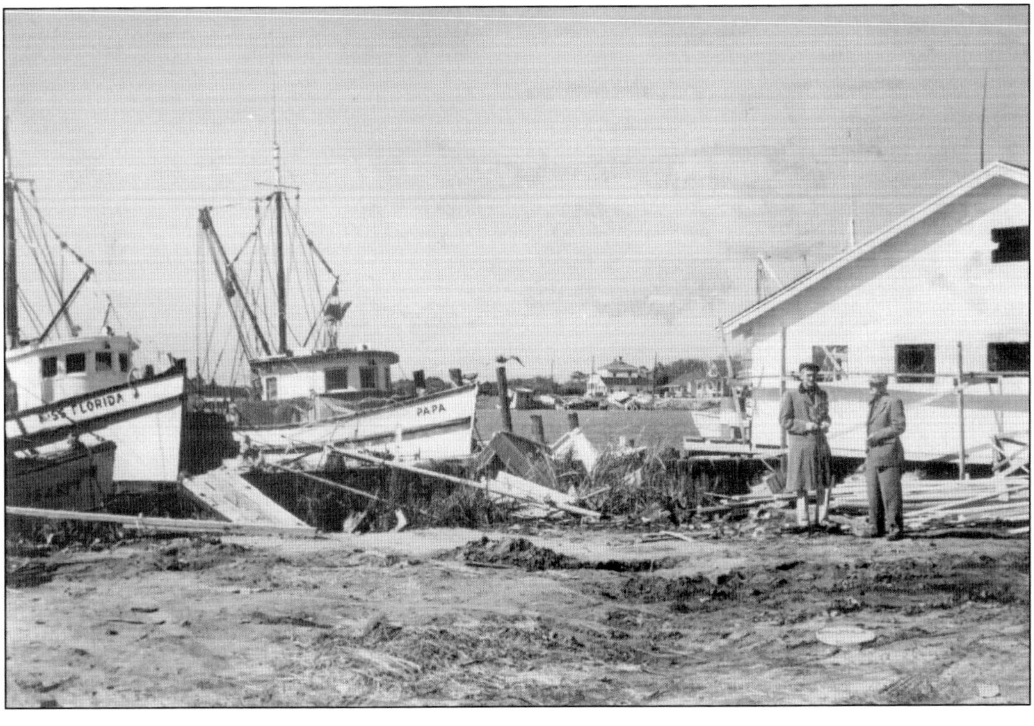

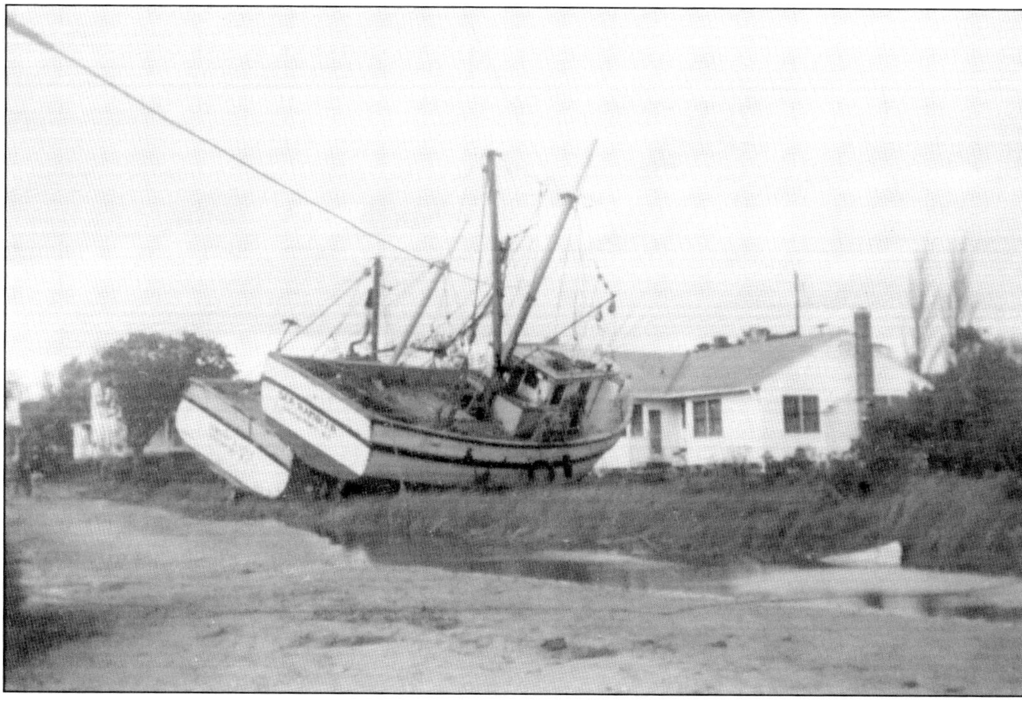

**Destructive Hurricane Hazel.** Two boats, *Dorothy & Leila* and *Sea Rambler*, came ashore a few feet from Merritt Moore's house. New docks were built after Hurricane Hazel destroyed so much of the waterfront. (Courtesy of Lewis J. Hardee Jr.)

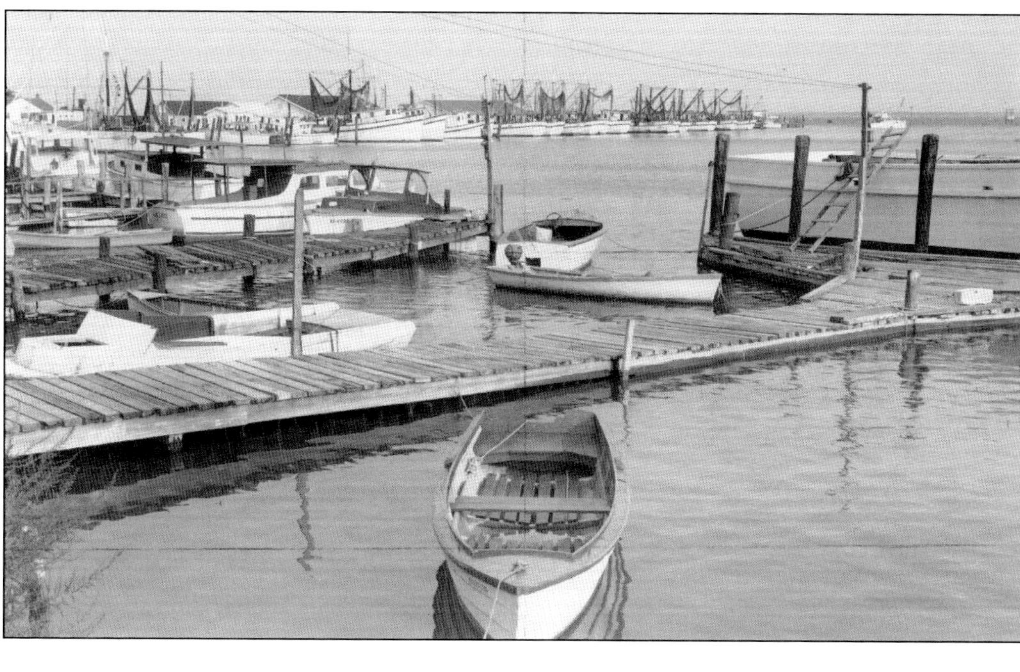

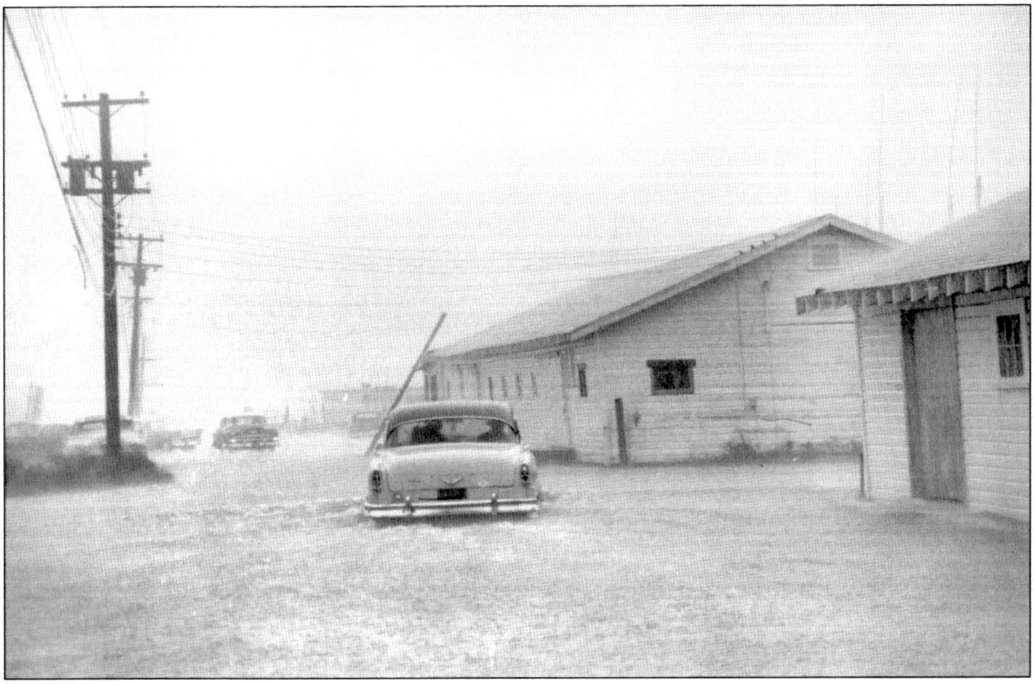

**SOUTHPORT STORM.** Severe, destructive weather is not uncommon on the coast, and this a storm that caused major flooding. (Courtesy of Lewis J. Hardee Jr.)

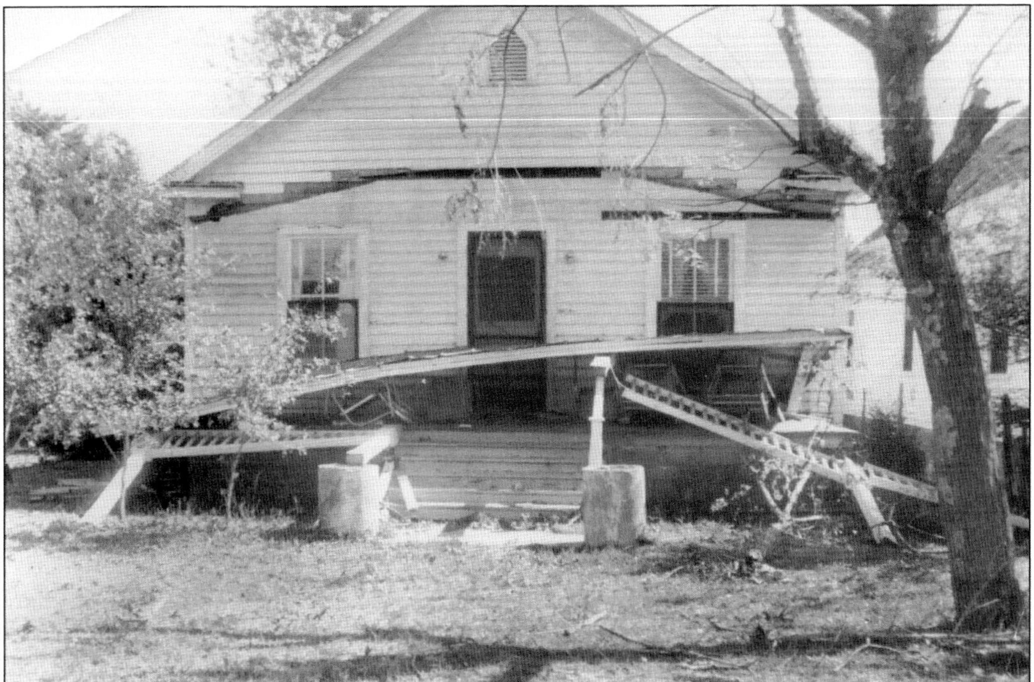

**HURRICANE HELENE, 1958.** The storm of 1957 caused major flooding in Southport. A year later, Hurricane Helene blew into town and tore the porch off of Alta Wescott Dosher's (the grandmother of Lewis J. Hardee) house on Atlantic Avenue. (Courtesy of Lewis J. Hardee Jr.)

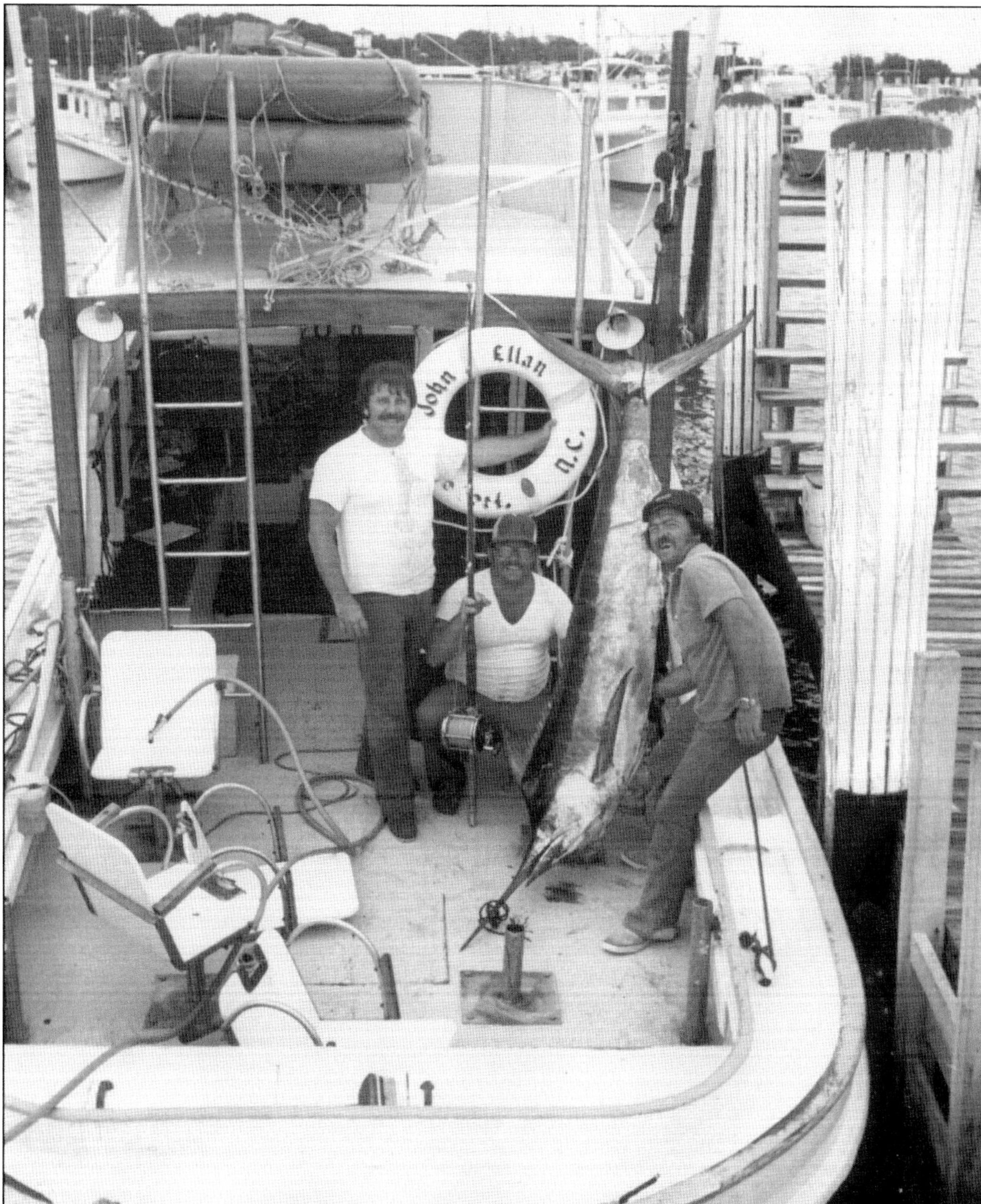


**Rescue Mission.** From left to right, Ralph Freeman, Marty Martin, and Charlie Perry pose aboard the *John Ellan* with a huge marlin they caught in a fishing tournament. During the tournament, another boat, the *Martha Ellan* went down offshore, prompting the trio to rescue eight men out of the water. Leaving the tournament caused them to be disqualified, but they were presented with a plaque recognizing their bravery for the rescue. Charlie Perry owns the American Fish Company and has been in the marine construction business for over 30 years. (Courtesy of Charlie Perry.)

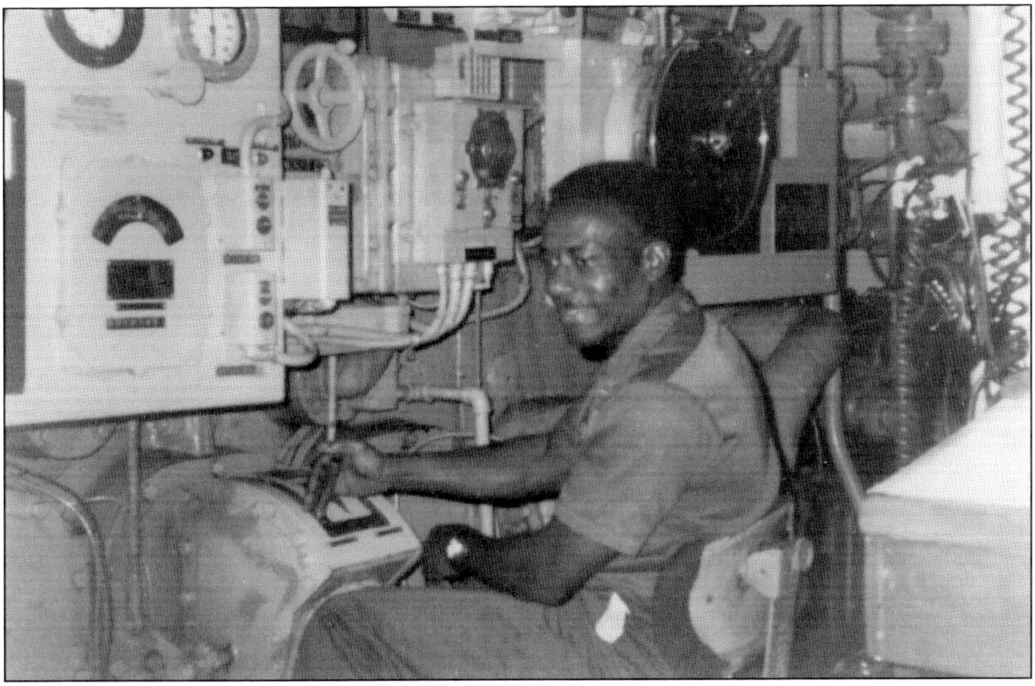

**Engineer Operating a Tugboat.** Southport native Tom L. Frink, an Army veteran of the Korean War, was hired as a deckhand aboard one of the Army tugboats at the Military Ocean Terminal–Sunny Point (MOTSU) in 1967. After two years of study, he earned an assistant engineer rating. He lost his job in July 1976 due to a workforce reduction but was back at MOTSU three months later as a security guard and patrol boat operator. He obtained his US Coast Guard board operator license and was back on a tug in 1985 as an assistant engineer. He now holds a Coast Guard assistant engineer license. Below is the Sunny Point Army tugboat from around 1955. (Courtesy of Tom L. Frink.)

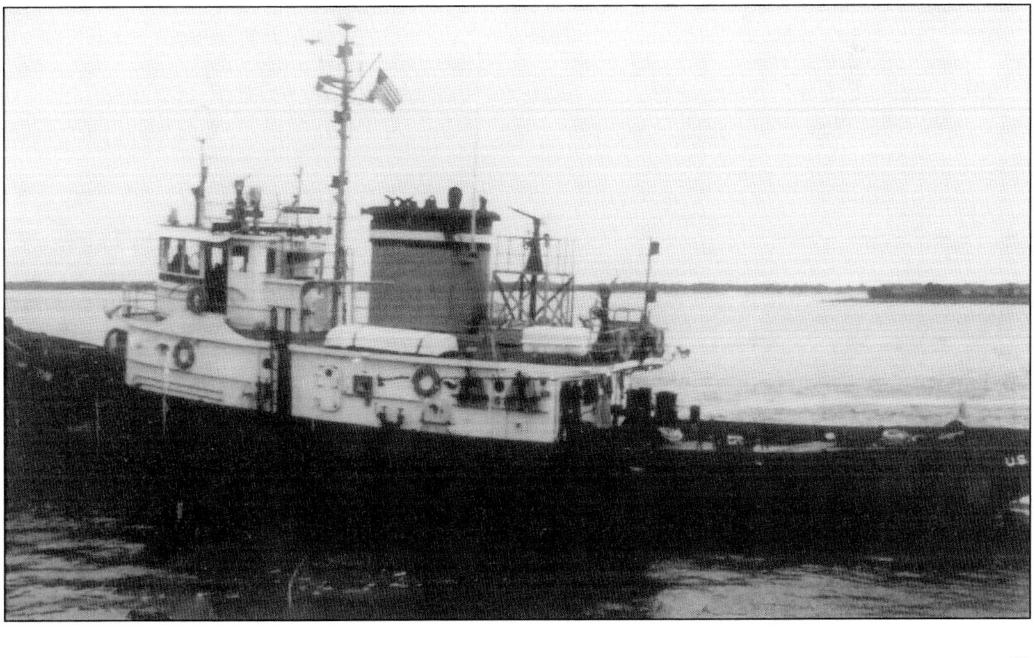

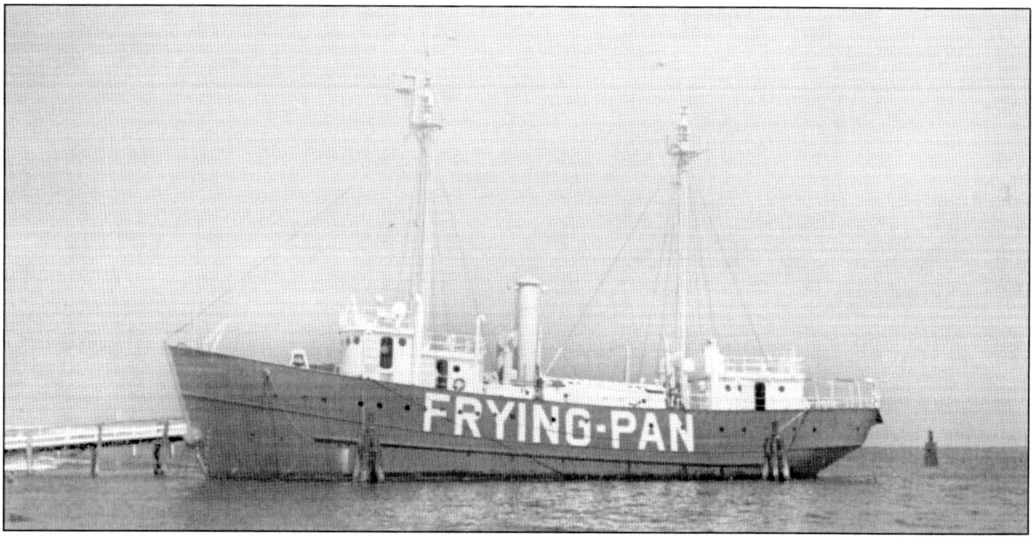


**Frying Pan Lightship.** The *Frying Pan* lightship arrived at the Southport waterfront in October 1967 and was to be converted into a nautical museum. It was stationed at the foot of Howe Street and was later replaced by a light tower. (Courtesy of Norfrette Bellamy.)

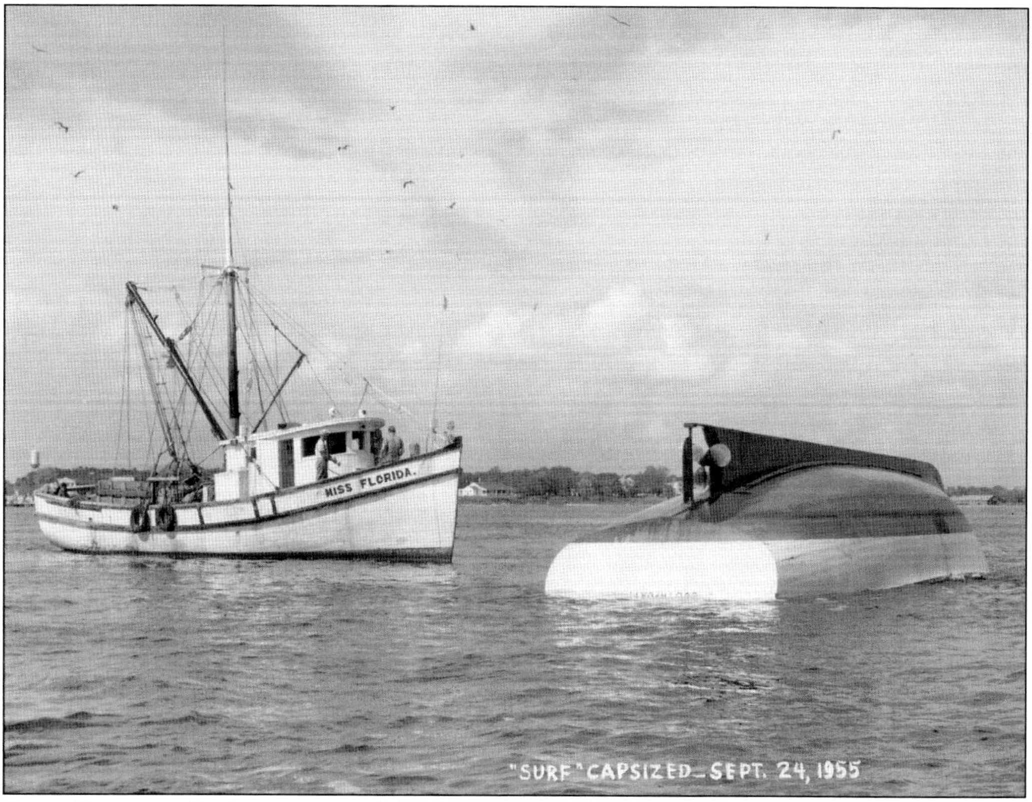


**Surf, Capsized.** *Surf* was a part of the fifth and final fleet of the Lewis Hardee Sr. boats. In September 1955, the new boat caught an anchor in its net at Battery Island, and the strong river current caused the boat to capsize. There were no injuries, and the next day a diver from Wilmington helped to right it. (Courtesy of Lewis J. Hardee Jr.)

# *Three*

# SCHOOL MEMORIES

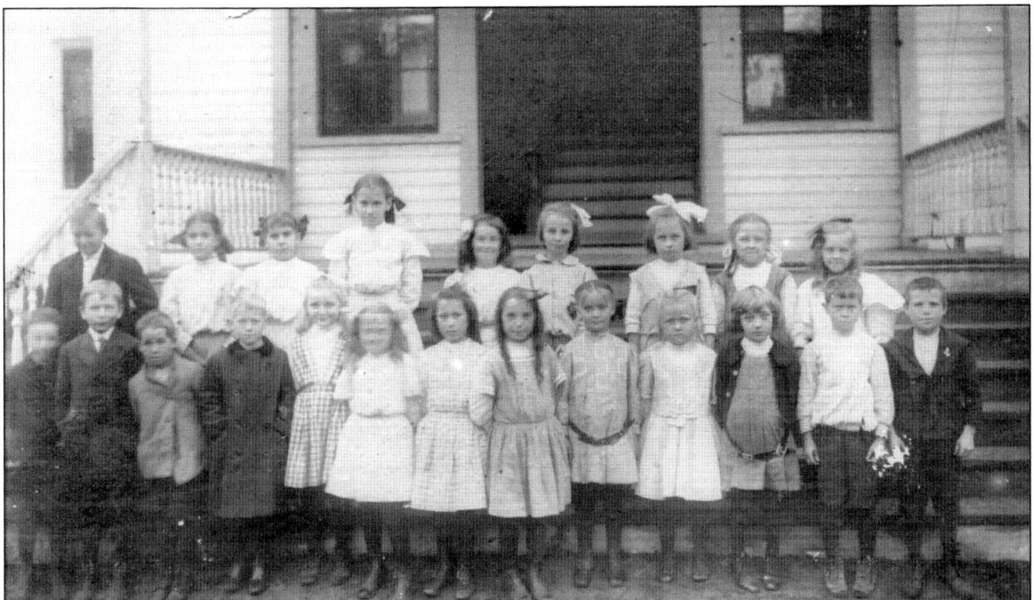

**ELEMENTARY STUDENTS.** This 1908 class picture was taken in front of the art gallery building. (Courtesy of Andrea P. Clemmons.)

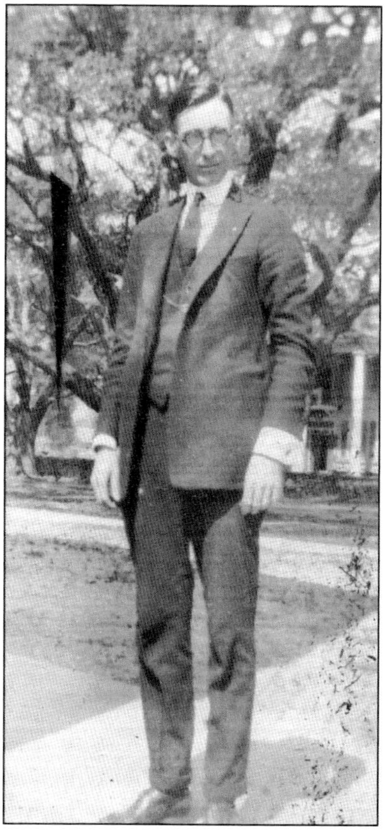

**THE PRINCIPAL.** H.D. Smith was the principal of Southport High School in 1923. (Courtesy of Andrea P. Clemmons.)

**SOUTHPORT HIGH SCHOOL JUNIOR CLASS, 1923.** Before the new brick building was constructed on Nash Street, Southport High School students had a picture taken at the Masonic Building (Army-Navy Club building) next to the Methodist church. (Courtesy of Andrea P. Clemmons.)

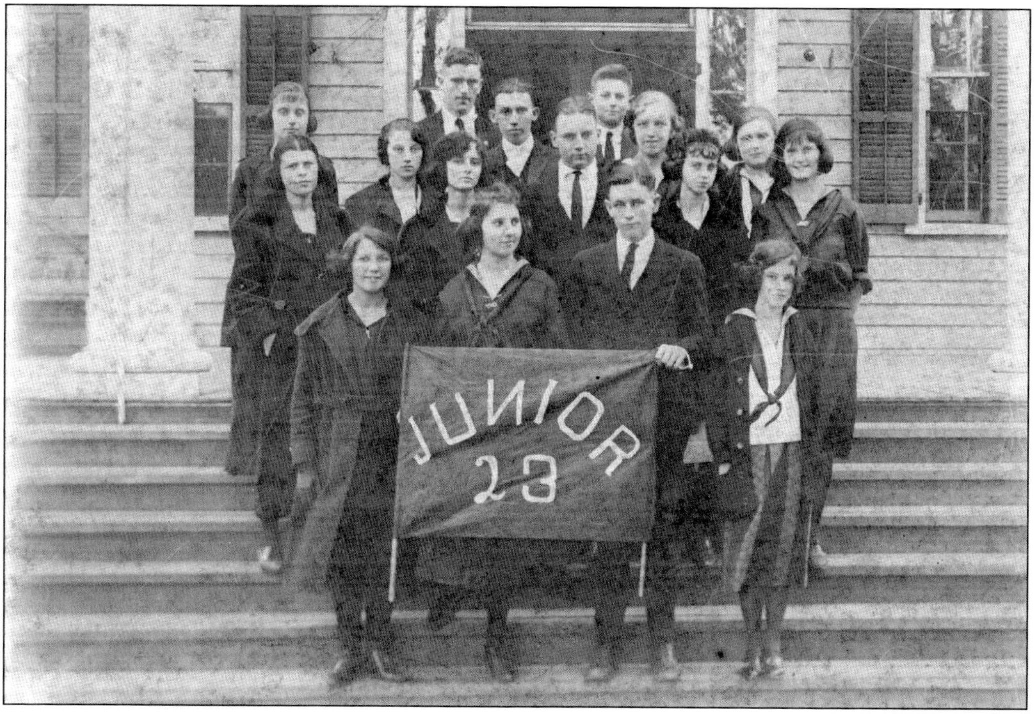

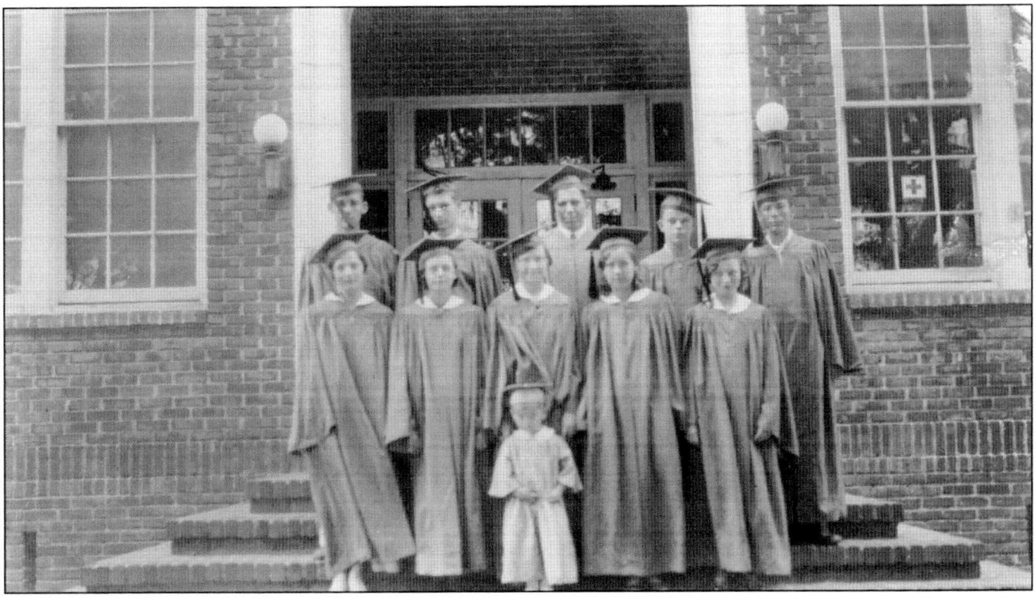

**Southport High School Graduating Class, 1932.** This class included, from left to right, (front row) Jessie Mae Russ, Dorothy Dosher, Catherine Fullwood, Gertrude Holden, and Eunice Larsen; (second row) Farnk Niernsee, Ike Robinson, Reggie Drew, Joe Jelks, and Billie Price; little Billy Bowling was the class mascot. (Courtesy of Lewis J. Hardee Jr.)

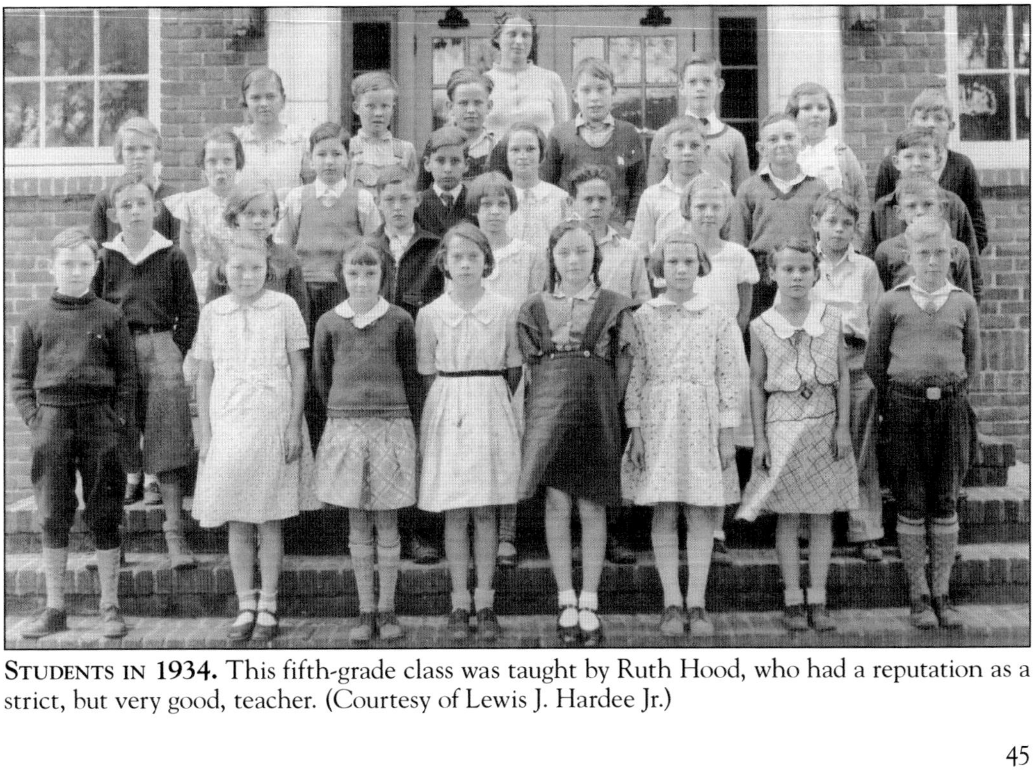

**Students in 1934.** This fifth-grade class was taught by Ruth Hood, who had a reputation as a strict, but very good, teacher. (Courtesy of Lewis J. Hardee Jr.)

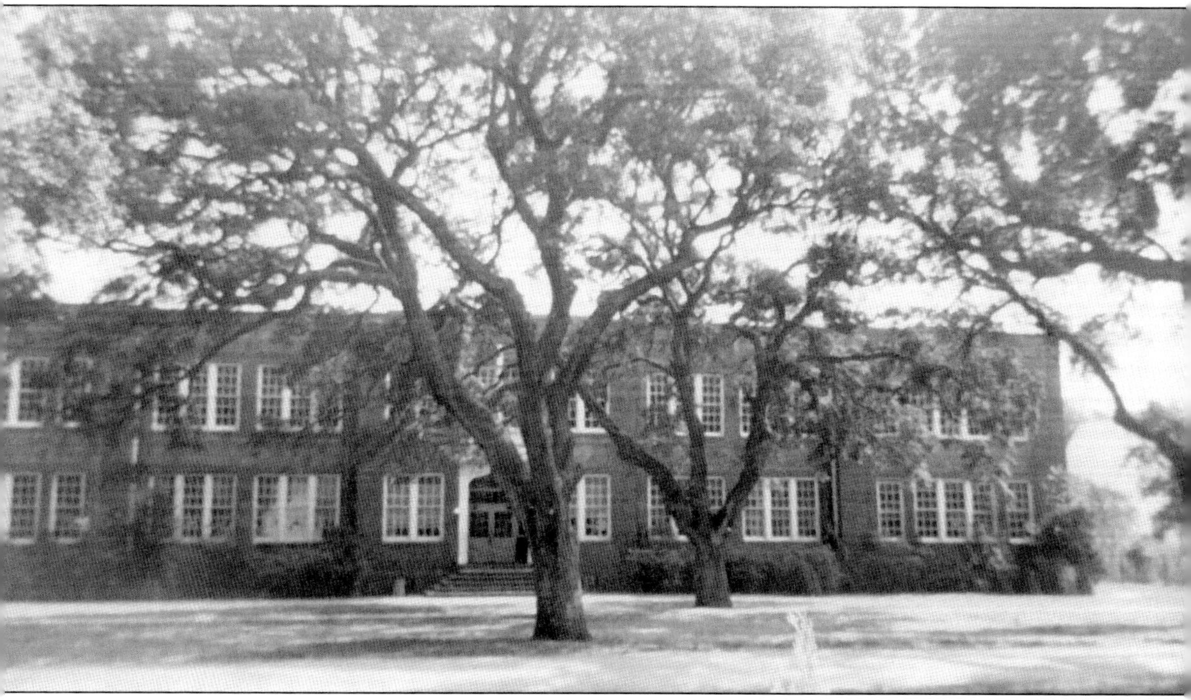

**SOUTHPORT HIGH SCHOOL.** The school was built in 1922. It was called a high school even though it included grades 1 through 12. After the school was destroyed by fire in 1969, many of the white students attended the black high school, Brunswick County Training School (BCTS). Today, the post office stands on the site of the former Southport High School. (Courtesy of Andrea P. Clemmons.)

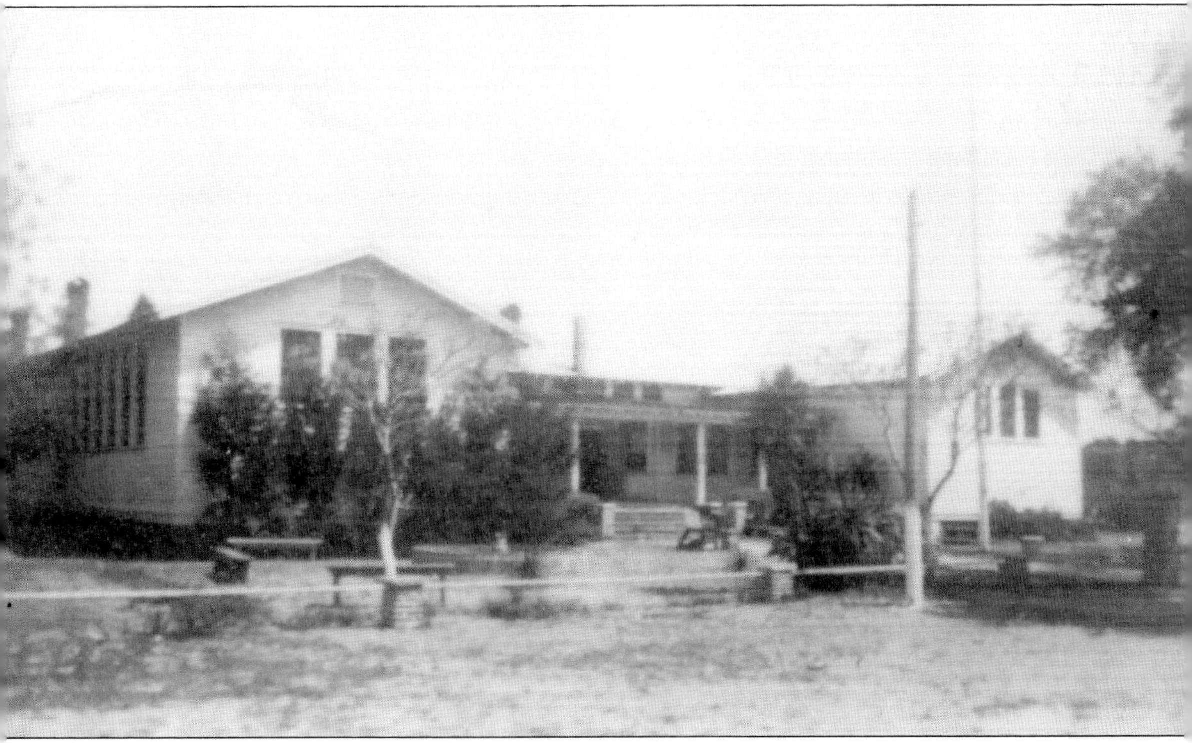

**Brunswick County Training School.** The Brunswick County Training School, a high school for blacks, was established on Lord Street in the fall of 1925, with Alvin C. Caviness as principal. In the late 1960s, BCTS remained the only school in the county offering 12 grades to black students. (Courtesy of Sarah P. Joyner.)

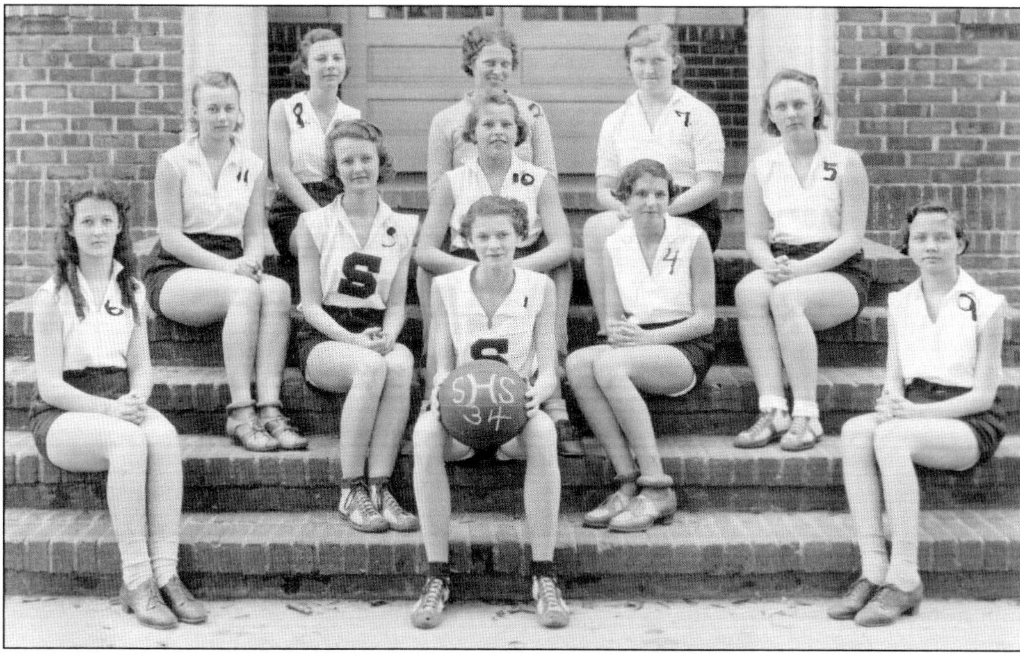


**1934 Southport High School Girls' Basketball Team.** Posing for the team picture are, from left to right, (first row) Lois Jane Bussels, Lib Watson, and Josephine Smith; (second row) Helen Rourk, Leila Hubbard, Earline Rogers, Marion Norment, and Evelyn Loughlin; (third row) Maybelle Reynolds, Ruth Hood, and Mary Holiday. (Courtesy of Lewis J. Hardee Jr.)

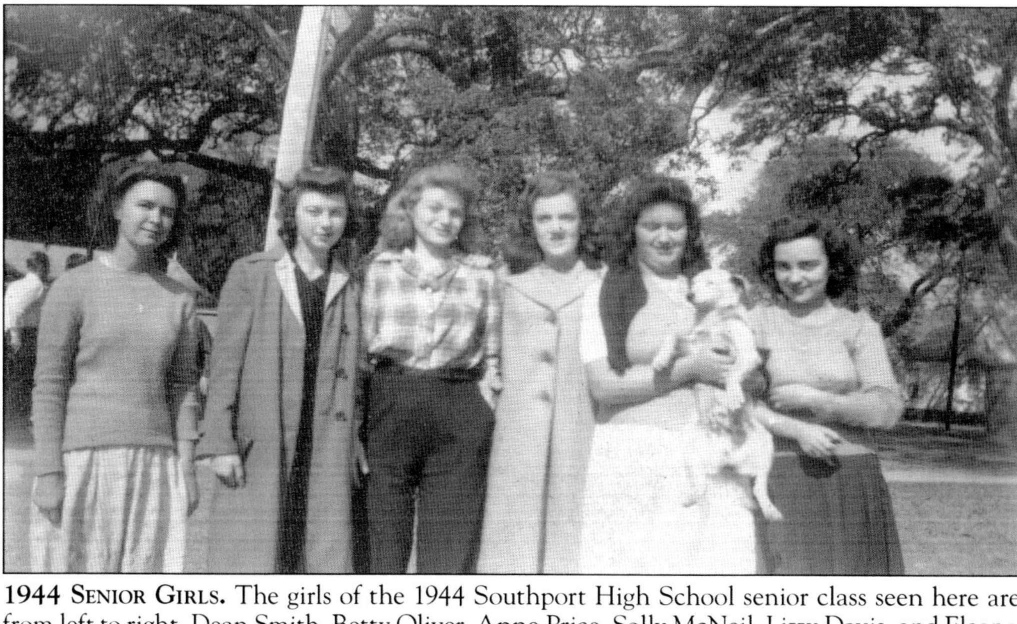

**1944 Senior Girls.** The girls of the 1944 Southport High School senior class seen here are, from left to right, Dean Smith, Betty Oliver, Anne Price, Sally McNeil, Lizzy Davis, and Eleanor Reese. (Courtesy of Andrea P. Clemmons.)

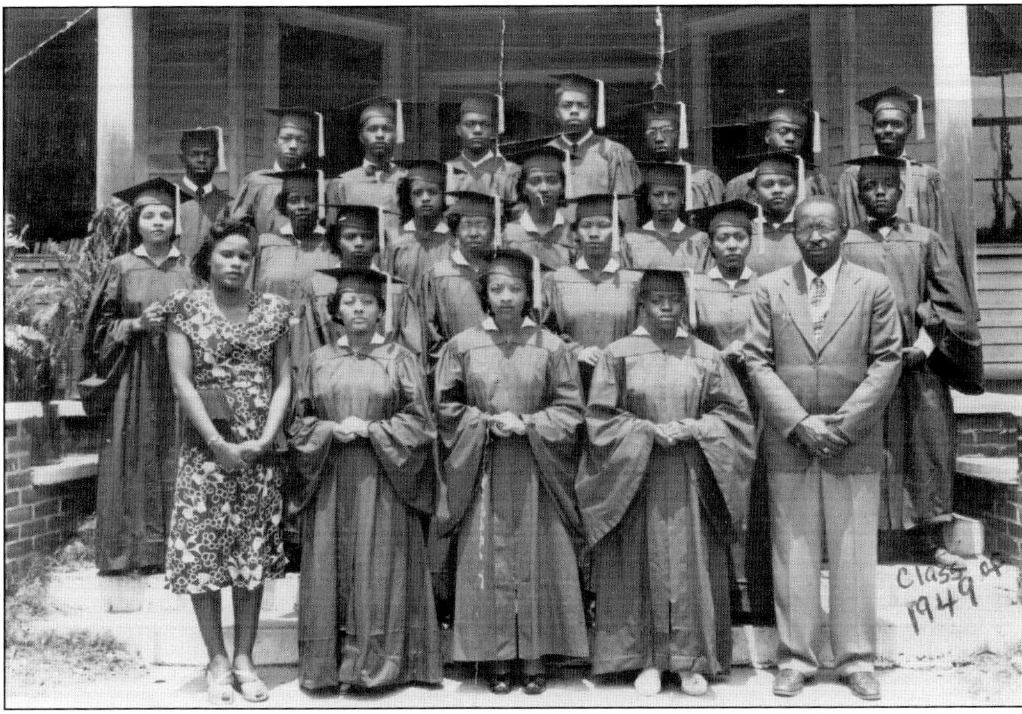


**CLASS OF 1949.** This is the senior class of Brunswick County Training School. Principal Caviness is in the first row on the far right, and Marjorie Clemmons is in the center of the first row. (Courtesy of Marjorie Clemmons.)

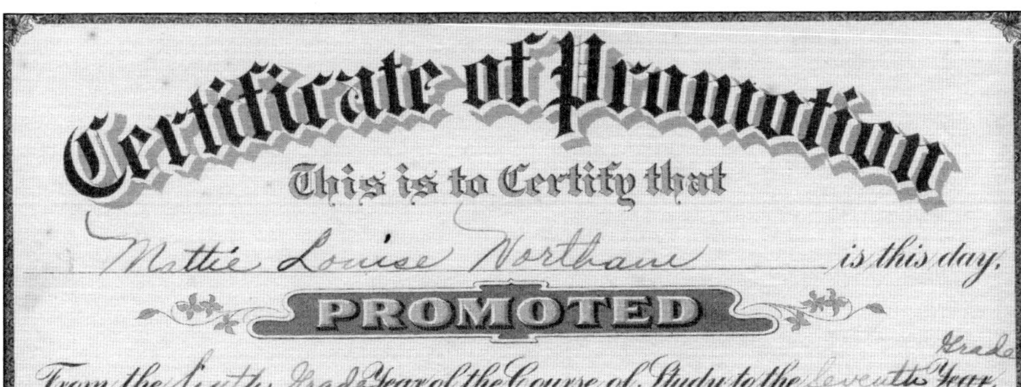

Certificate of Promotion

This is to Certify that

Mattie Louise Northam is this day,

PROMOTED

From the Sixth Grade Year of the Course of Study to the Seventh Grade Year.

Dated at B. C. T. S. this 27th day of May 1927

James W. Barbour Jr. Principal

Pocahontas O. Brown Teacher.

**PROMOTED TO THE SEVENTH GRADE.** This certificate shows the promotion of Mattie Louis Wortham from the sixth grade to the seventh grade at Brunswick County Training School on May 27, 1927. (Sharon Claudette Smith.)

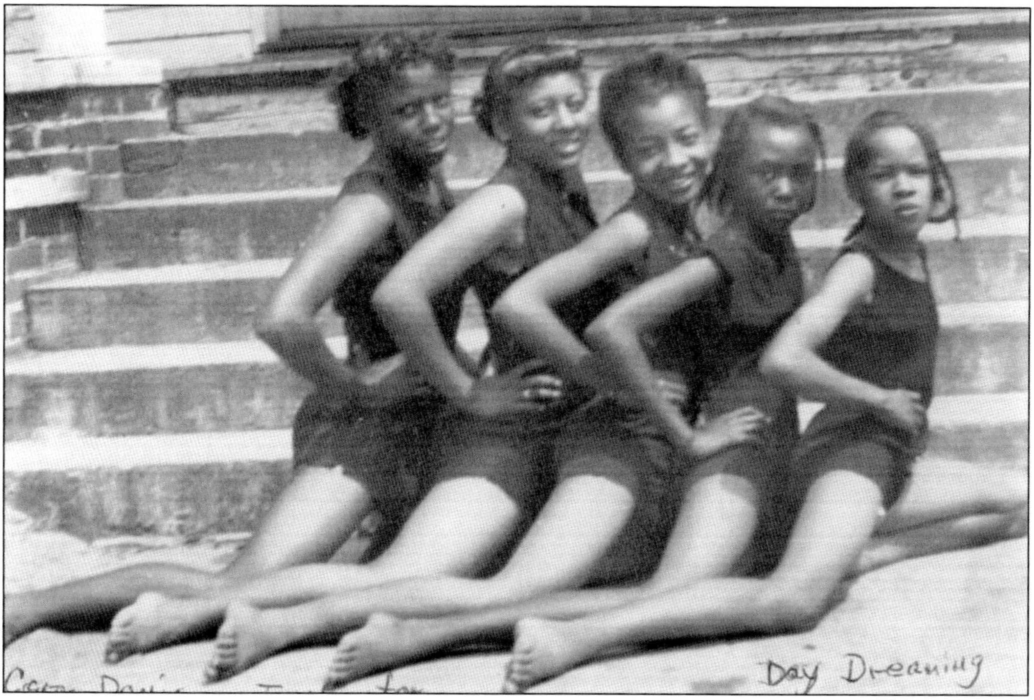


**DAYDREAMING.** Cora Mebane's BCTS dance group from the 1940s included, from left to right, Faye Ray Brown, Anna Mae Eagles, Marjorie Clemmons, Deloris Green, and Ernestine Clemmons. (Courtesy of Marjorie Clemmons.)

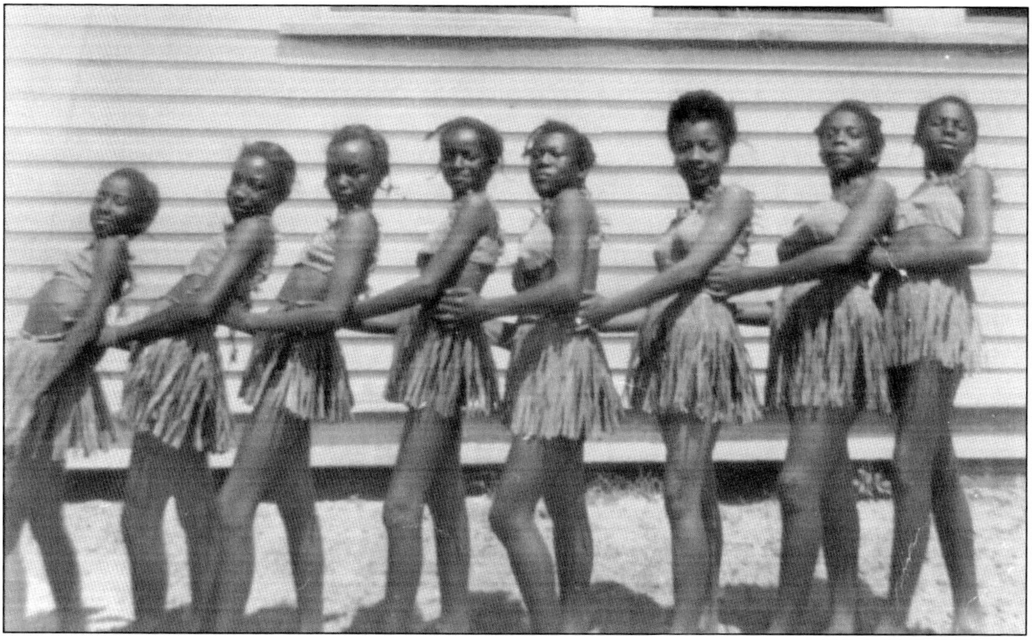

**BRUNSWICK COUNTY TRAINING SCHOOL DANCE GROUP.** Another of Cora Mebane's dance groups from the 1940s included, from left to right, Carleen Jackson, Louise Williams Davis, Anna Mae Eagles, Odessa Jackson, Peggy Parker, Marjorie Clemmons, Rose McAfee, and Rosa Galloway. (Courtesy of Marjorie Clemmons.)

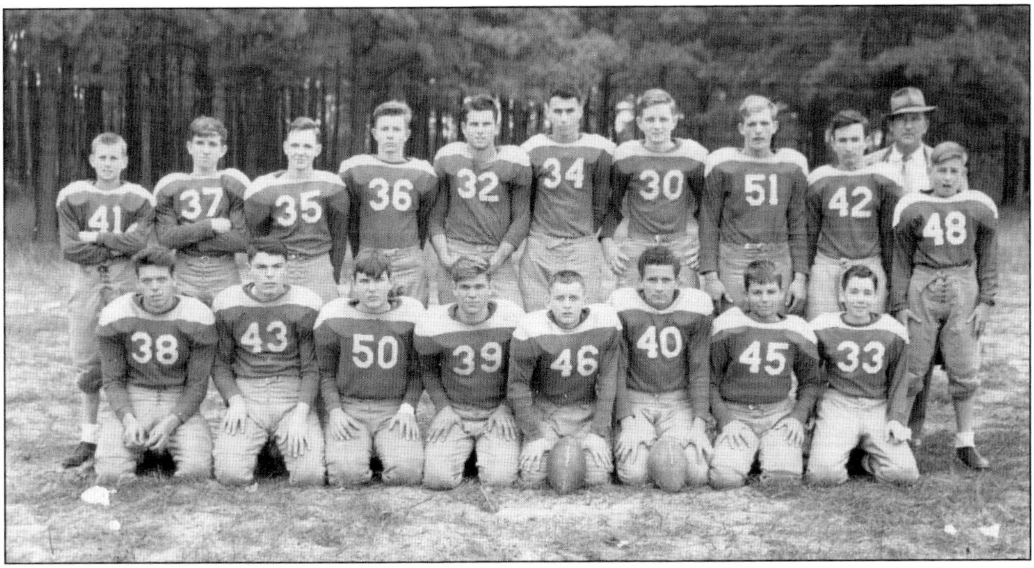


**SOUTHPORT HIGH SCHOOL FOOTBALL TEAM.** The 1950 team included, from left to right, (first row) Boyce Spencer, Myrle Muncy, Roy Daniel, Abbie Dosher, Ronnie Brunson, Gene Watts, Dillian Webb, and Jack Russ; (second row) Joe Cochran, Richard Dosher, Red Ward, Sonny Hickman, Doug Watts, Ronnie Hood, Coopie Burriss, Jerry Spencer, Billy Cullis, Ralph Molicheck, and coach H.J. Sanders. (Courtesy of Trudy M. Young.)

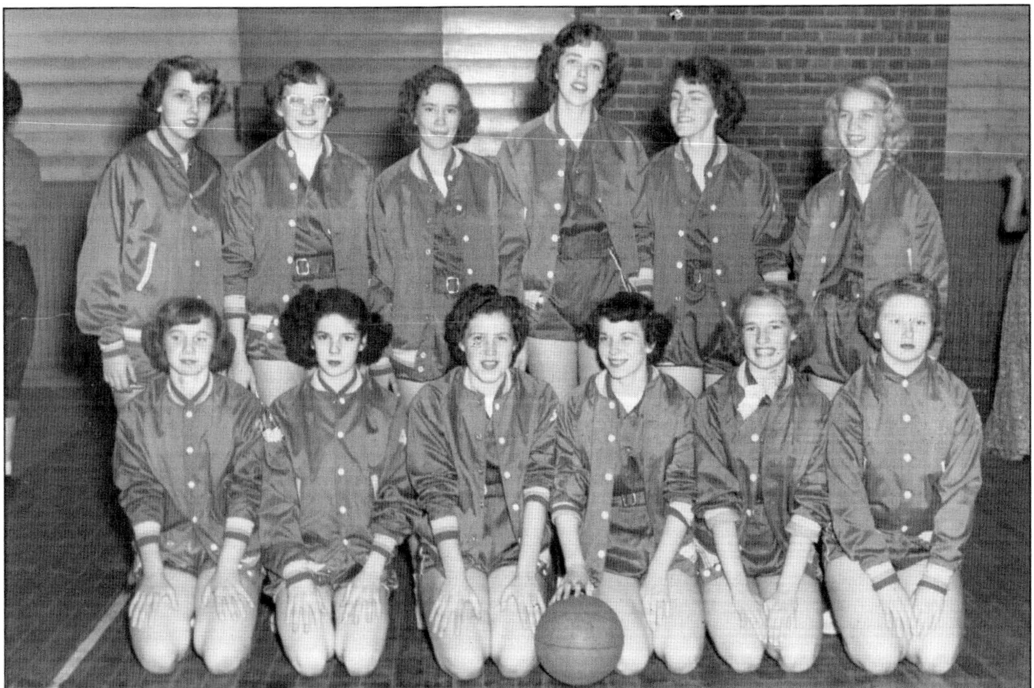

**SOUTHPORT HIGH SCHOOL GIRLS' BASKETBALL TEAM, 1950.** This team included, from left to right, (first row) Latitia Hickman, Sylvia Floyd, Jacque Larsen, Janice Trunnel, Remona Williamson, and Tillie Thorsen; (second row) Nancy Swan, Stuart Arrington, Alice Brown, Trudy McNeil, Julia Smith, and ? Potter. (Courtesy of Trudy M. Young.)

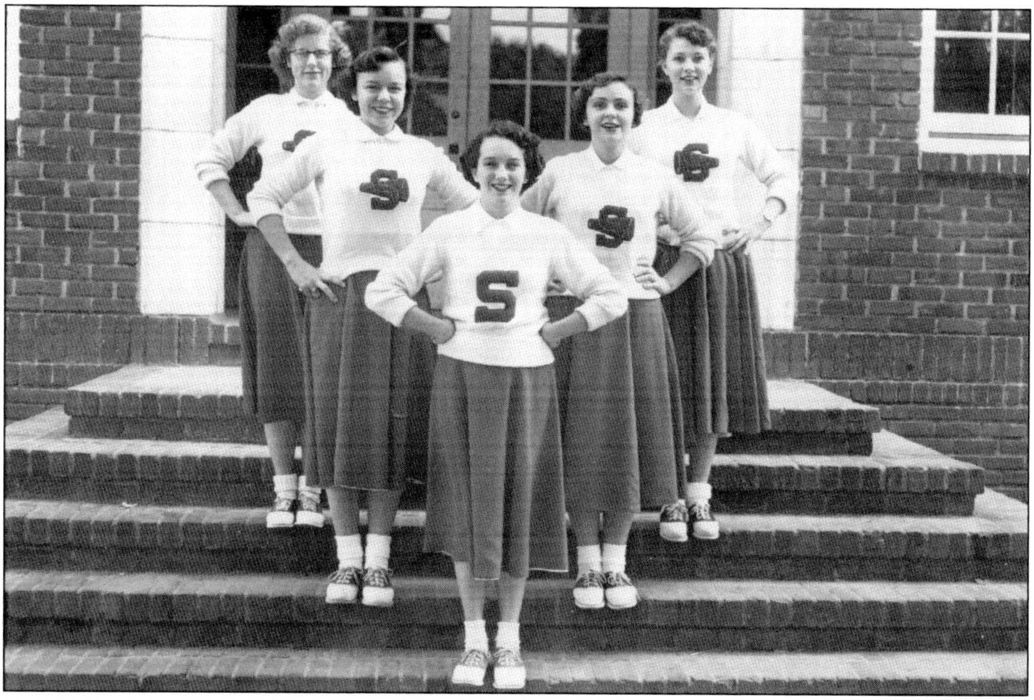

**Cheerleaders.** These young ladies cheered for Southport High School during the 1952–1953 school year. (Courtesy of Trudy M. Young.)

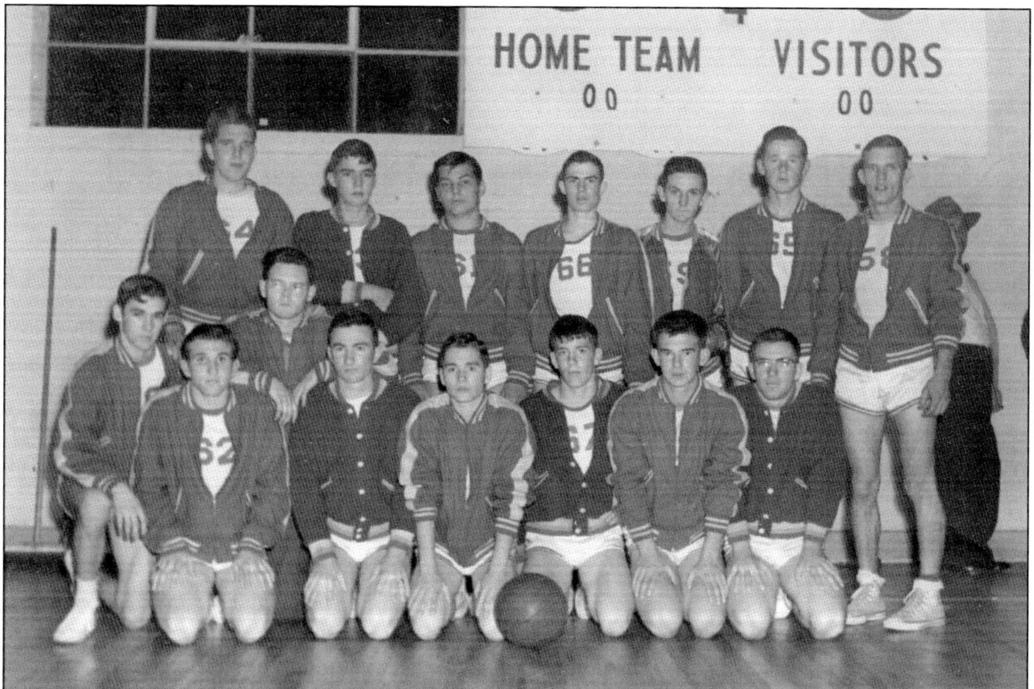


**Southport High School Boys Basketball Team, 1952–1953.** Joe Young, the husband of Trudy M. Young, is in the back row, second from the right. (Courtesy of Trudy M. Young.)

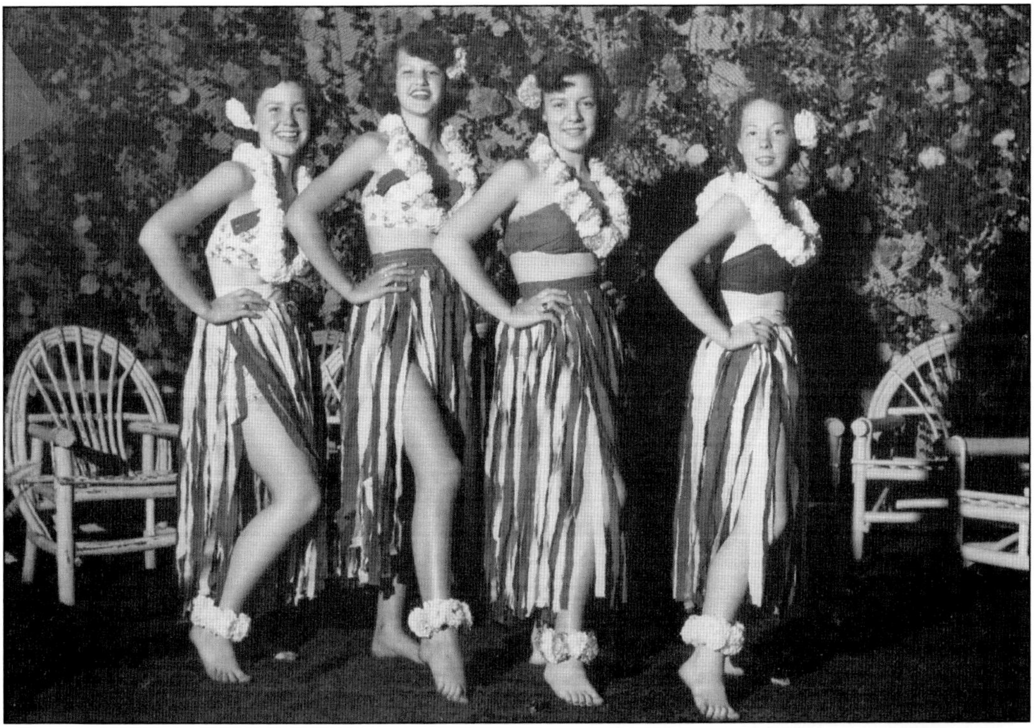

**Hula Girls.** Southport High School Class Night, a program held at the school the night before graduation, is shown here in 1953. Trudy McNeil sang "A Little Grass Shack in Hawaii" while the junior class girls danced the hula. Students wore their Junior-Senior Banquet (now known as prom) dresses and suits. The seniors marched down the aisle and up to the stage as the juniors stood on each side of the aisle holding long ropes of flowers and singing " 'Tis May the Month of Roses." From left to right are Jacque Larsen, Libby Caster, Barbara Johnson, and Omega Ward. (Courtesy of Trudy M. Young.)

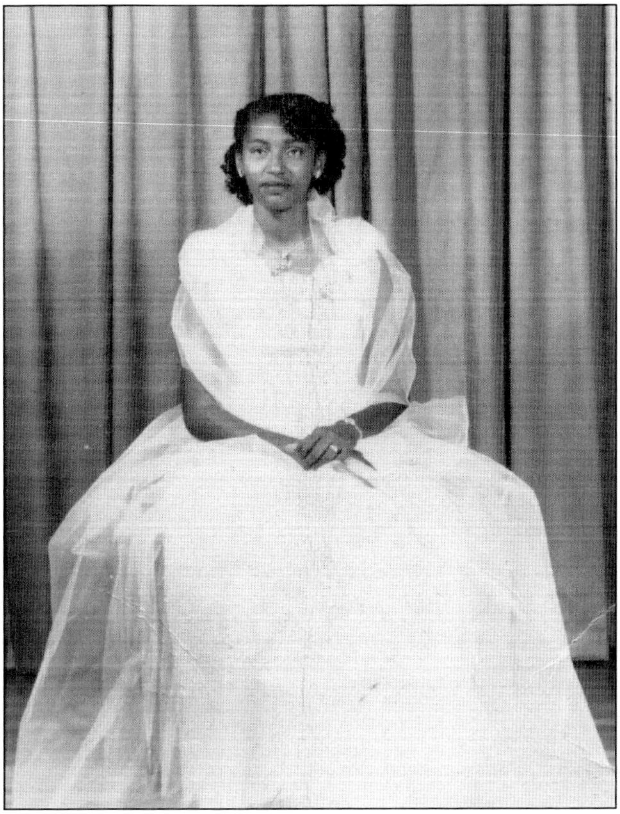

**Brunswick County Training School Prom, 1952.** Rebecca Brown poses at the Junior-Senior Prom held in the gymnasium at Brunswick County Training School. (Courtesy of Rebecca B. Smith.)

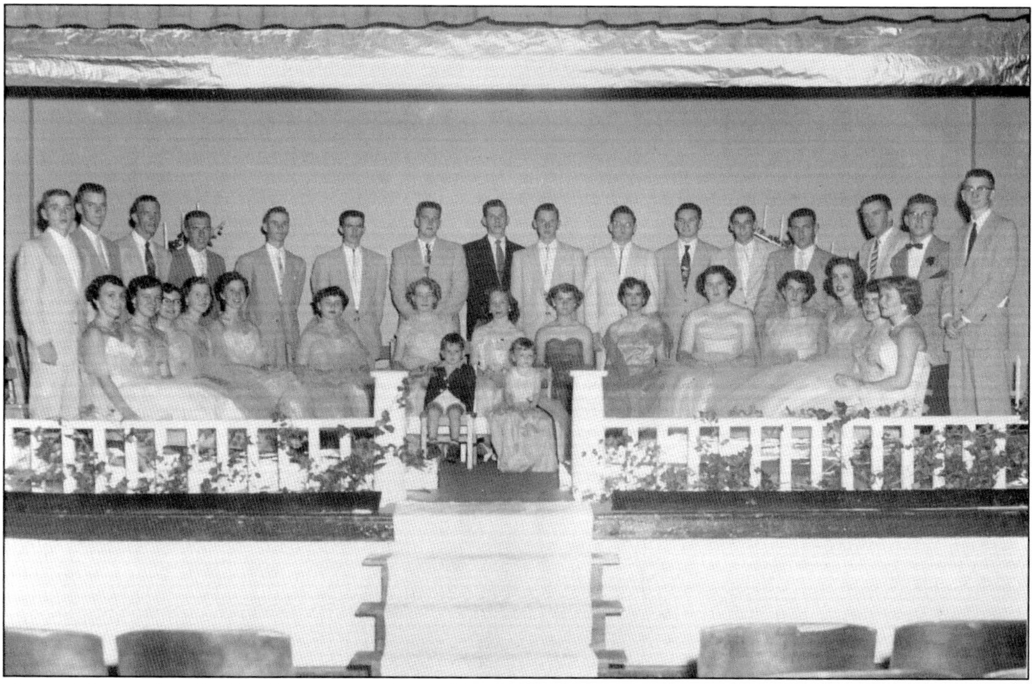

**Class Night.** Trudy McNeil is seated third from the right, and Joe Young is standing eighth from the right at the 1954 Southport High School Class Night. (Courtesy of Trudy M. Young.)

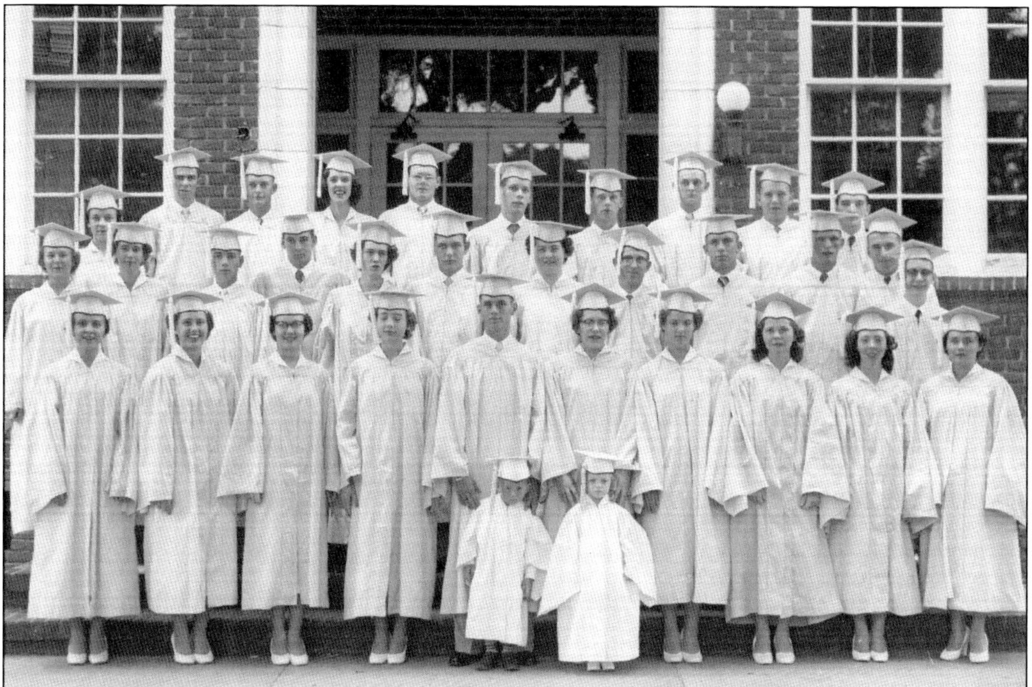

**Graduating Class, 1954.** This Southport High School senior class photograph includes Trudy McNeil in the back row, third from the left, and Joe Young in the back row, fourth from the right. (Courtesy of Trudy M. Young.)

**PRINCIPAL AND SECRETARY.** A.C. Caviness was principal of the Brunswick County Training School for 41 years and was dedicated to providing quality education to all students. Malissa Brown worked as his secretary and later retired from the US Postal Service. She married Kenneth Bellamy and together they had four children. (Courtesy of Sarah P. Joyner.)

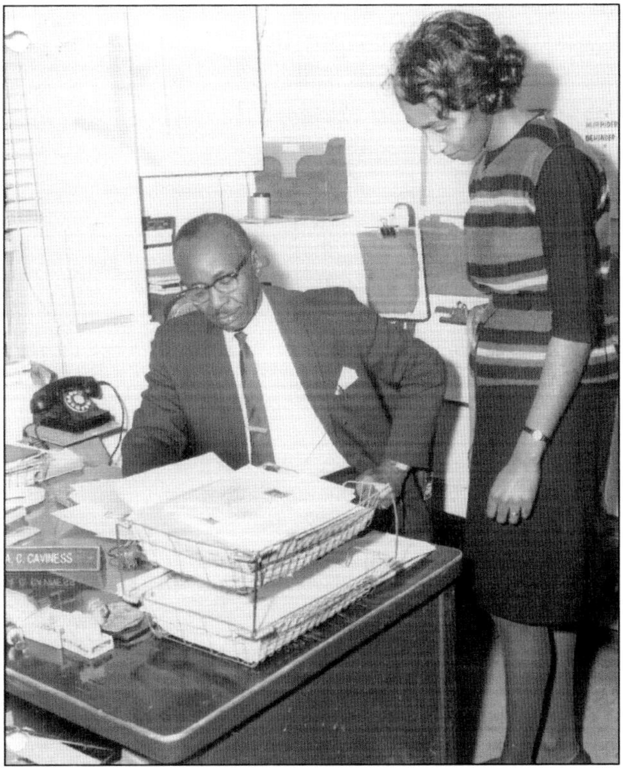


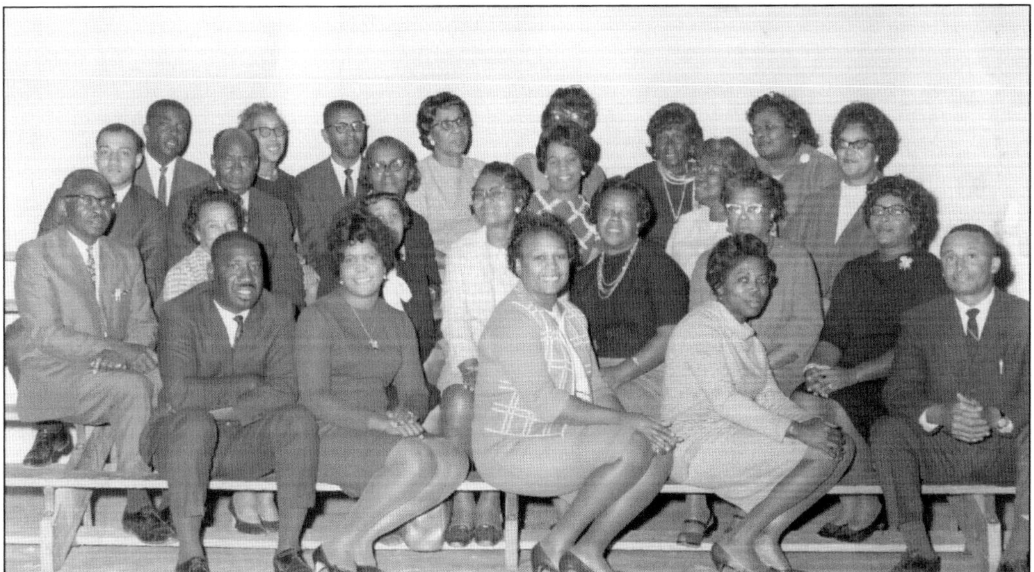

**BRUNSWICK COUNTY TRAINING SCHOOL FACULTY.** The faculty pictured here includes, from left to right, (first row) Mr. Davis, Mrs. Miller, Mrs. Mitchell, Mrs. Gore, and Mr. Francis; (second row) principal Caviness, Mrs. Clemmons, Mrs. Swain, two unidentified, Mrs. Price, and Mrs. Bryant; (third row) Mr. Parker, Mr. Green, Mrs. Horton, Mrs. Parker, Mrs. Breelove, and Mrs. Sidberry; (fourth row) Mr. Evans, Mrs. Mebane, Mr. Frink, Mrs. Green, Mrs. Young, Mrs. Caviness, and Mrs. Davis. (Courtesy of Sarah P. Joyner.)

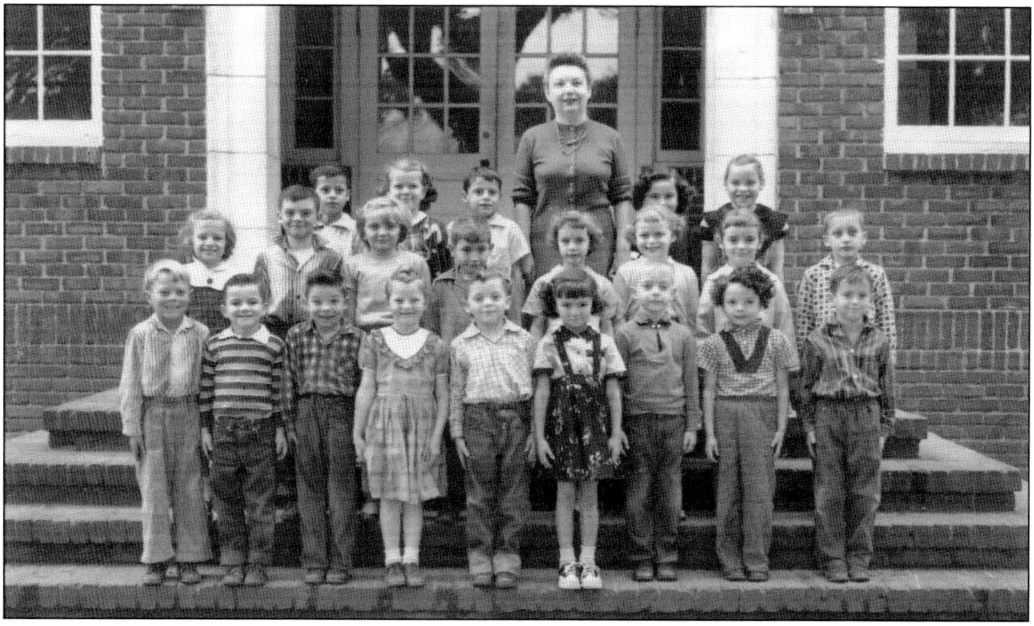

**First-Grade Class, 1960s.** Mary Lee Norment's class from Southport High School included Scarlett Price, the first child on the left in the second row. (Courtesy of Andrea P. Clemmons.)

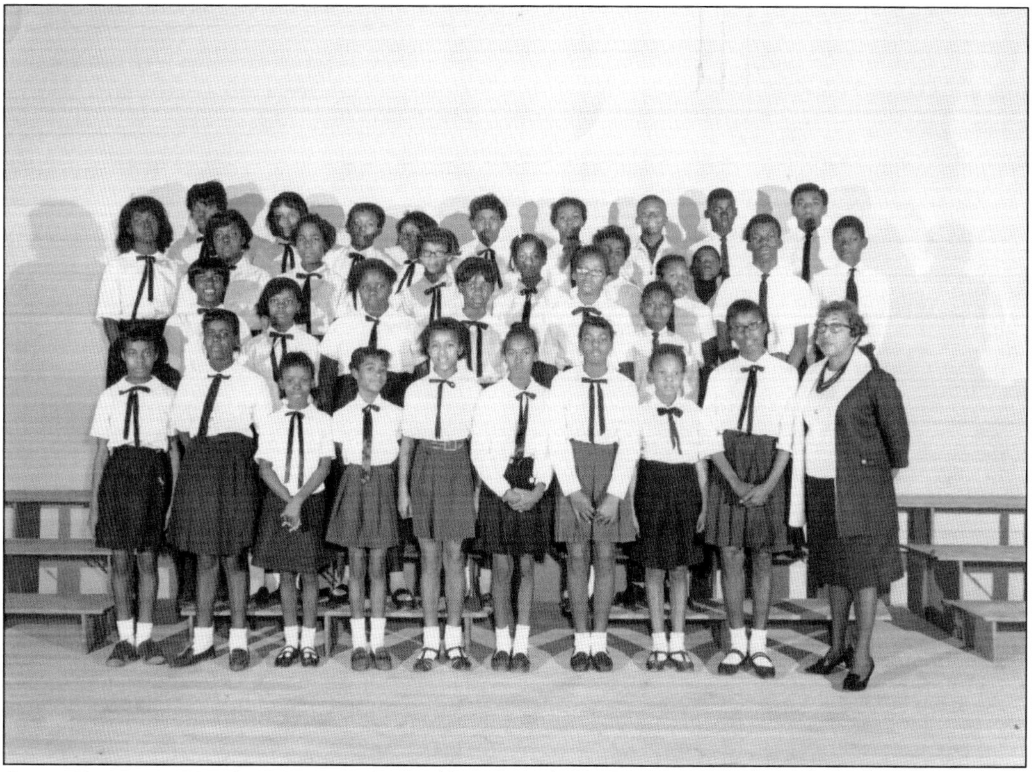

**Class Picture.** Teacher Cora Mebane (first row, far right) and a Brunswick County Training School class pose in the gymnasium in the 1960s. (Courtesy of Sarah P. Joyner.)

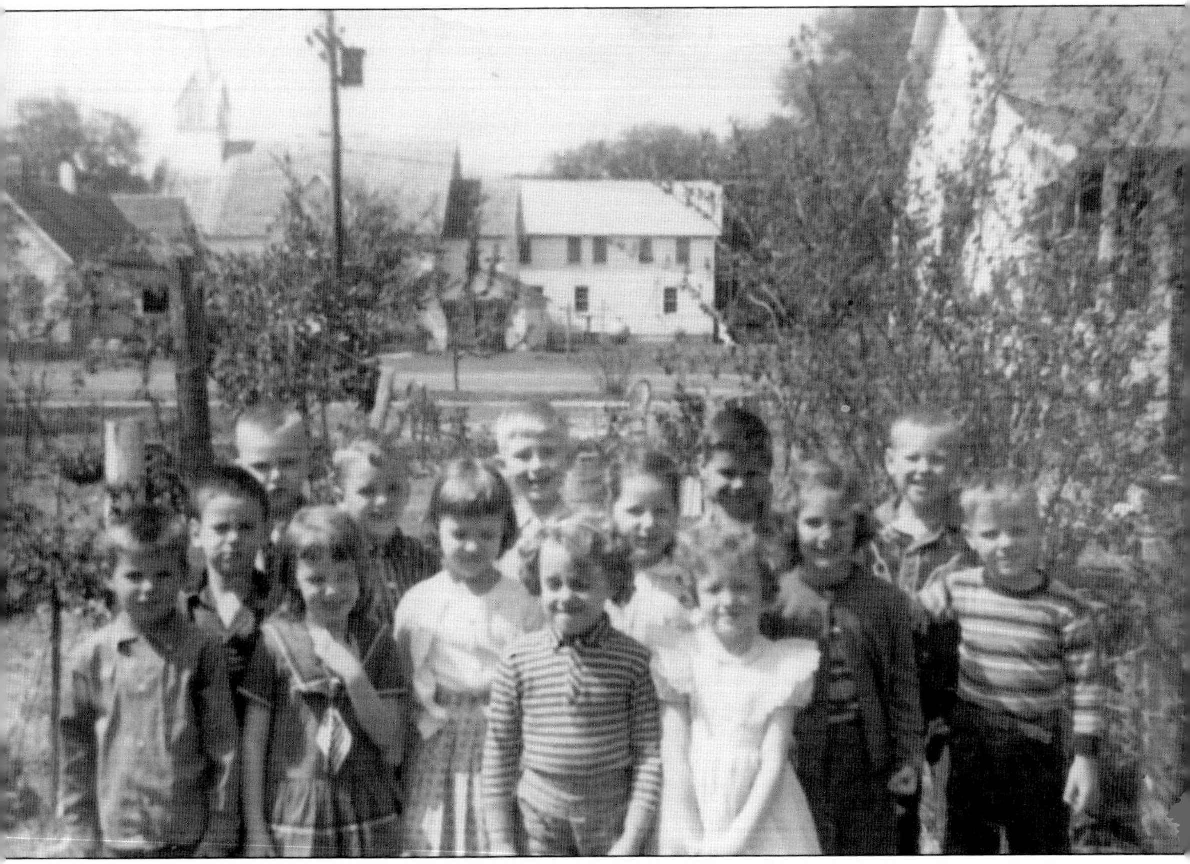

**KINDERGARTEN.** Mrs. Russ's 1960 kindergarten class poses for a class picture outdoors. Andrea Clemmons is in the front row on the far right in the white dress. The Methodist church is on the left in the background. (Courtesy of Andrea P. Clemmons.)

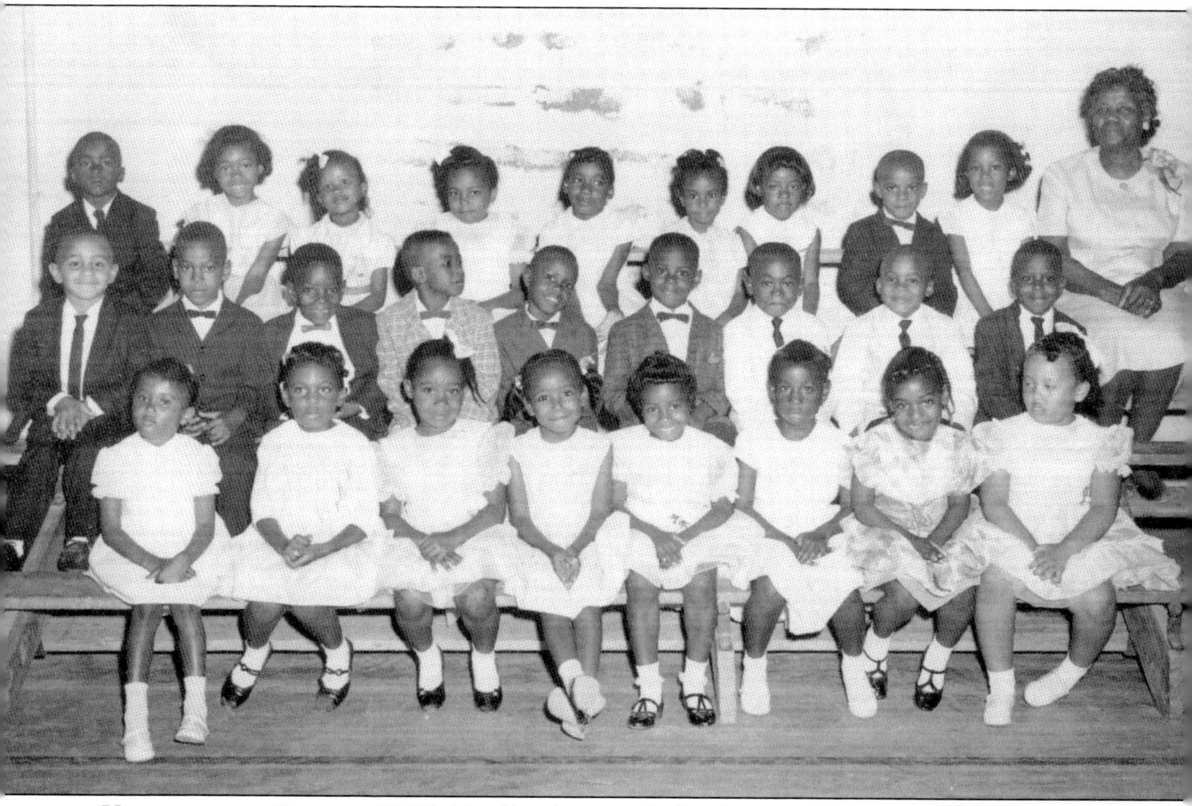

**KINDERGARTEN CLASS, C. 1965.** Mrs. Breelove taught kindergarten for many years at Brunswick County Training School. In this kindergarten class photograph, author Sharon Claudette Smith is pictured in the front row, second from the left. (Courtesy of Rebecca B. Smith.)

BRUNSWICK COUNTY SCHOOLS
P. O. Box 848
Southport, North Carolina

March 15, 1967

Dear Parent:

Your school system's desegregation plan under the Civil Rights Act of 1964 is being continued for the coming school year. The purpose of the plan is to eliminate the dual structure of separate schools for children of different races.

The plan requires <u>every</u> student or his parent to choose the school the student will attend in the coming school year. It does not matter which school the student is attending this year, and it does not matter whether that school was formerly a white or a Negro school You and your child may select any school you wish.

A choice of school is required for each student. A student cannot be enrolled at any school next school year unless a choice of schools is made. This year there will be a 30-day choice period, <u>beginning March 15, 1967</u>, and <u>ending, April 15, 1967</u>.

A choice form listing the available schools and grades is enclosed. This form must be filled out and returned. You may mail it in the enclosed enveloped, or deliver it by hand to any school or to the address above any time during the 30-day choice period. No one may require you to file your choice form before the end of the choice period. No preference will be given for choosing early during the choice period.

No principal, teacher, or other school official is permitted to influence or dissuade anyone from choosing a school where a desegregated education can be obtained. No one is permitted to favor or penalize any student or other person because of a choice made. <u>Once a choice is made, it cannot be changed except</u> for serious hardship.

Also enclosed is an explanatory notice giving full details about the desegregation plan. It tells you how to exercise your rights under the plan, and tells you how teachers, schoolbuses, sports, and other activities are being desegregated.

Your School Board and the school staff will do everything we can to see to it that the rights of all students are protected and that our desegregation plan is carried out successfully.

Sincerely yours,

George F. Williams

George F. Williams, Superintendent,
Brunswick County Schools

**DESEGREGATION PLAN OF 1967.** This letter was given to every parent in 1967, accompanied by a detailed outline of the desegregation plan for the schools. (Courtesy of Marjorie Clemmons.)

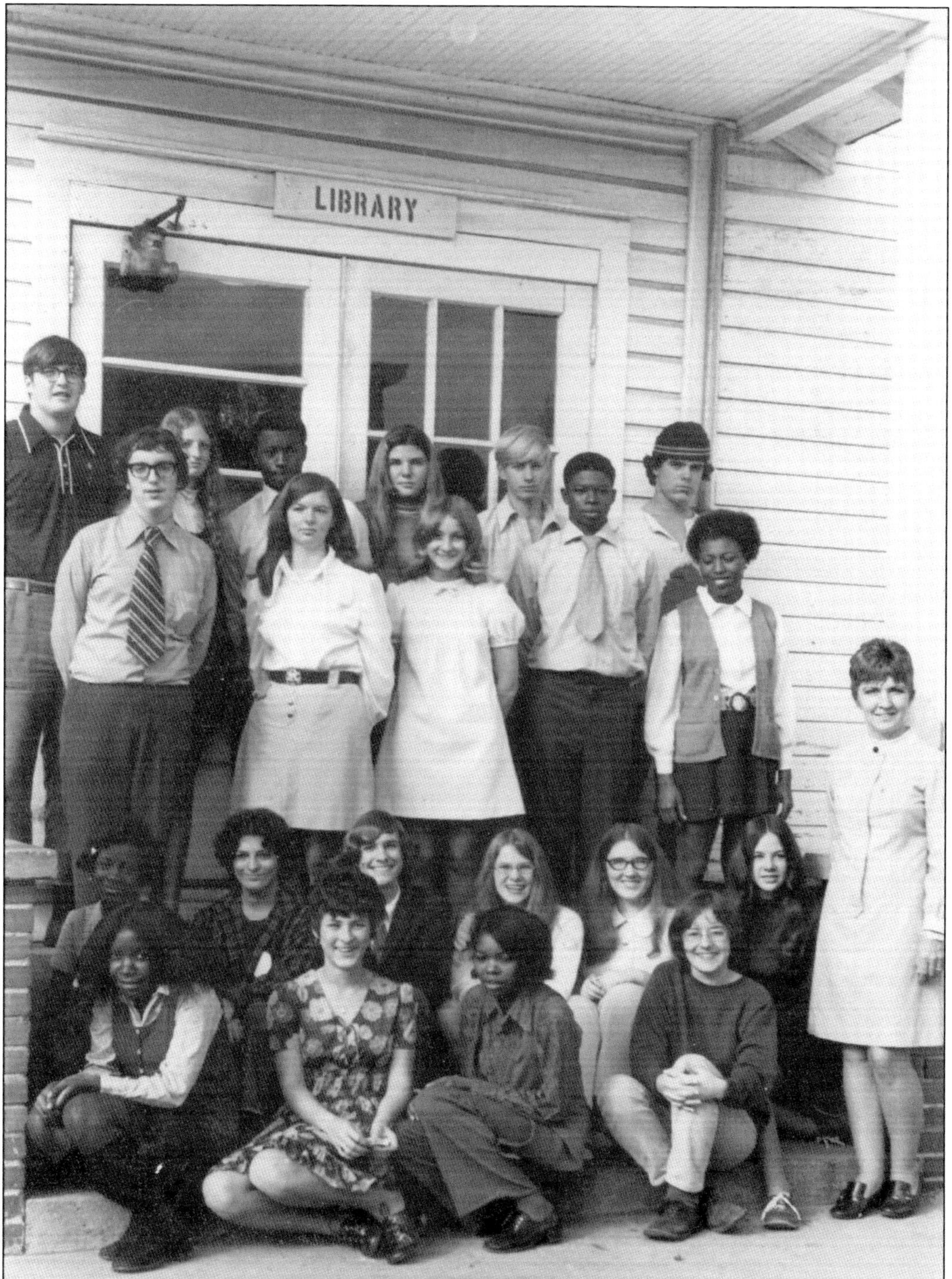


**Spanish Class, 1971.** Mrs. Sinclair (first row, far right) taught Spanish at Brunswick County Southport High School and at South Brunswick High School. She was adored by her students. Andrea Clemmons is in the back row, second from the left. (Courtesy of Andrea P. Clemmons.)

*Four*

# Family Fun and Friends

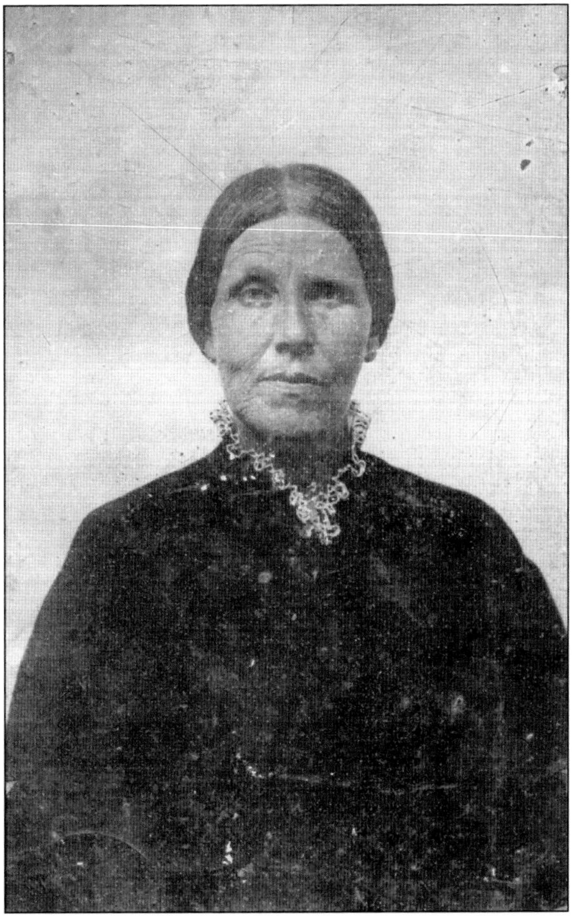

**Susan Dunbar Davis Dosher.** This photograph from the 1860s or 1870s shows Susan Dunbar Davis Dosher, who married Charles Gause Dosher and had three sons and two daughters. One son, Frederick, died at the age of 17, and another, Charlie, drowned at sea, but the third son, James Henry Dosher, was Trudy M. Young's great-grandfather, making Susan Dunbar Davis Dosher her great-great-grandmother. (Courtesy of Trudy M. Young.)

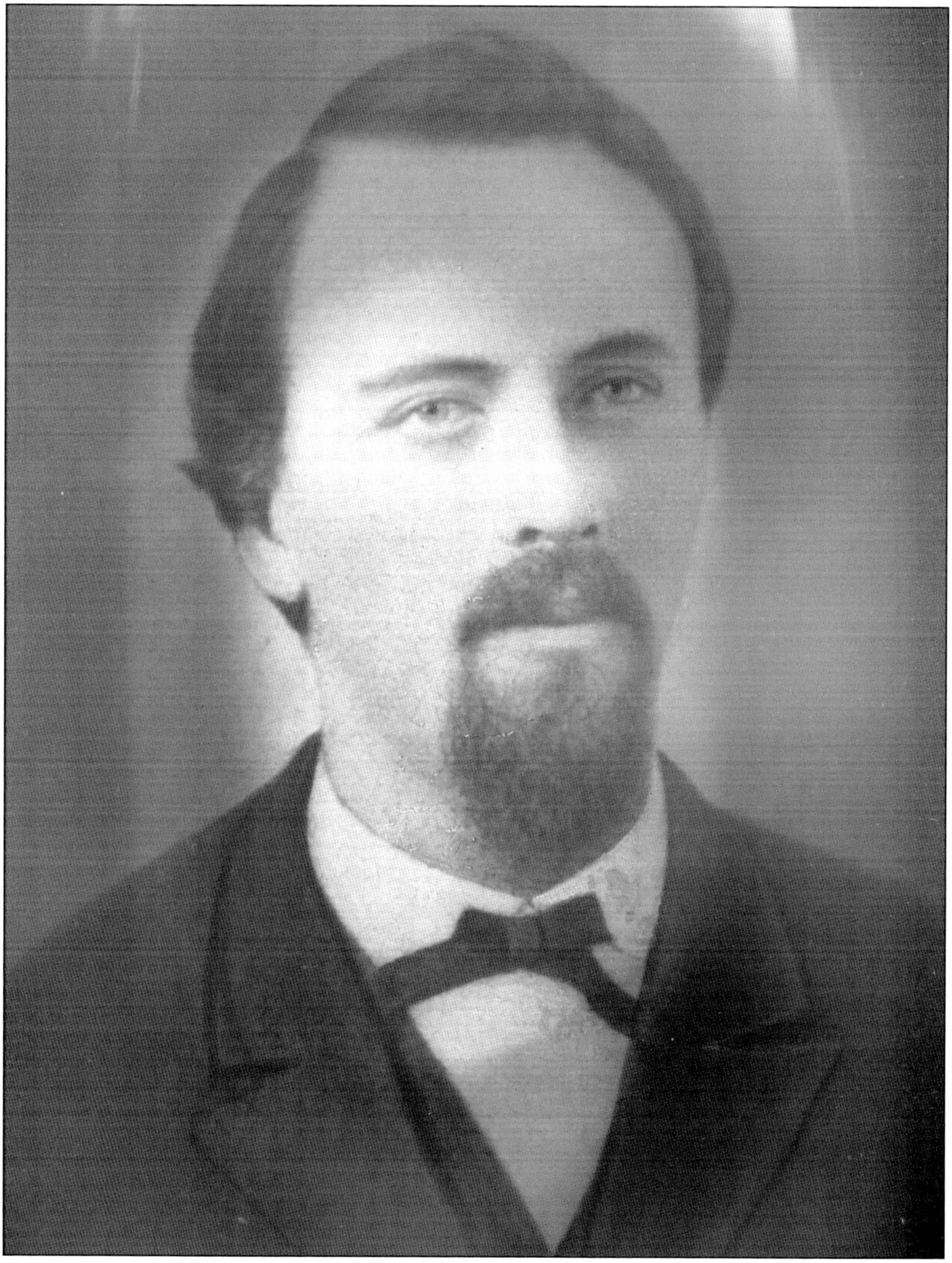

**KEEPER OF THE LIGHTHOUSE.** James Henry "Sonny" Dosher, the third son of Susan Dunbar Davis Dosher and Charles Gause Dosher, poses for his wedding portrait in the mid-1860s. He and his wife, Rebecca Guthrie, had nine children: Annie, Gertrude (Trudy M. Young's grandmother), Susan, Fred, Zeb, Milton, Lillian, Katie, and Esther. James Henry was keeper of the lighthouse, "Old Baldy," for over 30 years, and he and Rebecca were members of Trinity United Methodist Church. He was born on July 13, 1843, and died on June 23, 1934. (Courtesy of Trudy M. Young.)

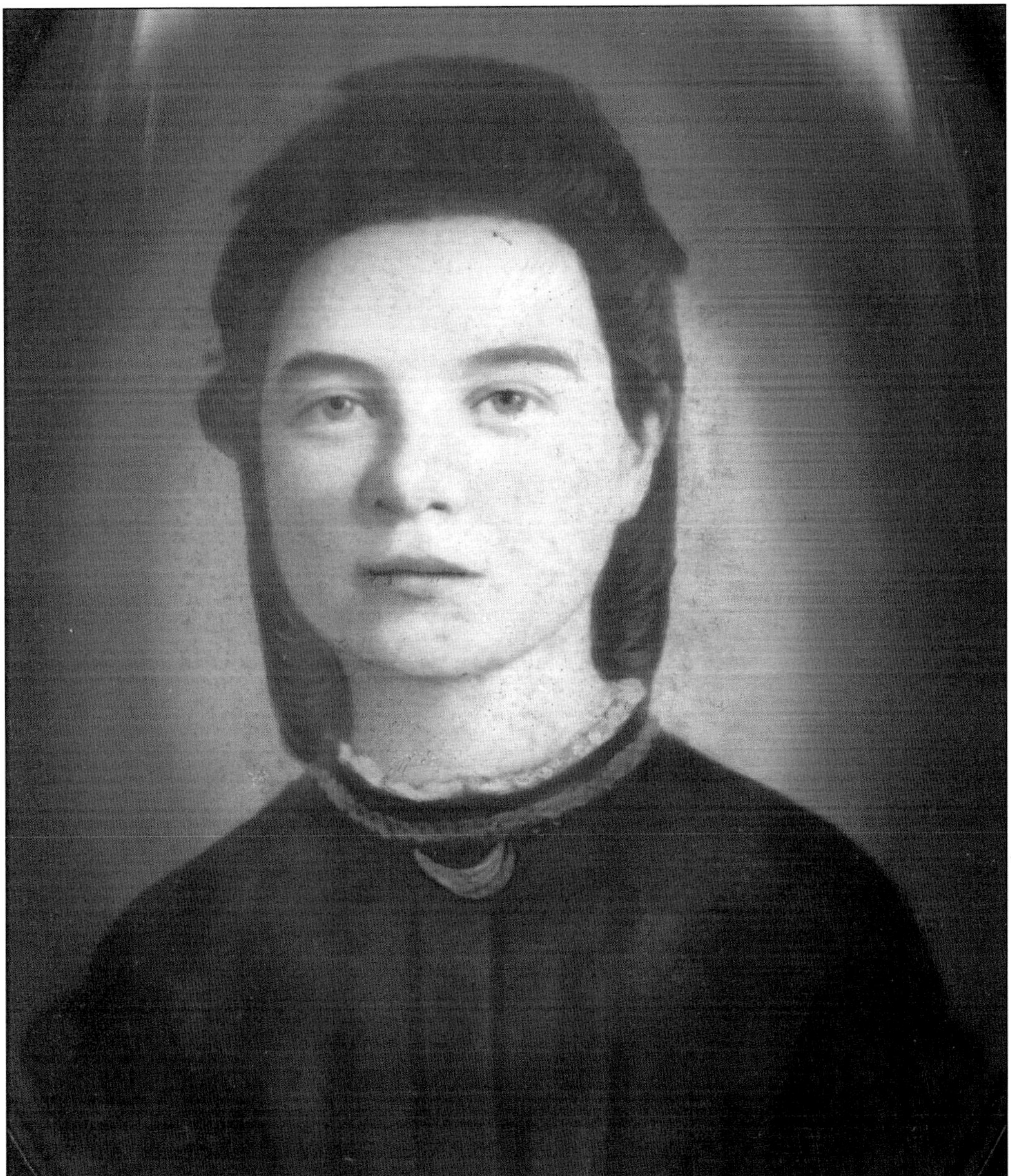

**WEDDING PORTRAIT, 1860s.** Rebecca Guthrie was the daughter of Archibald M. Guthrie, and her mother's last name was Crapon. She was born on October 4, 1848, and married James Henry Dosher in the mid-1860s. Rebecca had nine children and died on January 25, 1916. (Courtesy of Trudy M. Young.)

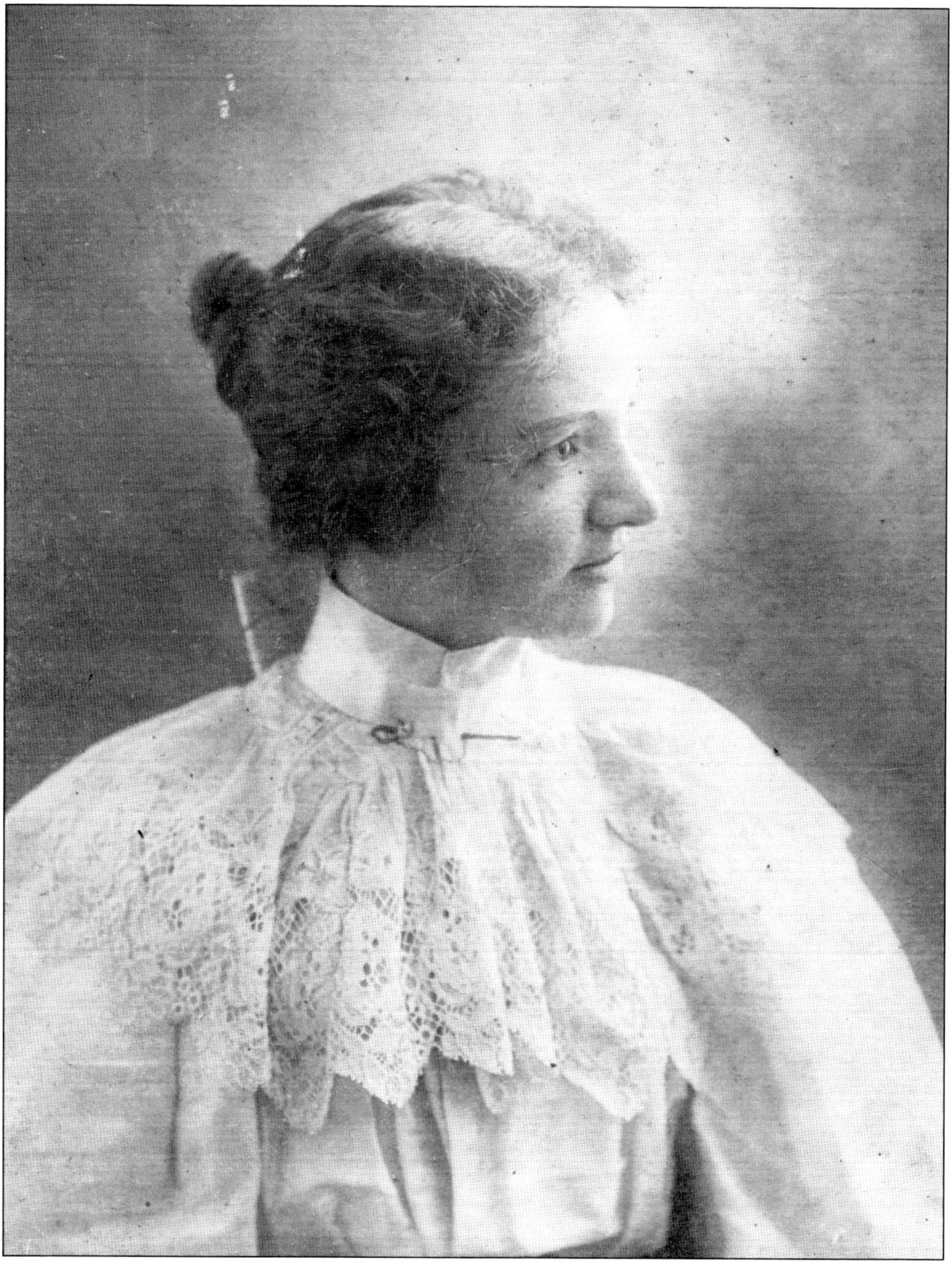

**GERTRUDE DOSHER GAUSE PORTRAIT.** This portrait of Gause was taken in the early 1900s. Gertrude married Charles Eyden Gause, and they had one daughter, also named Gertrude Gause. (Courtesy of Trudy M. Young.)

**GERTRUDE GAUSE, 1920S.** This portrait was taken of Gertrude Gause, the only child of Charles E. and Gertrude Dosher Gause, when she was about 16 years old. She married James Augustine "Gus" McNeil, and they had three children: Sarah Ann "Sally," Gertrude "Trudy," and James Augustine "Jim" (or "Buddy") McNeil Jr. (Courtesy of Trudy M. Young.)

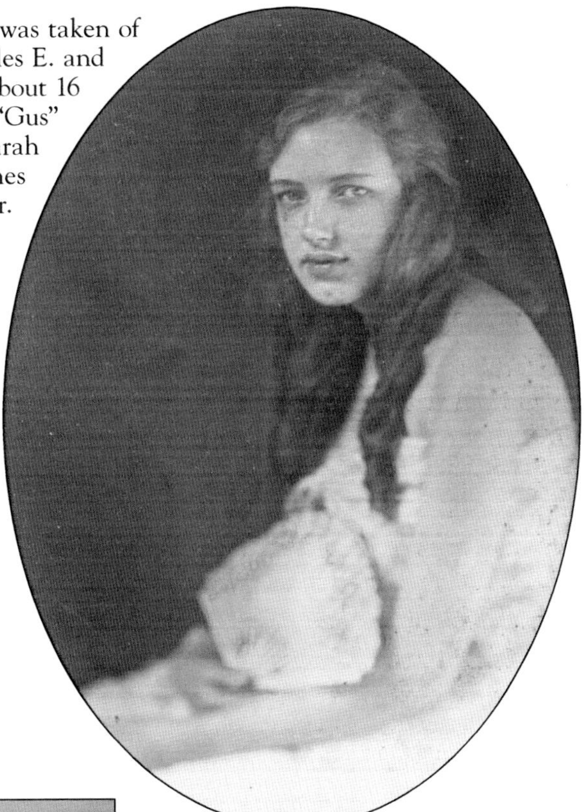

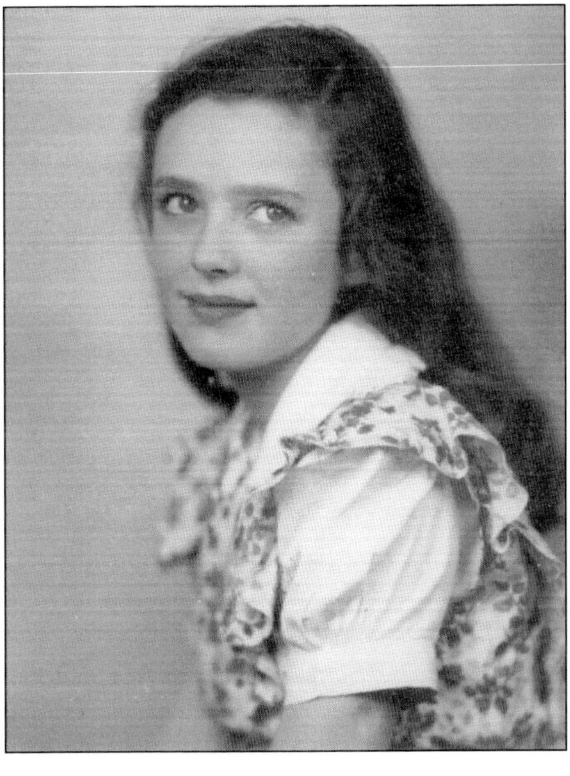

**THE FIFTH GENERATION FROM SUSAN DUNBAR DAVIS DOSHER.** This portrait of Gertrude McNeil (now Trudy M. Young) was taken when she was 10. She is the great-great-granddaughter of Susan Dunbar Davis Dosher. (Courtesy of Trudy M. Young.)

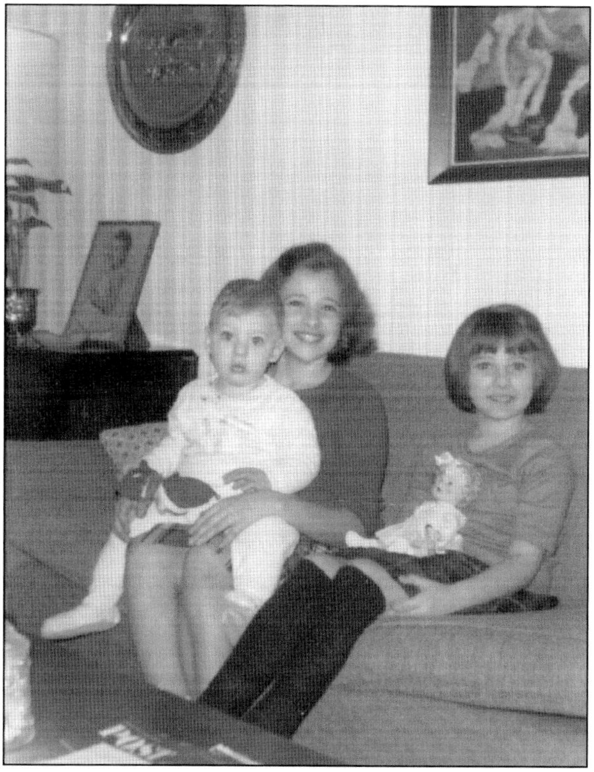

**THE SIXTH GENERATION FROM SUSAN DUNBAR DAVIS DOSHER.** Trudy M. Young's children, the sixth generation from Susan Dunbar Davis Dosher, pose in this family photograph from the 1966 Christmas holiday. Big sister Katherine holds her baby brother Erik, and Marie holds her doll. (Courtesy of Katherine Hufham.)

**TRUDY AND HER CHILDREN.** Trudy M. Young holds baby Erik, with Katherine (left) and Marie (right) by her side, in 1966. (Courtesy of Katherine Hufham.)

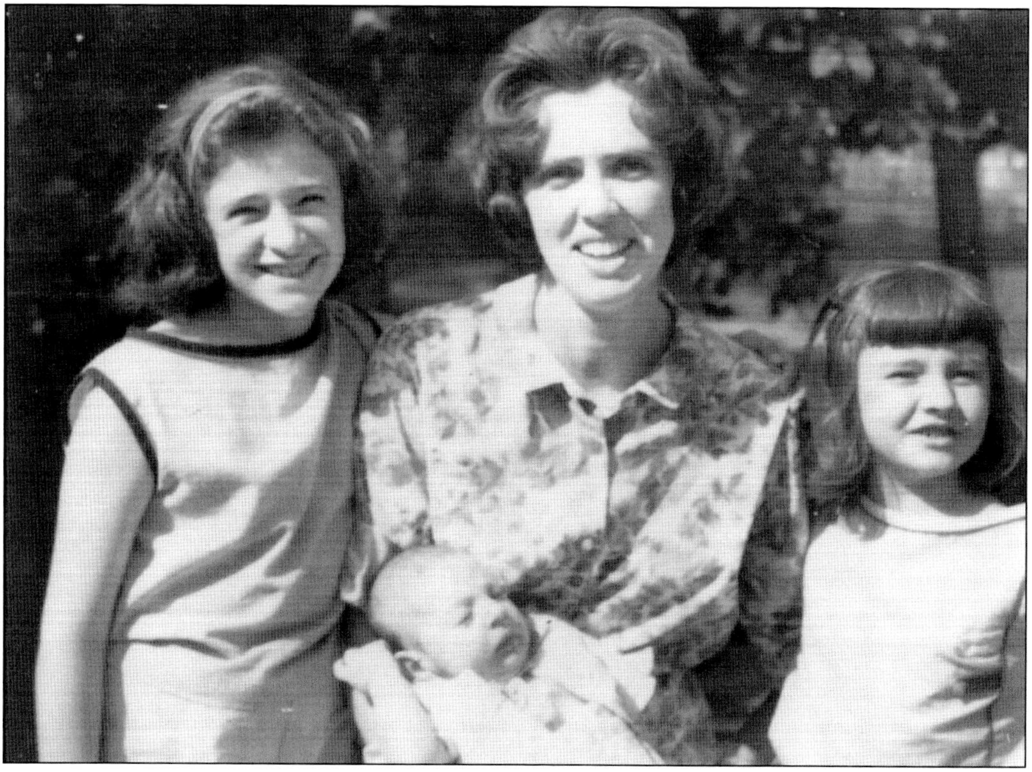

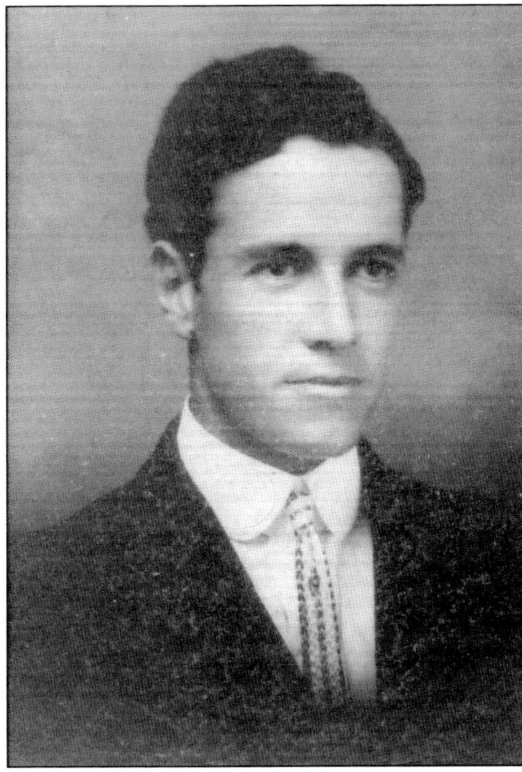

**Gus McNeil.** Gus McNeil opened the Standard Oil Company of New Jersey in Southport in the 1920s, which he operated for over 40 years. It was located on Howe Street by the water tower and later became Esso and Exxon. (Courtesy of Trudy M. Young.)

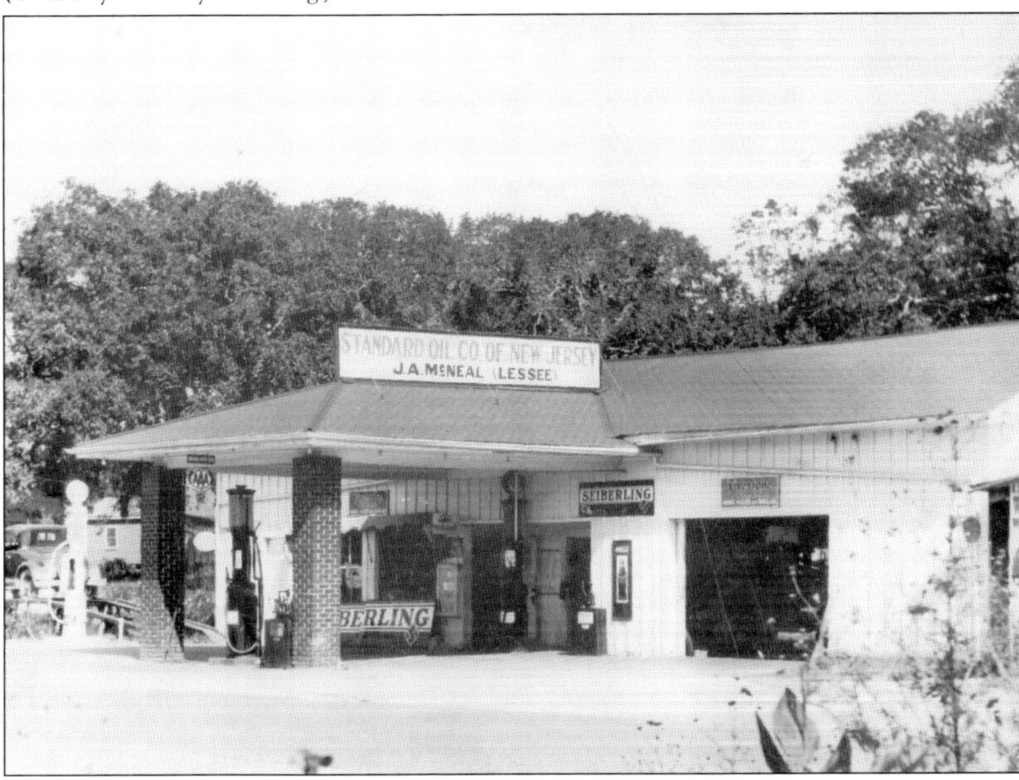

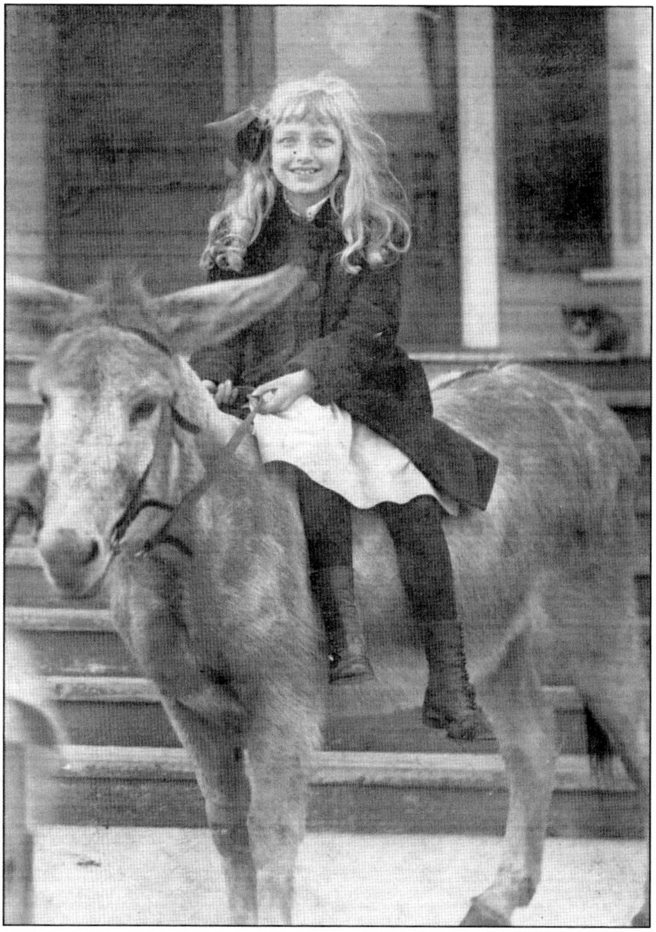

**Donkey Ride.** Little Gertrude Gause goes for a donkey ride in 1910 at the age of seven or eight. (Courtesy of Trudy M. Young.)

**Gertrude's Pony and Carriage, 1914.** Josephine Robbins (left) and Gertrude Gause pose in front of Gertrude's pony in 1914 as the family dog, Ned, watches from the carriage. (Courtesy of Trudy M. Young.)

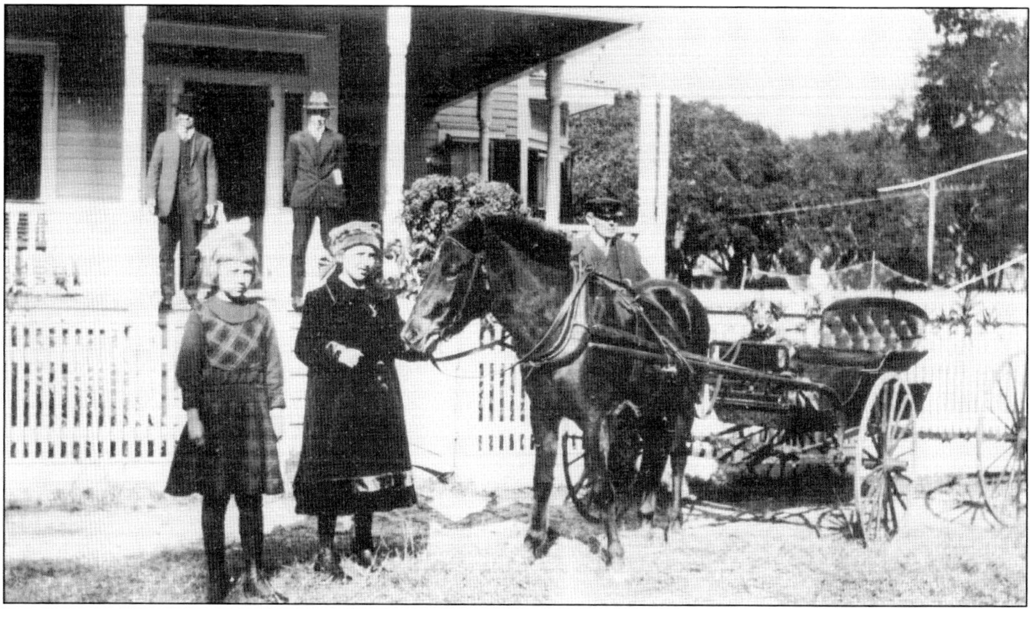

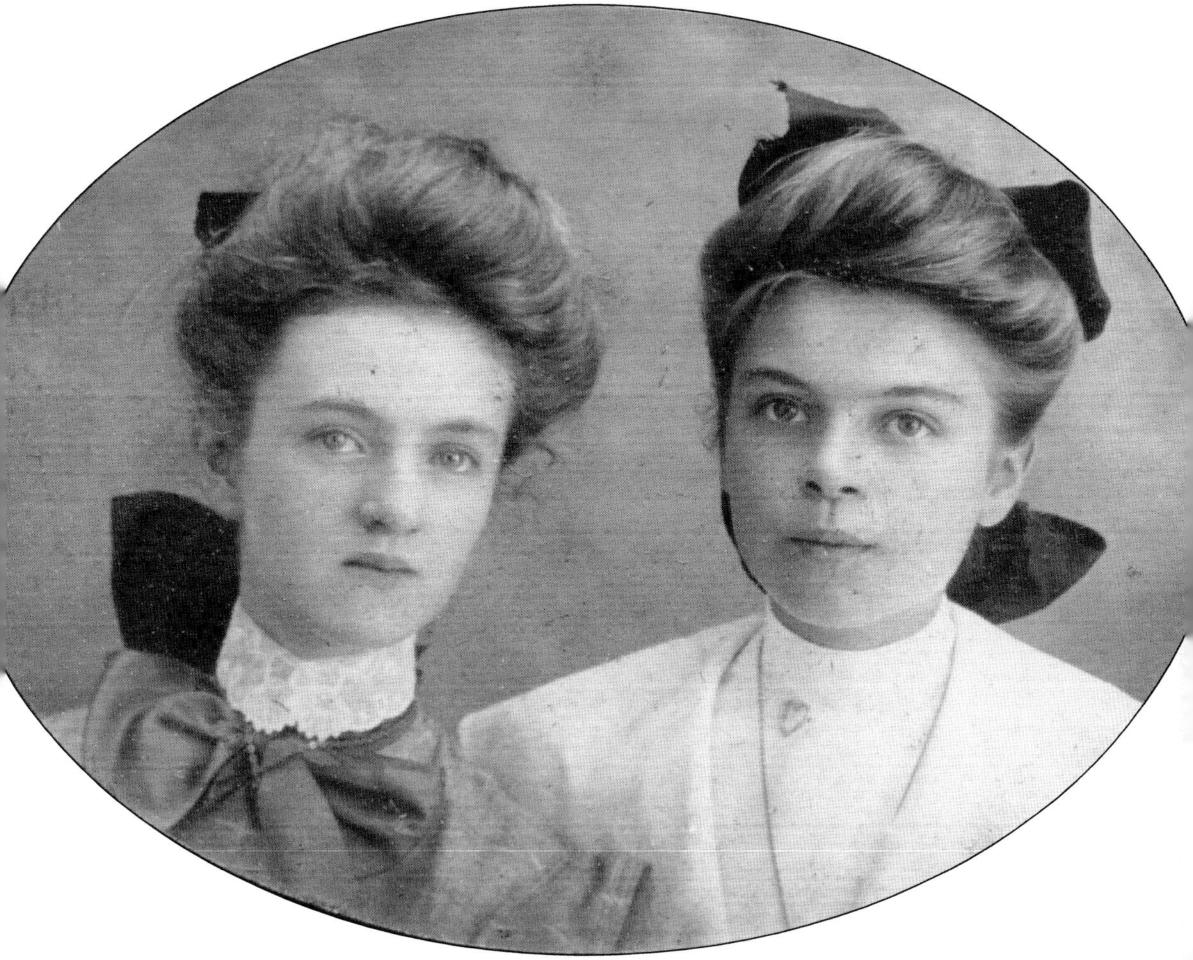

**KATIE DOSHER AND MAMIE BESSANT PORTRAIT.** This image, taken around 1915, is of Katie Dosher (left) and Mamie Bessant. Katie was the daughter of James Henry Dosher; she never married. Mamie was Katie's niece. (Courtesy of Trudy M. Young.)

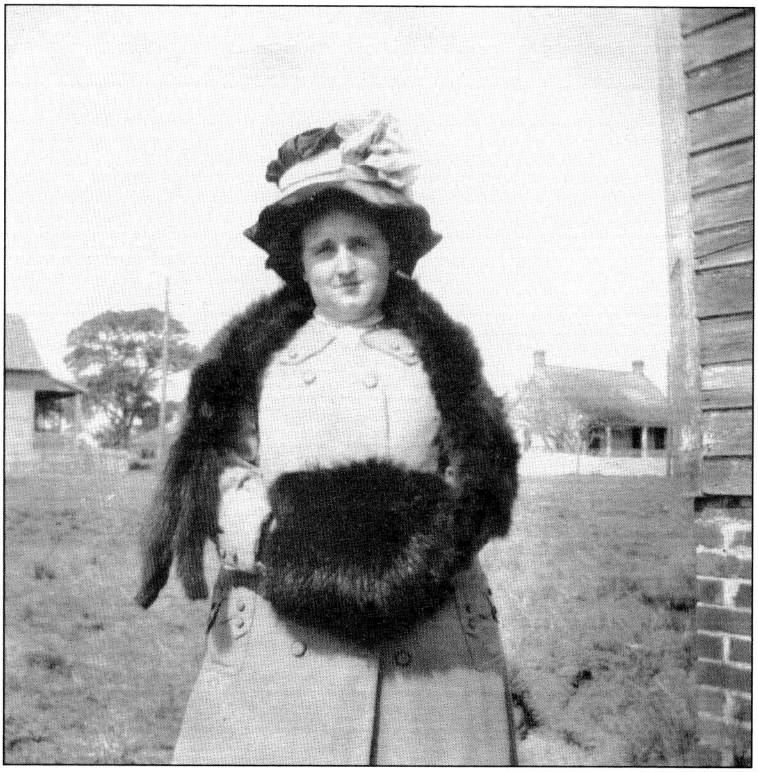

**MAMIE DANIELS.** This photograph of Mamie was taken around 1910. She was the second cousin to Trudy M. Young. (Courtesy of Trudy M. Young.)

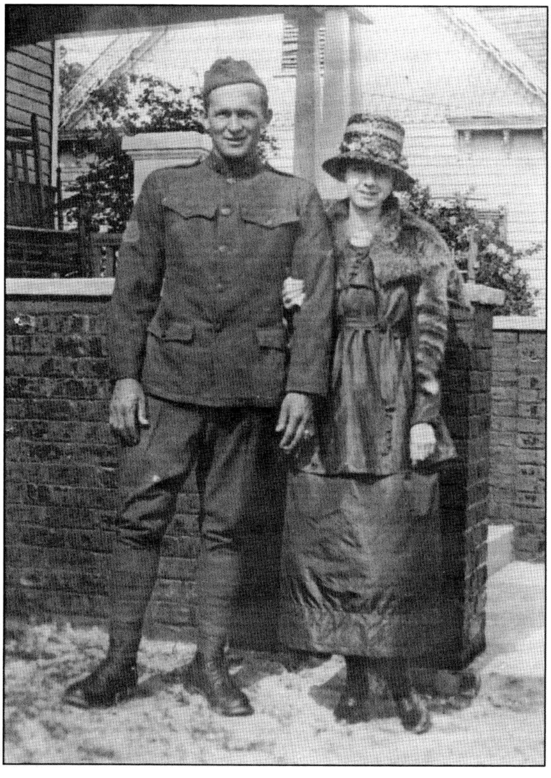

**JOHN AND ESTHER ERIKSEN.** John Eriksen was born in Norway in 1889 and married Esther Dosher, James Henry Dosher's youngest daughter, in December 1916. John served in World War I and later became mayor of Southport in the 1940s. (Courtesy of Trudy M. Young.)

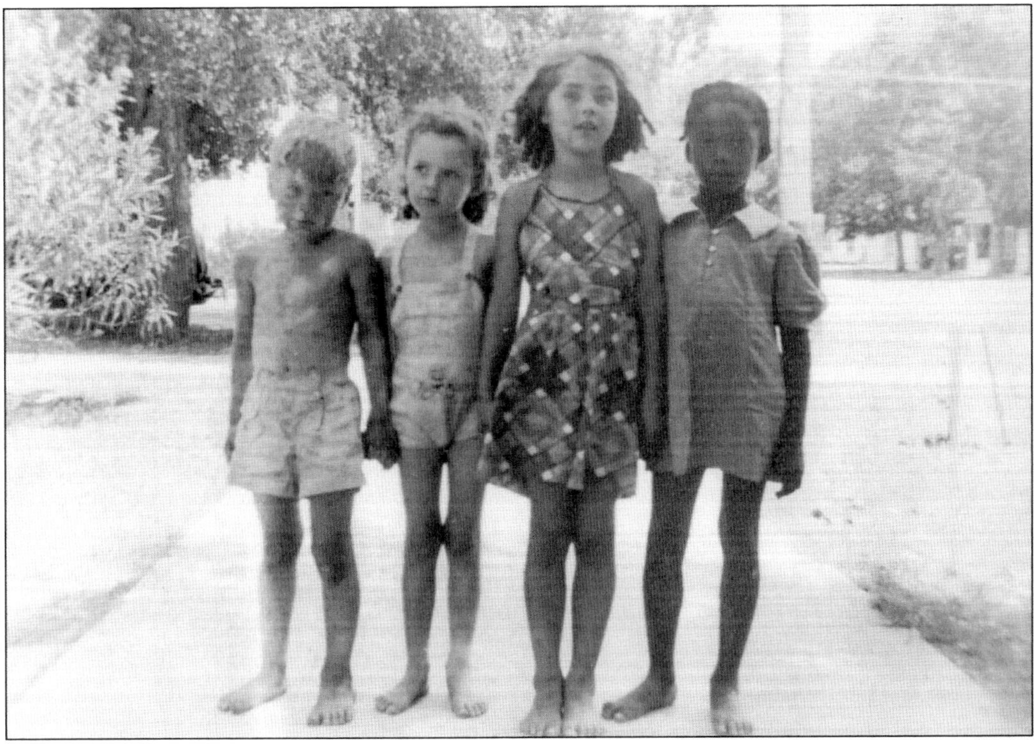

**CHILDHOOD FRIENDS.** Posing in front the McNeil home at the corner of Nash and Howe Streets in 1941 are, from left to right, Dickie Dozier, Trudy McNeil (now Trudy M. Young), Gloria Hewett, and Rosa Marie Galloway. (Courtesy of Trudy M. Young.)

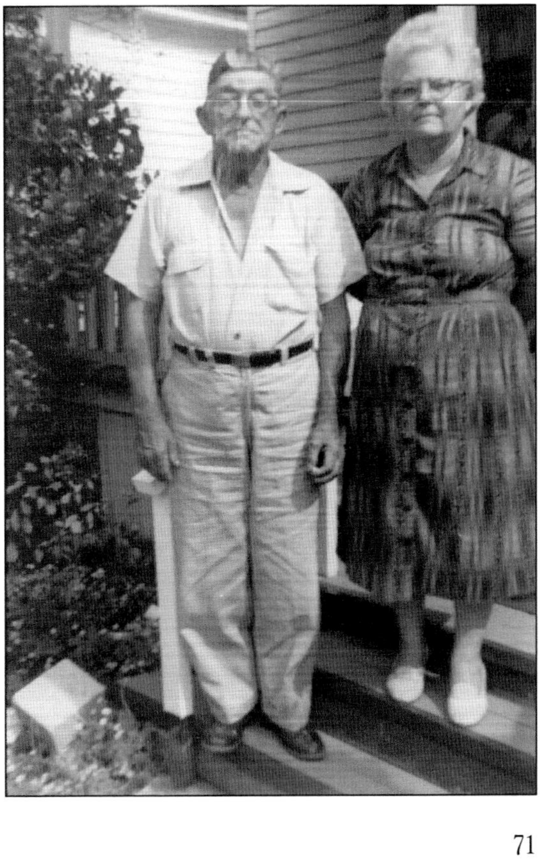

**DANIELS HOME.** Ed Daniels and his wife, Carrie, stand in front of their home on Atlantic Avenue in October 1960. Ed worked as a meter reader for the City of Southport during the 1950s. (Courtesy of Trudy M. Young.)

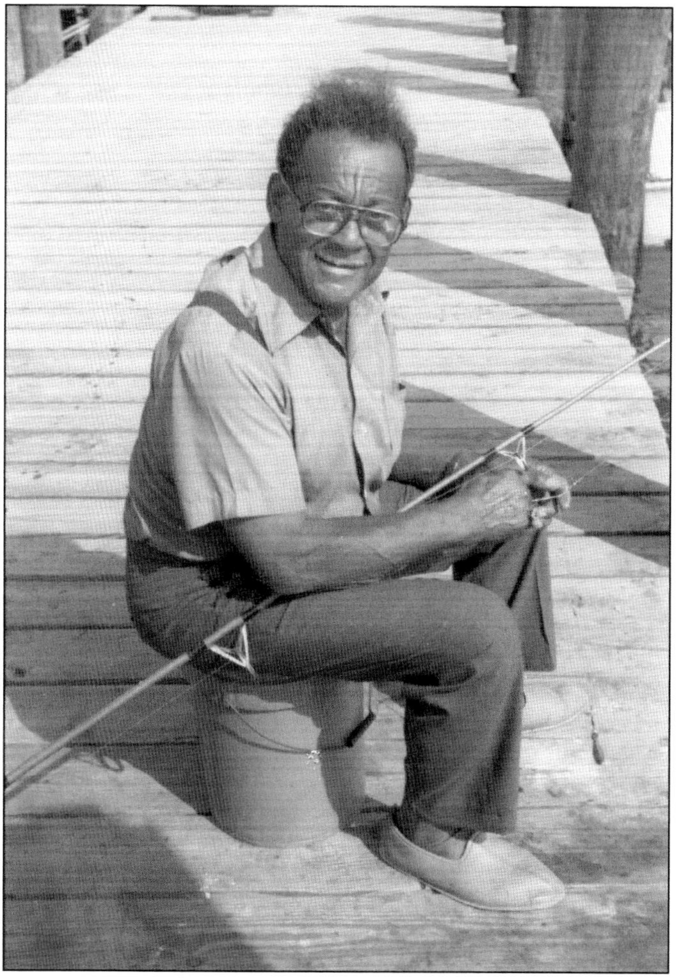

**Dexter Clemmons.** Dexter, a Southport native, was born in 1907. He opened Hi Way Cleaners during World War II; it was known to all as the "Pressing Club." Dexter was especially fond of children and was called the "cookie man." He would take cookies to children who lived in the neighborhoods where laundry was being delivered to homes. His son Lorenzo and daughter-in-law Marjorie worked alongside him, and he retired after nearly 50 years in the business. (Courtesy of Marjorie Clemmons.)

**Hi Way Cleaners.** Clemmons ran Hi Way Cleaners, located at 508 Howe Street, for 50 years. When he retired, he turned it over to his son Lorenzo Clemmons and Lorenzo's wife, Marjorie. (Courtesy of Marjorie Clemmons.)

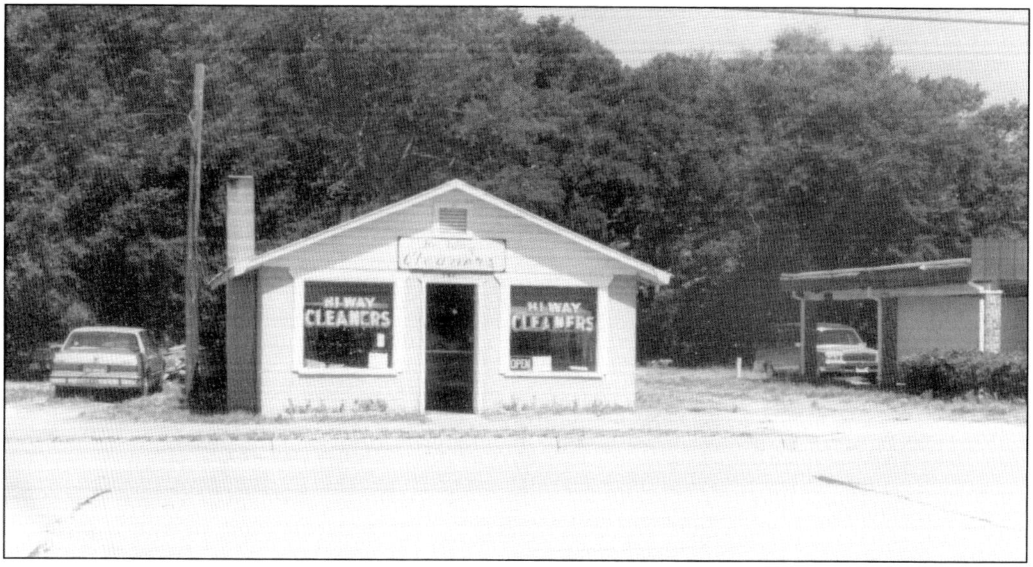

**BABY MICHAEL.** Baby Michael, the grandson of Dexter Clemmons, plays in his high chair in 1954. (Courtesy of Marjorie Clemmons.)

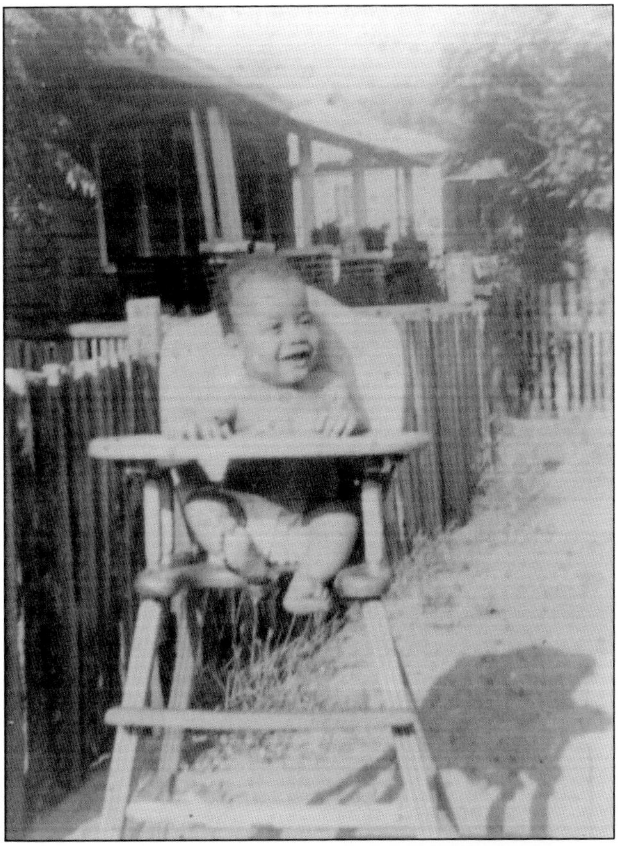

**BIG FLOUNDER CATCH.** Michael Clemmons poses with a big haul of flounder in the 1970s. It was not unusual to catch this many fish during that time period before overfishing set in. (Courtesy of Andrea P. Clemmons.)

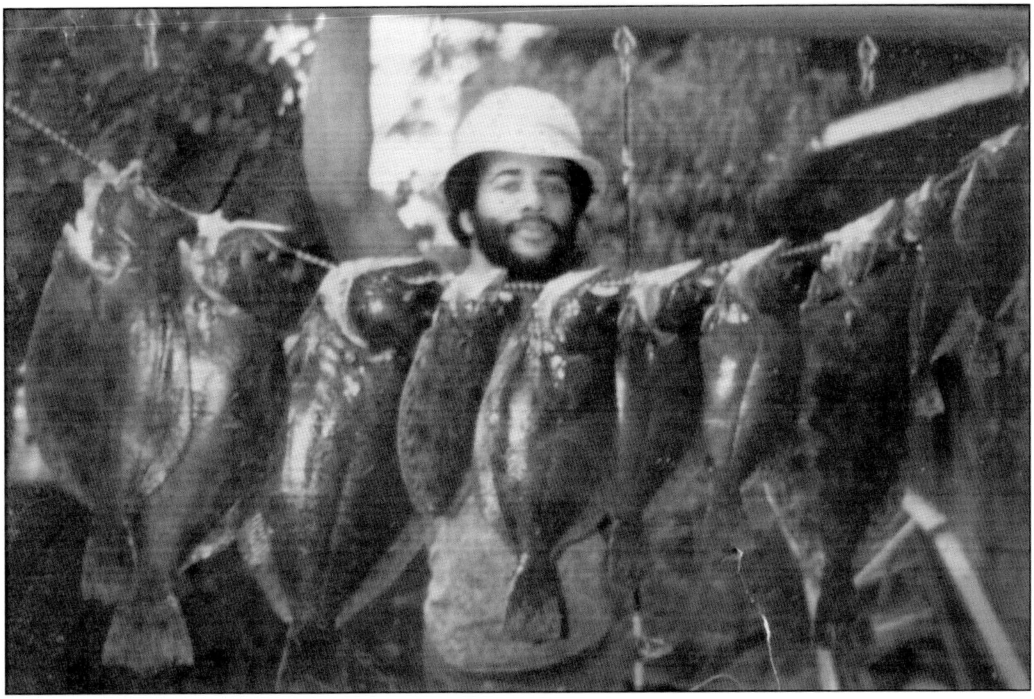

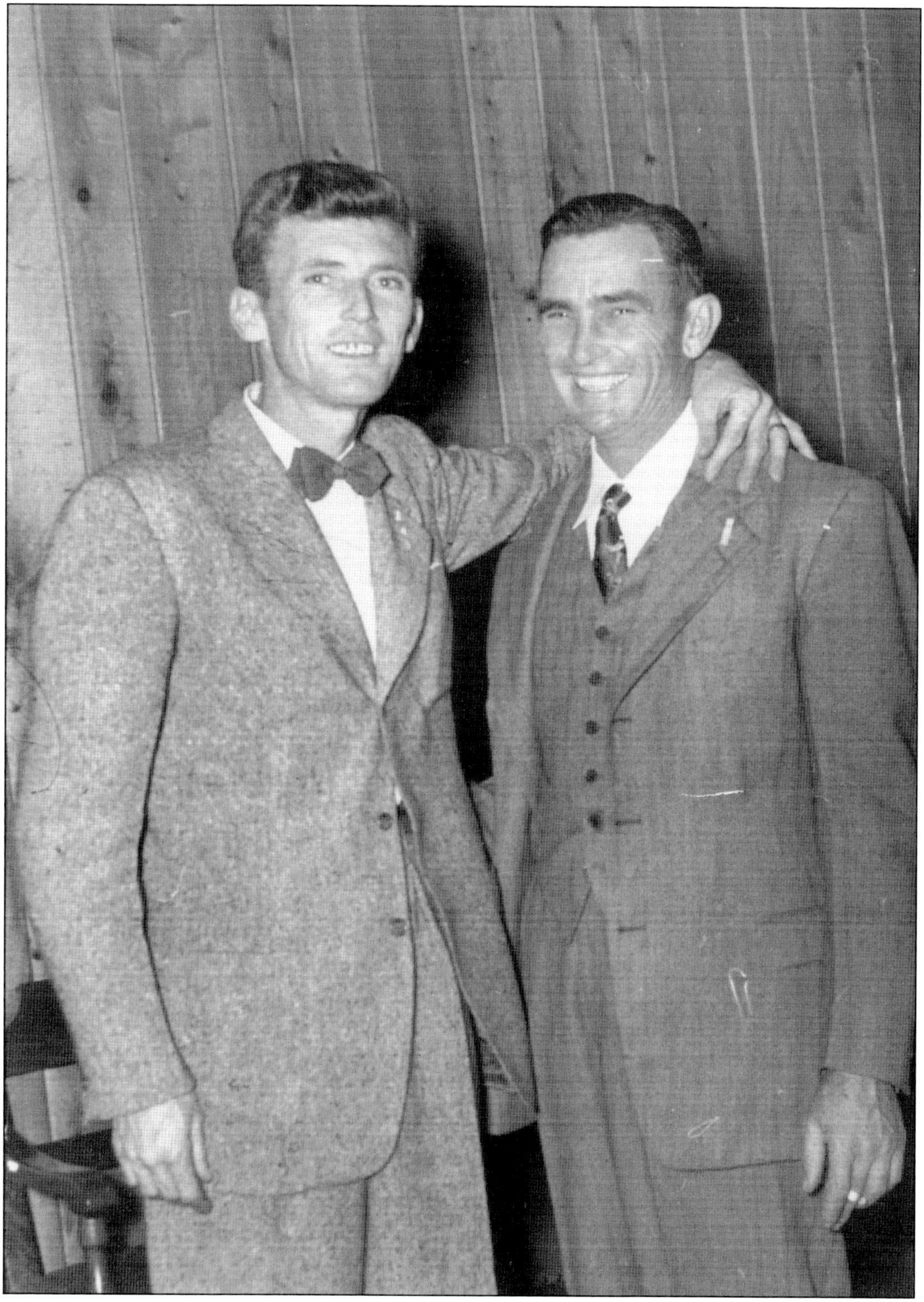

**Friends.** Dallas Pigott and Merritt Moore pose together at the United Services Organization (USO) in 1950. Both men worked for Lewis Hardee Sr. and had their own shrimp houses on the waterfront later on. (Courtesy of Jimmy Moore.)

**USO DEDICATION, 1942.** The new USO building, officially called the Federal Community Building, was dedicated on Saturday, April 25, 1942. (Courtesy of Trudy M. Young.)

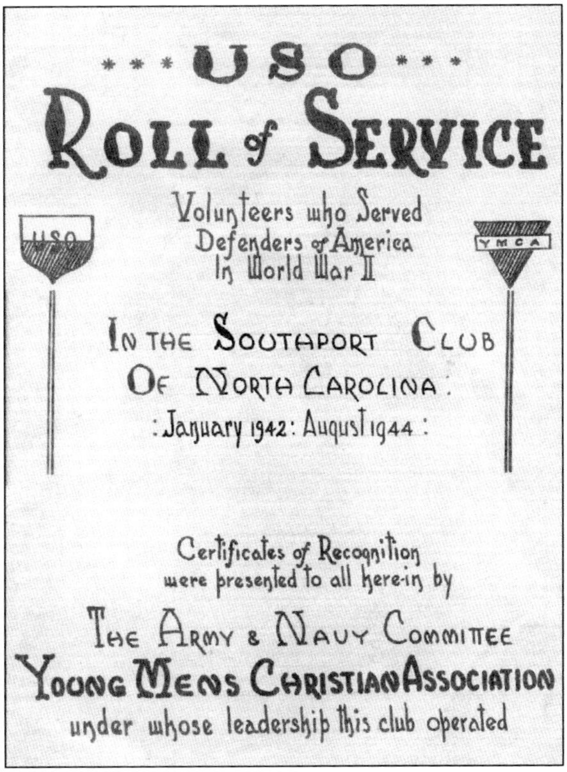
USO
ROLL of SERVICE
Volunteers who Served
Defenders of America
In World War II

IN THE SOUTHPORT CLUB
OF NORTH CAROLINA
: January 1942 : August 1944 :

Certificates of Recognition
were presented to all here-in by
THE ARMY & NAVY COMMITTEE
YOUNG MENS CHRISTIAN ASSOCIATION
under whose leadership this club operated

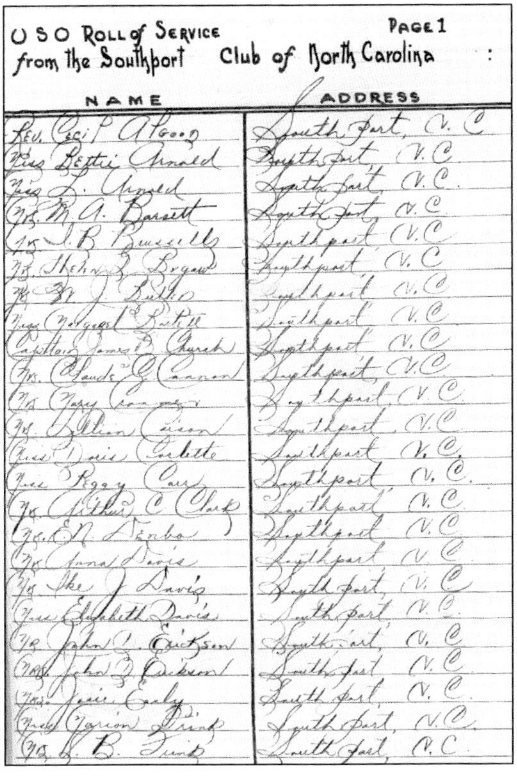
USO ROLL of SERVICE PAGE 1
from the Southport Club of North Carolina

| NAME | ADDRESS |
| --- | --- |
| Rev. Cecil Atwood | Southport, N.C. |
| Miss Bettie Arnold | Southport, N.C. |
| Miss L. Arnold | Southport, N.C. |
| Mrs. M. A. Barrett | Southport, N.C. |
| [illegible] | Southport, N.C. |
| [illegible] | Southport, N.C. |
| [illegible] | Southport, N.C. |
| [illegible] | Southport, N.C. |
| Captain James D. Church | Southport, N.C. |
| Mrs. Claude G. Cannon | Southport, N.C. |
| [illegible] | Southport, N.C. |
| [illegible] | Southport, N.C. |
| [illegible] | Southport, N.C. |
| Miss Peggy Carr | Southport, N.C. |
| Mrs. Arthur C. Clark | Southport, N.C. |
| Mrs. E. N. Denbo | Southport, N.C. |
| [illegible] Davis | Southport, N.C. |
| Mrs. Ike J. Davis | Southport, N.C. |
| Miss Elizabeth Davis | Southport, N.C. |
| Mrs. John C. Erickson | Southport, N.C. |
| Mrs. John J. Dickson | Southport, N.C. |
| Mrs. Jessie Early | Southport, N.C. |
| Mrs. Marion Frink | Southport, N.C. |
| Mrs. L. B. Frink | Southport, N.C. |

**USO ROLL OF SERVICE LIST.** An early copy of a USO service roll shows that many community members were involved. (Courtesy of Trudy M. Young.)

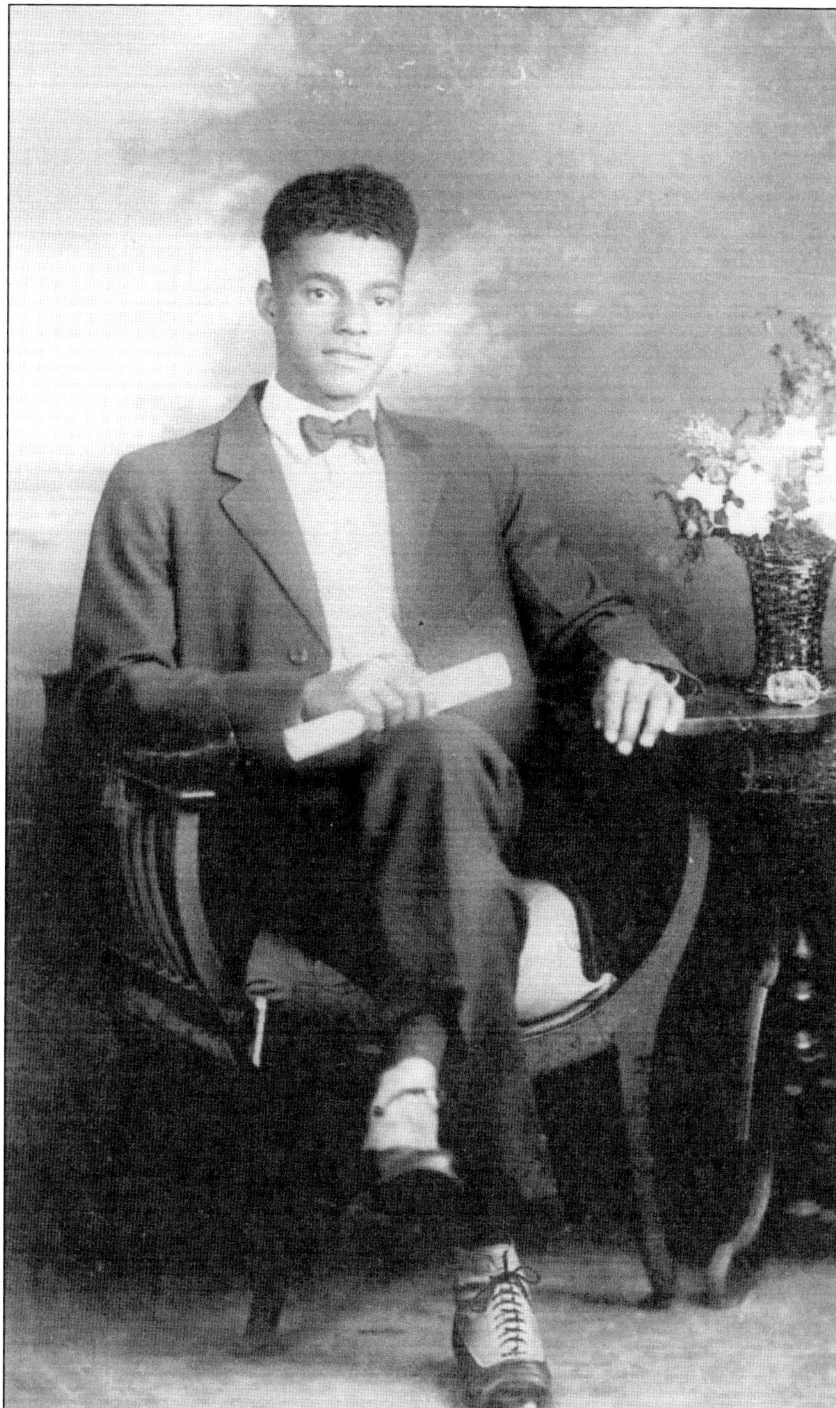

**Freddie Smith Sr., Early 1920s.** Freddie Smith Sr. worked as a cook on the *Merritt*, a US Army Corps of Engineers shallow draft dredge, the first of its kind anywhere. It was designed for use by the US Army Engineer District–Wilmington in the many shallow inlets and small harbors, where using pipeline dredges was impractical. (Courtesy of Joy Smith.)

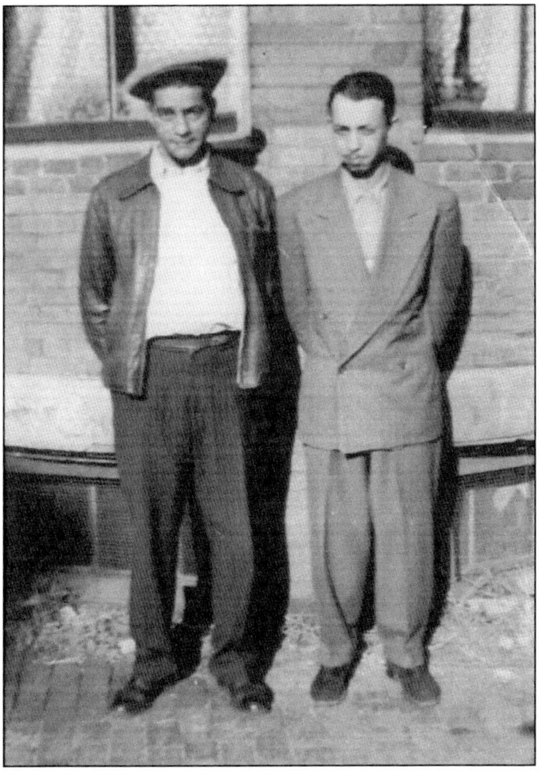

**Father and Son.** Freddie Sr. (left) and Freddie Jr. pose in the 1930s. (Courtesy of Joy Smith.)

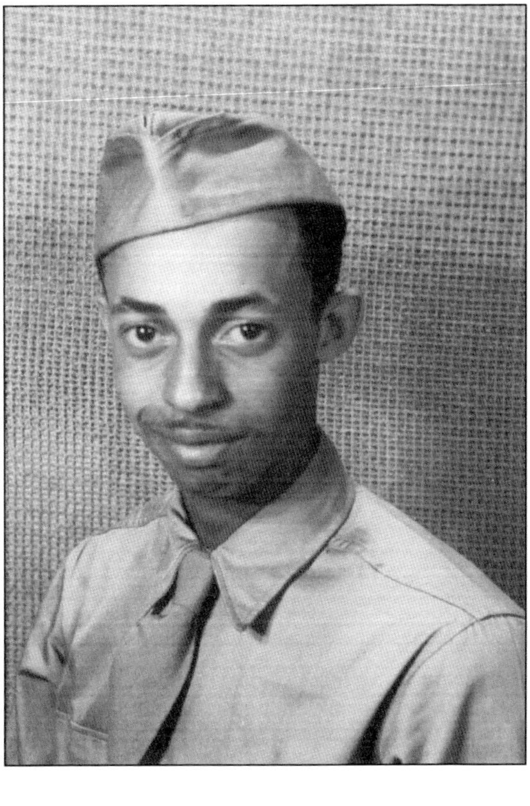

**Freddie Elmer Smith Jr.** Born in Southport on August 15, 1924, Freddie Smith Jr. attended Brunswick County Training School and later moved to Boston, where he attended the Boston Conservatory School of Music. He played trumpet, composed music, and was a jazz historian. He was also a businessman in Southport for years. At an early age, he joined St. James African Methodist Episcopal Zion Church. He also served in the Army and was employed at Military Ocean Terminal–Sunny Point (MOTSU) until his retirement in 1984. He died on March 14, 2002. (Courtesy of Joy Smith.)

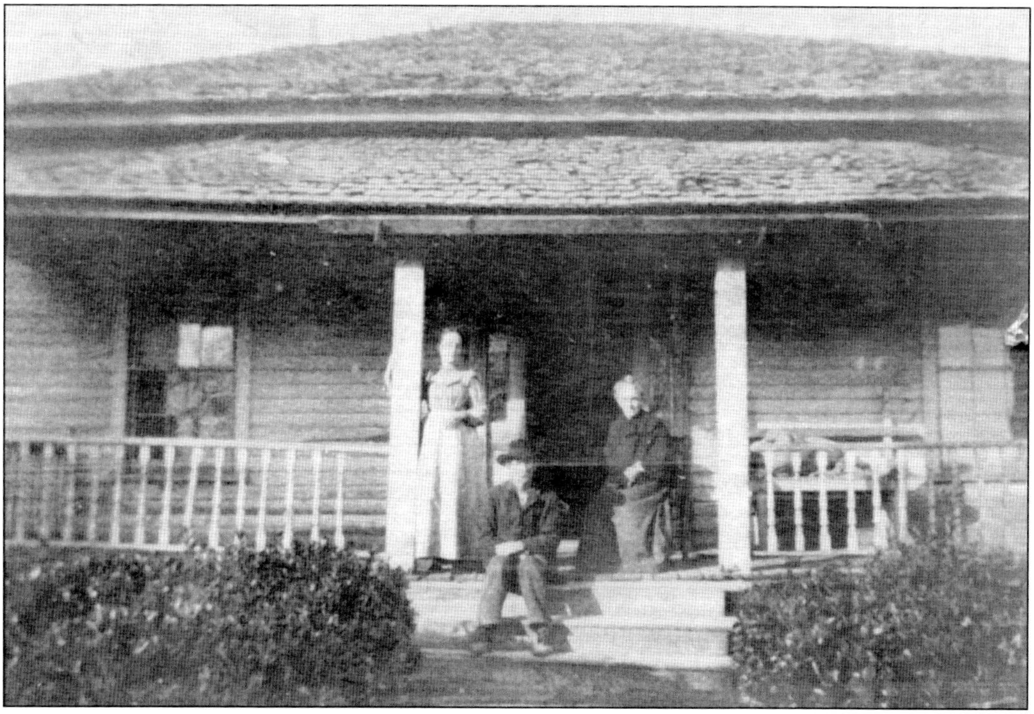

**Wescott Home.** John and Rebecca Drew Wescott sit in front of their home in 1900; standing is Clara Drew. (Courtesy of Lewis J. Hardee Jr.)

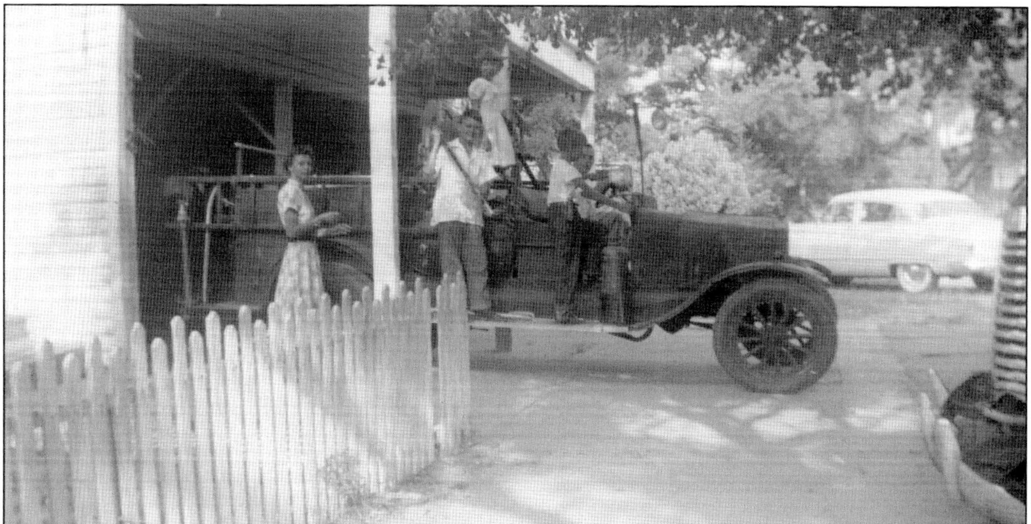

**Fire Truck, 1950s.** Members of the Hardee family play around on a Model T fire truck at the Southport Firehouse. (Courtesy of Lewis J. Hardee Jr.)

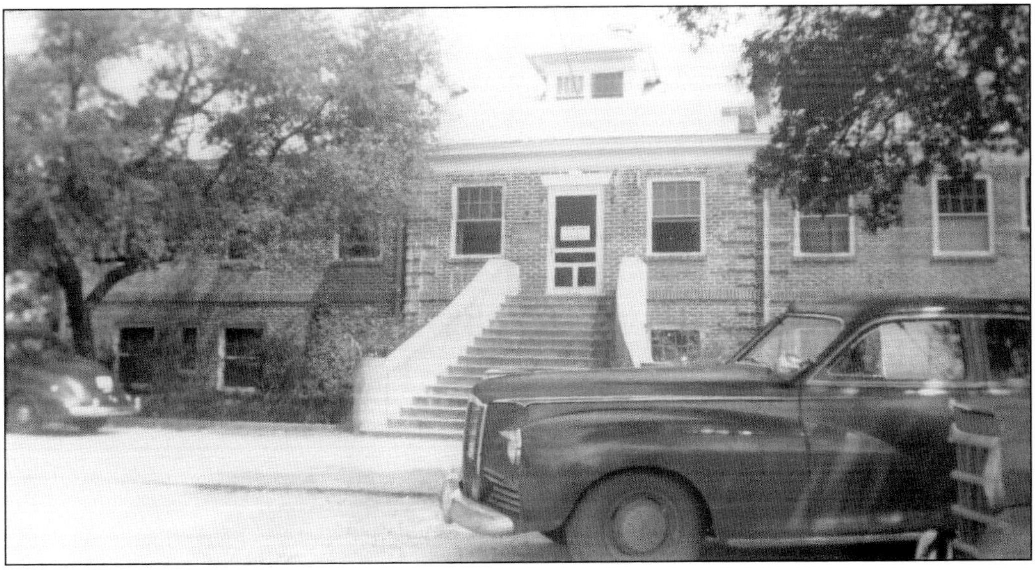

**DOSHER HOSPITAL, 1950S.** On June 2, 1930, Brunswick County Hospital opened in Southport. The hospital was renamed Dosher Memorial Hospital in honor of Dr. Julius Arthur Dosher shortly after his death in 1938. (Courtesy of Lewis J. Hardee Jr.)

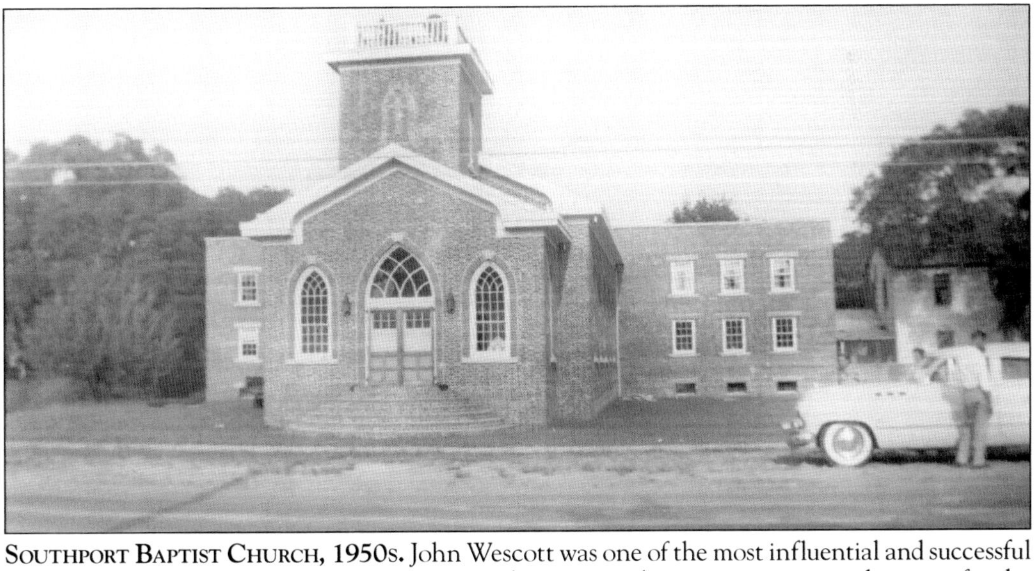

**SOUTHPORT BAPTIST CHURCH, 1950S.** John Wescott was one of the most influential and successful merchants in Southport. One of his most significant contributions was a major donation for the construction of the Baptist church, which was built at Franklin Square Park on the northeast corner of Nash and Howe Streets. (Courtesy of Lewis J. Hardee Jr.)

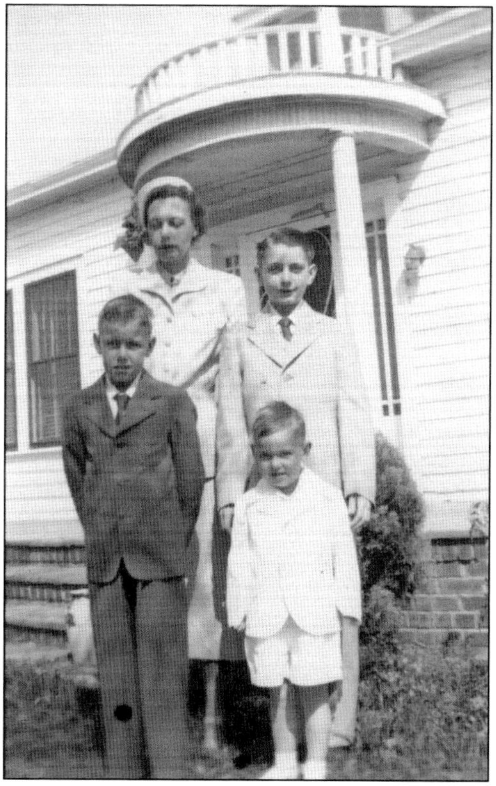

**Hardee Family, 1950s.** Dorothy Dosher was born in Southport in 1915 and was married to Lewis Hardee for 62 years; they had three sons. She stands in front of the Hardee home on Atlantic Avenue with her sons Mikael (front left), Don (front right), and Lewis Jr. (Courtesy of Lewis J. Hardee Jr.)

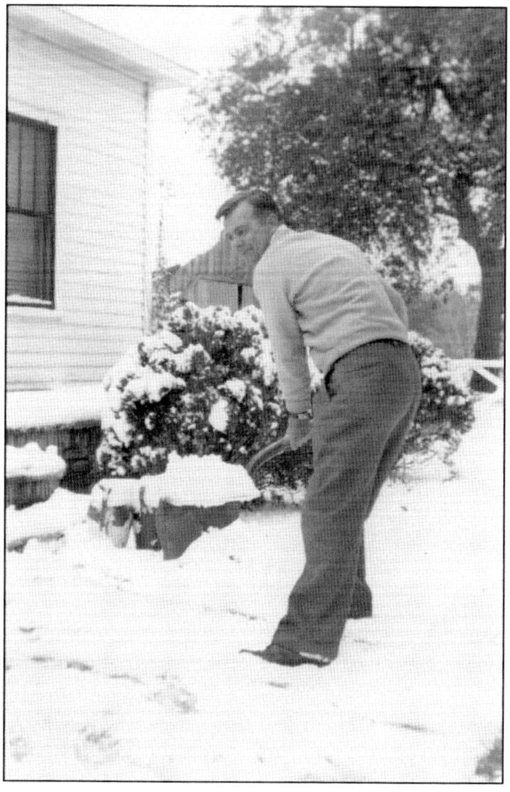

**Snow in Southport, 1951.** Lewis Hardee Sr. clears a path through the snow after the snowstorm of 1951. Southport rarely gets any of the white stuff, and this storm is still remembered by residents. (Courtesy of Lewis J. Hardee Jr.)

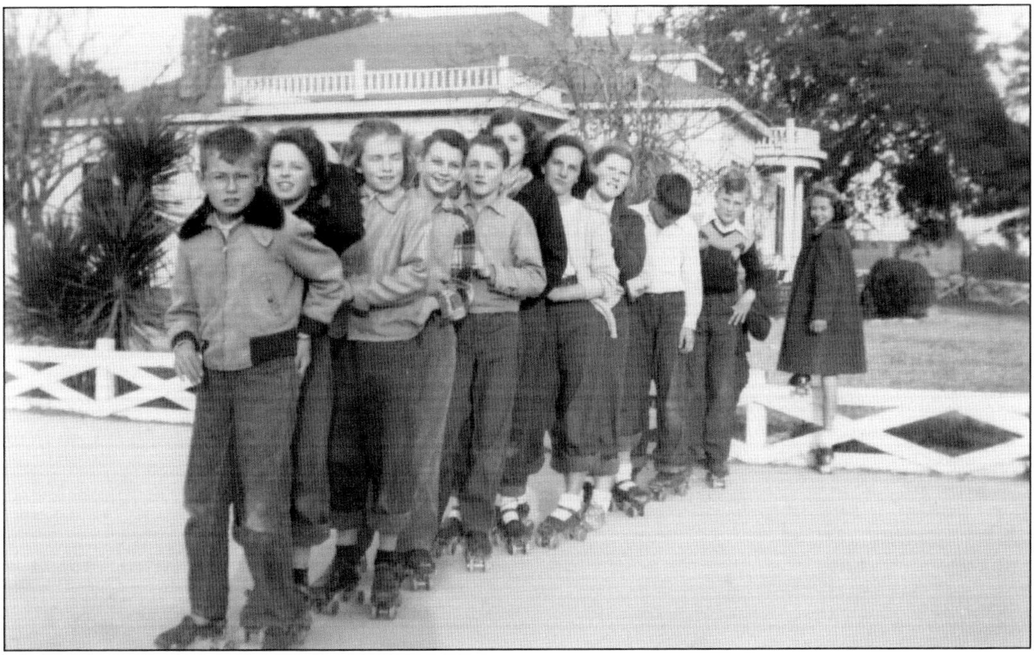

**SKATING PARTY.** Lewis J. Hardee Jr. is seen celebrating his birthday on January 17, 1951, with a skating party. The attendees included, from foreground to background, Mikael Hardee, "Butch" Harrelson, Betty McGlammery, Lewis J. Hardee Jr., Neil Lewis, Jean Thompson, Vivian McKeithan, Brookie Newton, Al Trunnell, John Sanders, and Lewis's mother Dorothy in the background. (Courtesy of Lewis J. Hardee Jr.)

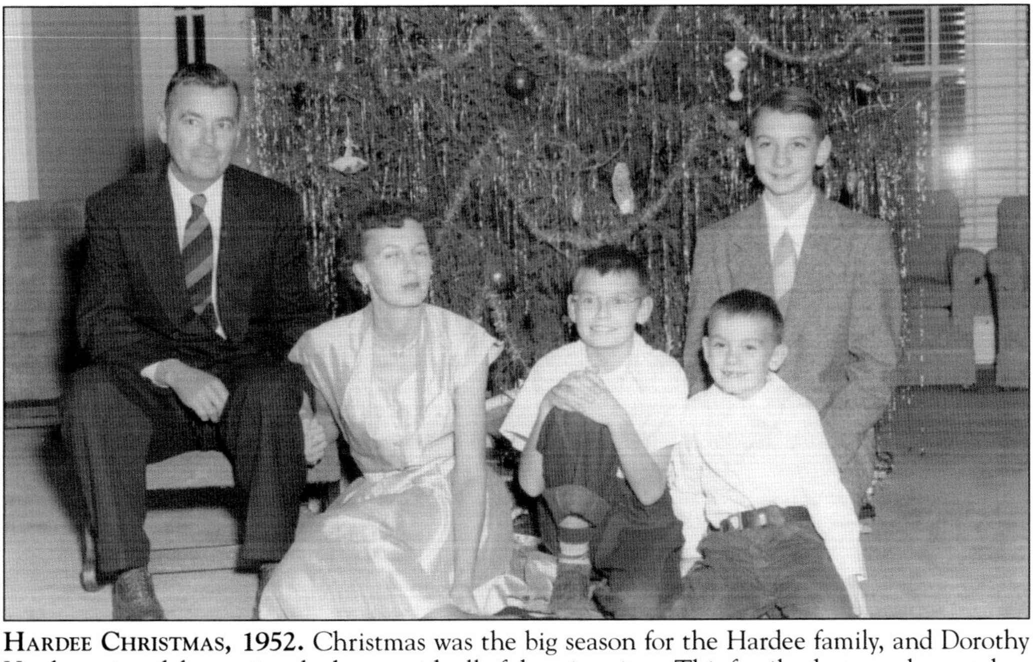

**HARDEE CHRISTMAS, 1952.** Christmas was the big season for the Hardee family, and Dorothy Hardee enjoyed decorating the house with all of the trimmings. This family photograph was taken in the living room in front of their beautifully decorated tree. Pictured from left to right are Lewis Hardee Sr., Dorothy, Mikael, Don, and Lewis Jr. (Courtesy of Lewis J. Hardee Jr.)

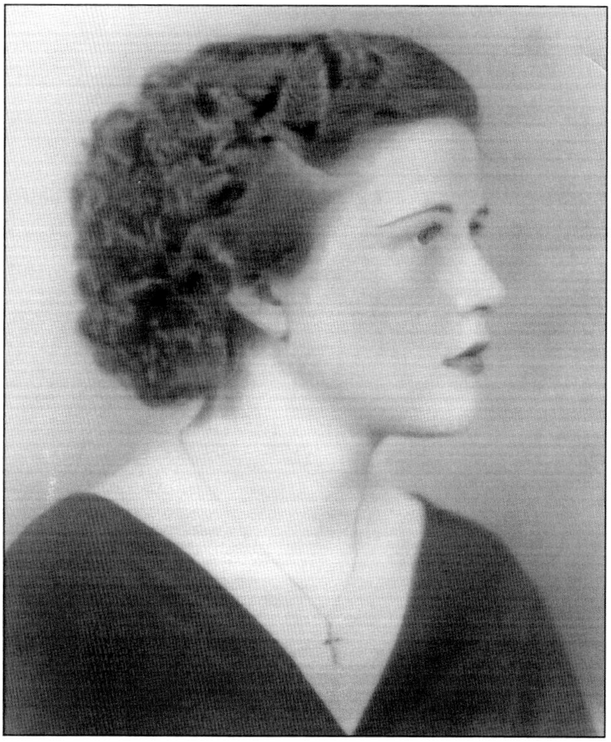

**Augusta's Portrait.** This 1916 image of Augusta Moore was taken when she was about 25 years old. She married Merritt Moore and they had three children: Paul, Jimmy, and Penny. (Courtesy of Jimmy Moore.)

**Shelling Butterbeans, 1950s.** Augusta Moore is seen teaching her daughter Penny how to shell butterbeans. (Courtesy of Jimmy Moore.)

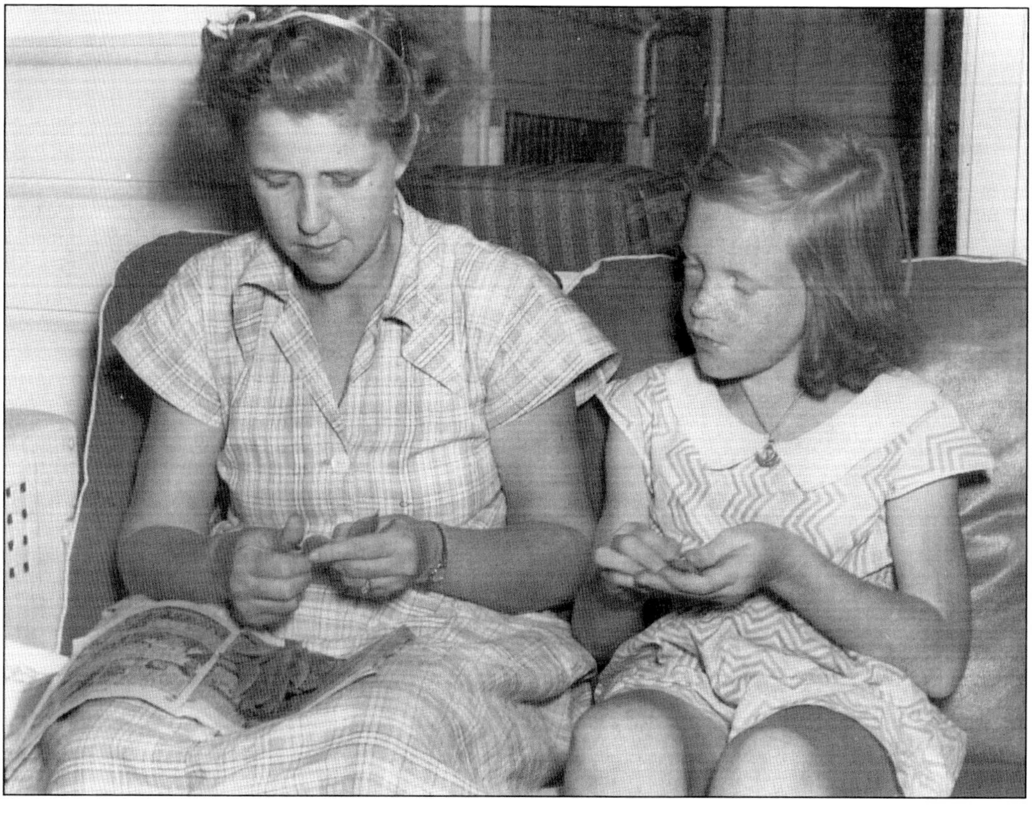

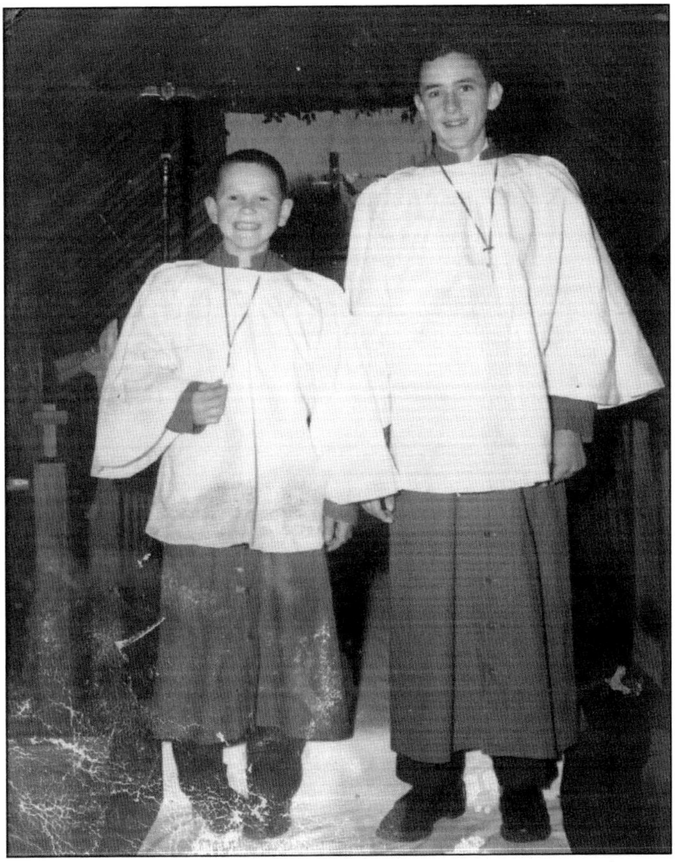

**Acolytes.** Jimmy (left) and Paul Moore are pictured serving as acolytes at St. Phillips Episcopal Church around 1952. The Moore family was actively involved in the church. (Courtesy of Jimmy Moore.)

**Four Generations.** Pictured from left to right are (first row) Jimmy, Penny, and Paul Moore; (second row) mother Augusta Moore, grandmother Mrs. Will S. Davis, great-grandparents Mr. and Mrs. R. Will Davis, grandfather Will S. Davis, and father Capt. Merritt Moore. (Courtesy of Jimmy Moore.)

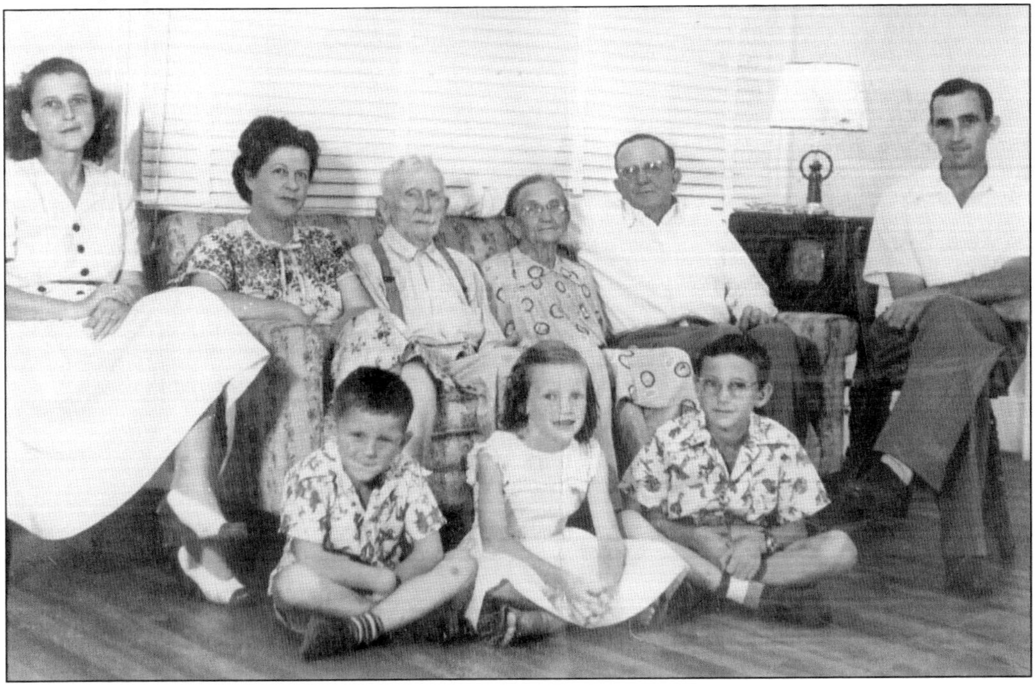

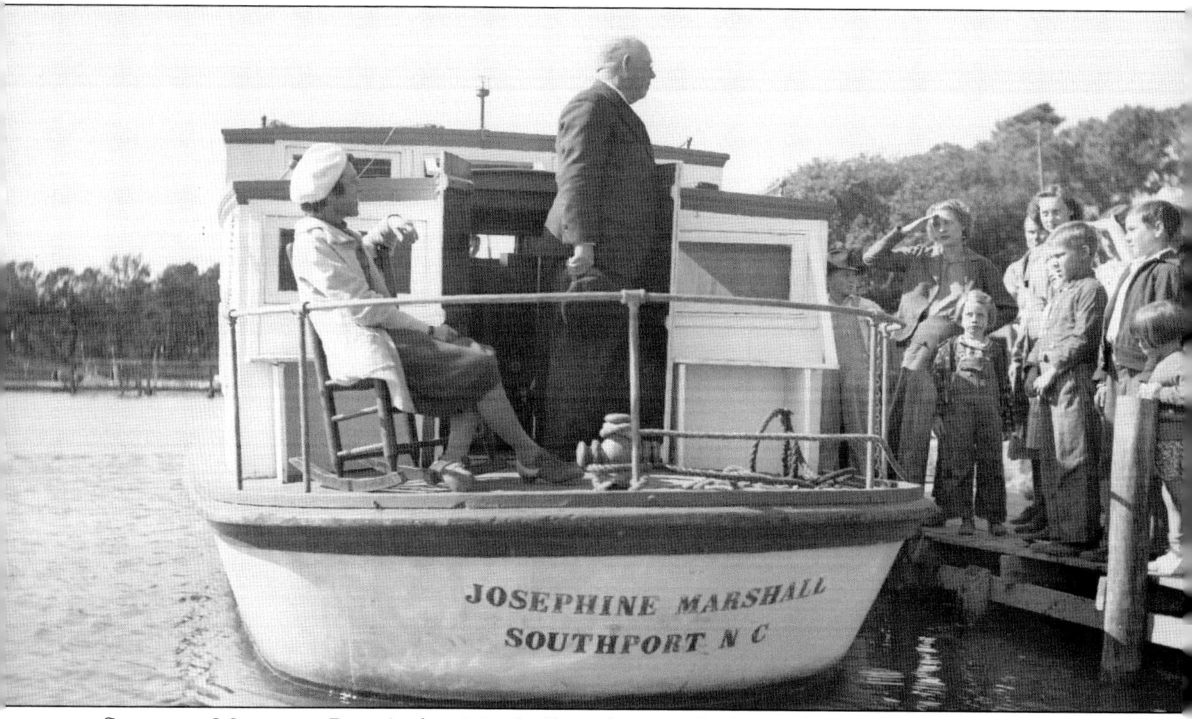


**SEAGOING MINISTER.** Rev. Arthur Marshall was born and educated in Ireland. He was ordained a deacon in 1912 and a priest in 1914. He operated the "Gospel Boat" out of Southport from 1938 to 1939 while a rector at St. Phillips Episcopal Church. The boat had a 90-horsepower engine given to Marshall by automobile magnate Walter P. Chrysler and could accommodate four: the pastor, his wife, and two crewmen. Floyd Gibbons donated a portable pipe organ for Marshall's services, and the boat stopped at more than 100 places in his circuit at least once a month, serving thousands of parishioners along the Intracoastal Waterway. It was the only such "floating church" in the United States. (Courtesy of the North Carolina State Archives.)

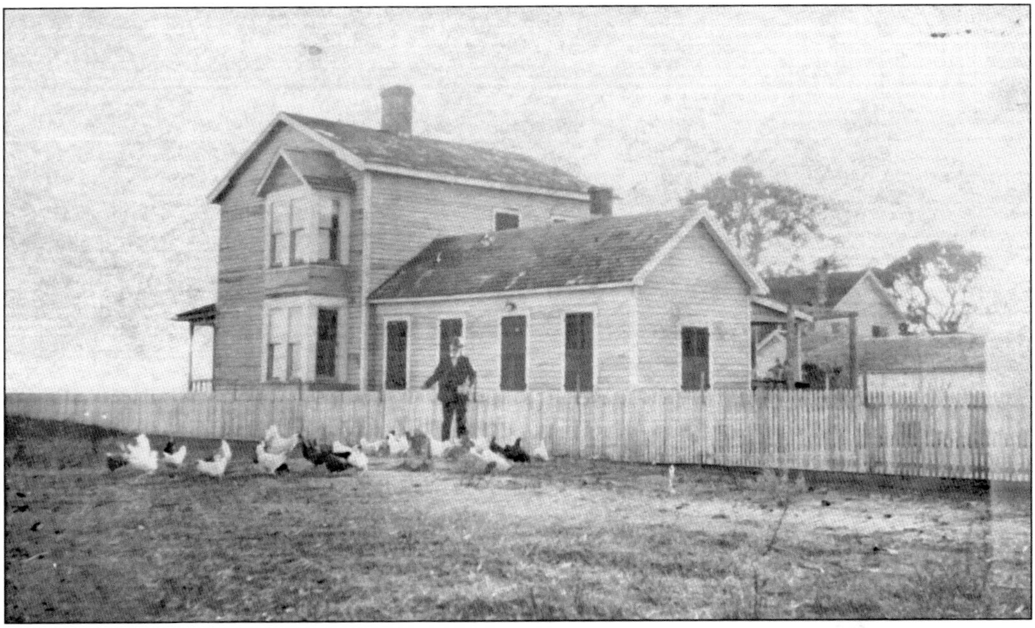

**Dr. Jens Berg's House.** This is a back view of what became Annie May Woodside's house, where Dr. Berg is feeding the chickens. This building was moved to 413 East Bay Street; it served as a fort hospital in 1808. Woodside inherited the house from her stepfather, Jens Berg, and lived in it until her death in 1981. (Courtesy of Andrea P. Clemmons.)

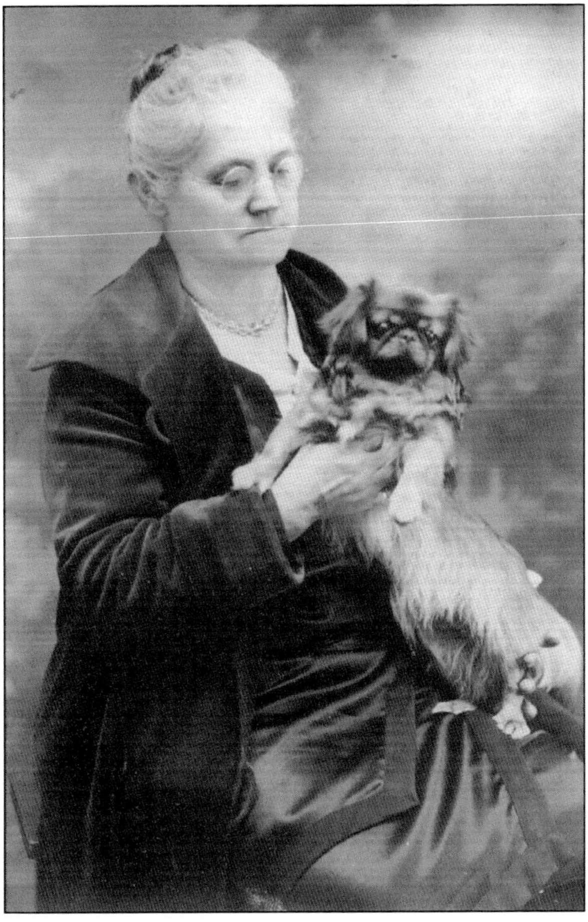

**Mary Anders Berg.** In 1902, Mary Anders married Dr. Jens Berg. She is the mother of Annie May Woodside, who was the first female superintendent in Brunswick County. (Courtesy of Andrea P. Clemmons.)

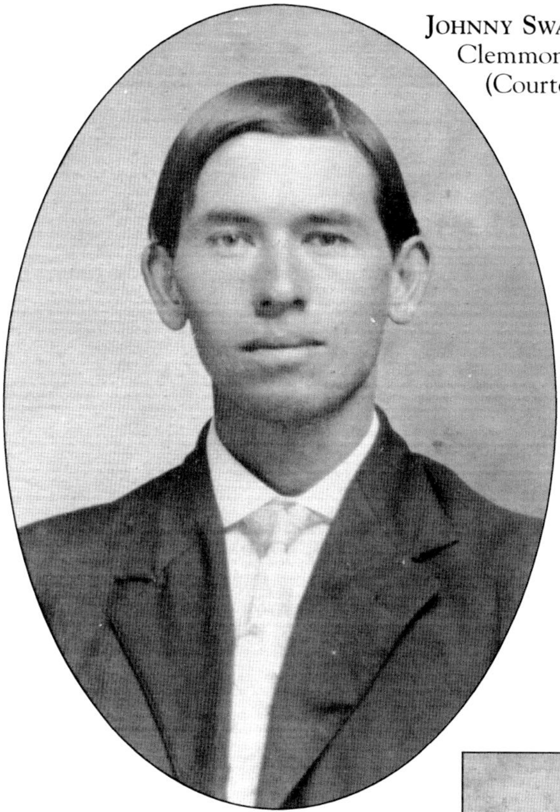

**JOHNNY SWAIN.** Swain, the third cousin to Andrea P. Clemmons, strikes a pose in this 1880 photograph. (Courtesy of Andrea P. Clemmons.)

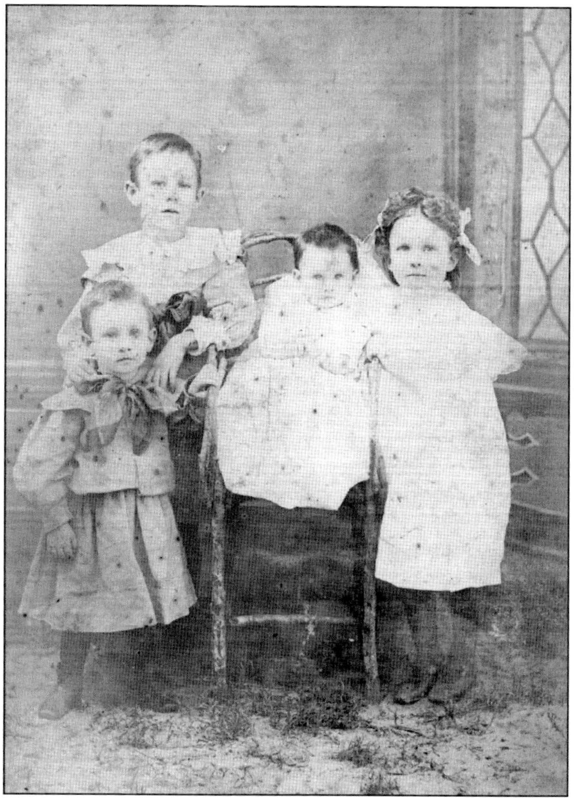

**THE PRICE CHILDREN.** The Price children pose for a photograph about 1898. From left to right are Dillard, John Dawson, baby Esther, and Laura Mae Price. (Courtesy of Andrea P. Clemmons.)

**JOHN DAWSON PRICE.** John Dawson Price poses with his daughter Carrie (left) and an unidentified girl in 1917. Carrie was born in 1912 and died very young in 1924. (Courtesy of Andrea P. Clemmons.)

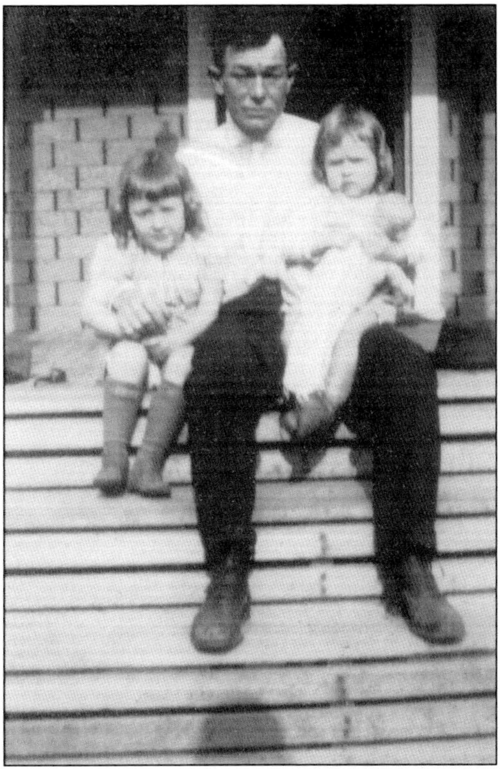

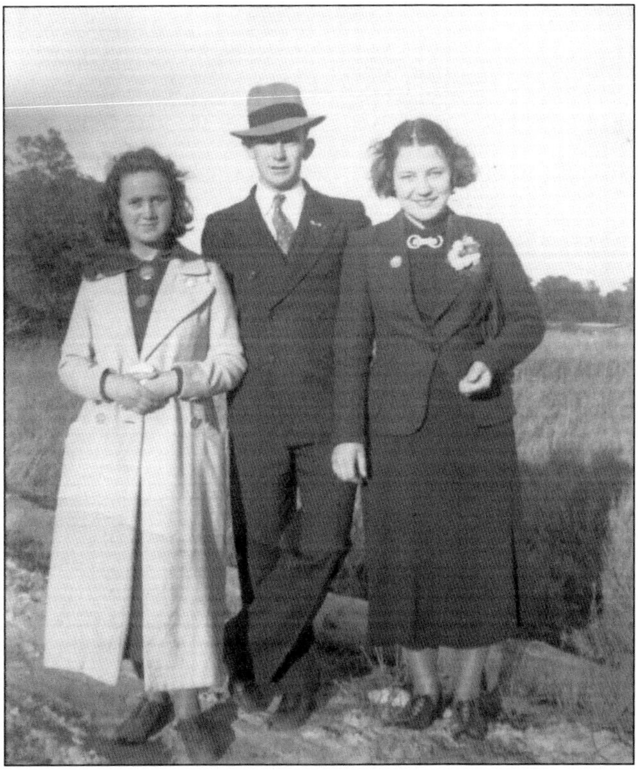

**FAMILY FARM.** Carrie Hewett, Leroy Price, and Fairlee Lewis pose on the Price family farm in the 1920s. (Courtesy of Andrea P. Clemmons.)

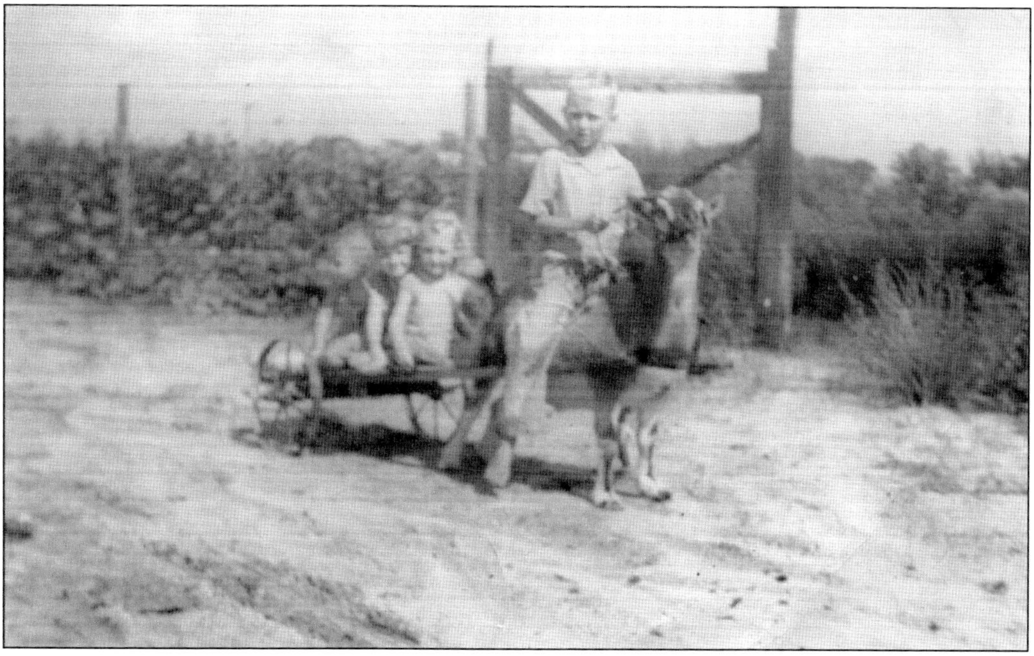

**GOAT EXPRESS.** James Price rides a goat pulling his sister Patsy (second to the right) and two other small riders. (Courtesy of Andrea P. Clemmons.)

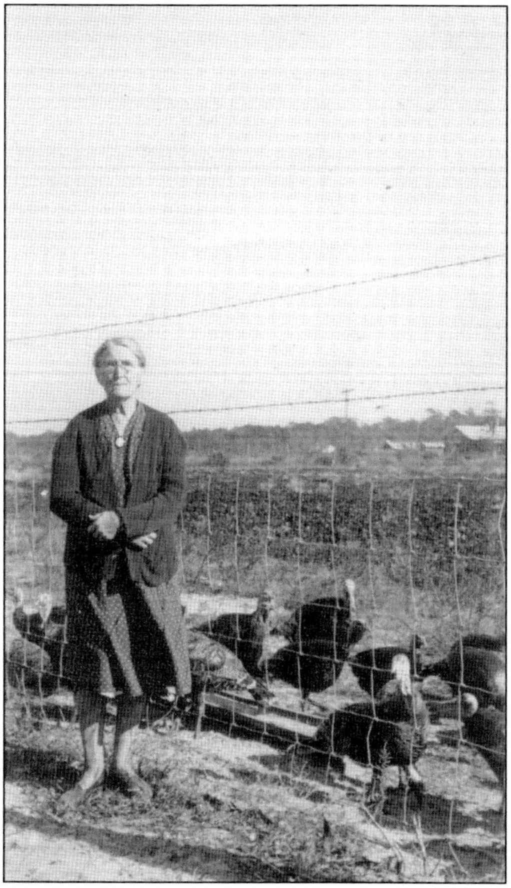

**ANDREA'S GRANDMOTHER.** Carrie Jeanette Price poses in front of her turkeys on the Price farm. In the background to the right is the County Home, which housed the elderly and mentally disabled. (Courtesy of Andrea P. Clemmons.)

**LEROY ON A DRAG HARROW.** Leroy Price drives a drag harrow on the 600-acre Price family farm in the 1930s. Pulled by a horse, a drag harrow was often used to loosen and even out the soil to prepare the ground for planting crops, similar to a cultivator. (Courtesy of Andrea P. Clemmons.)

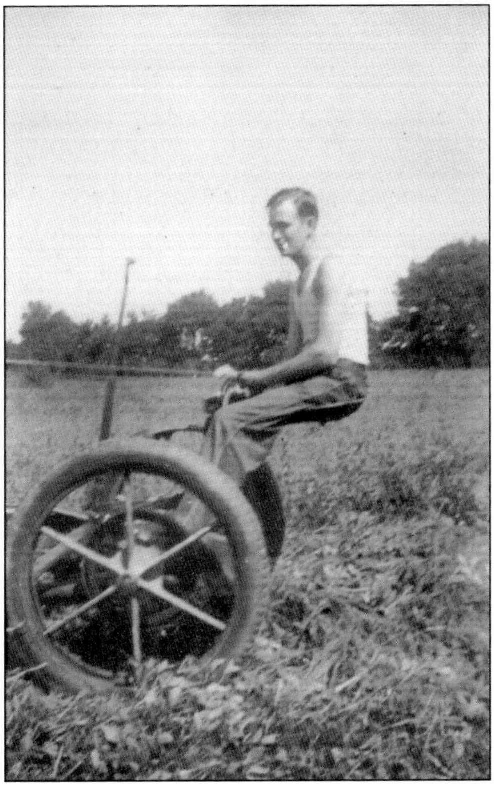

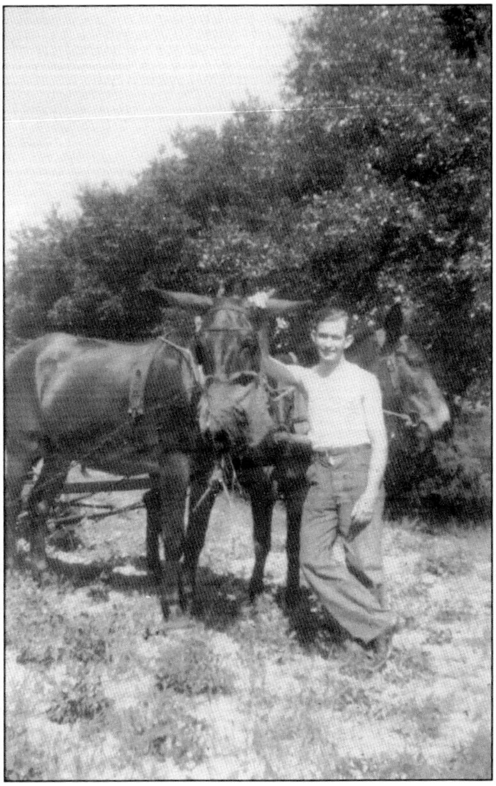

**LEROY ON THE FARM.** Leroy Price rubs his horse's ear on the Price farm in 1930s. (Courtesy of Andrea P. Clemmons.)

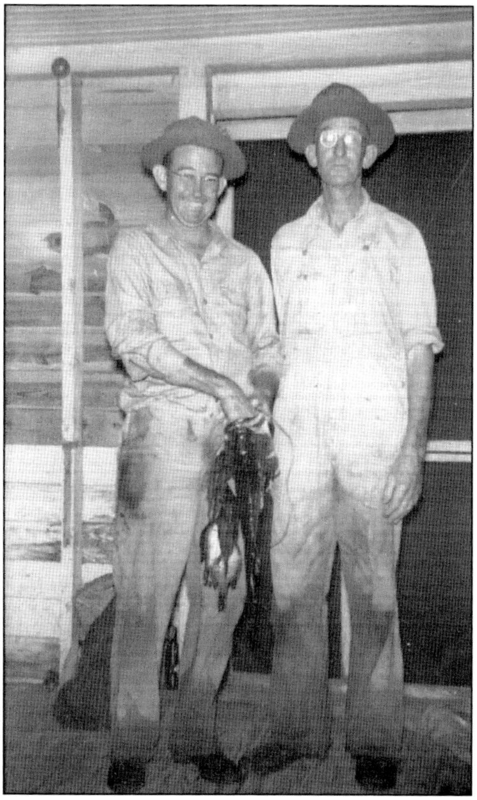

**Catfish for Dinner.** Leroy (left) and Dillard Price arrive home with several fish in the 1940s. (Courtesy of Andrea P. Clemmons.)

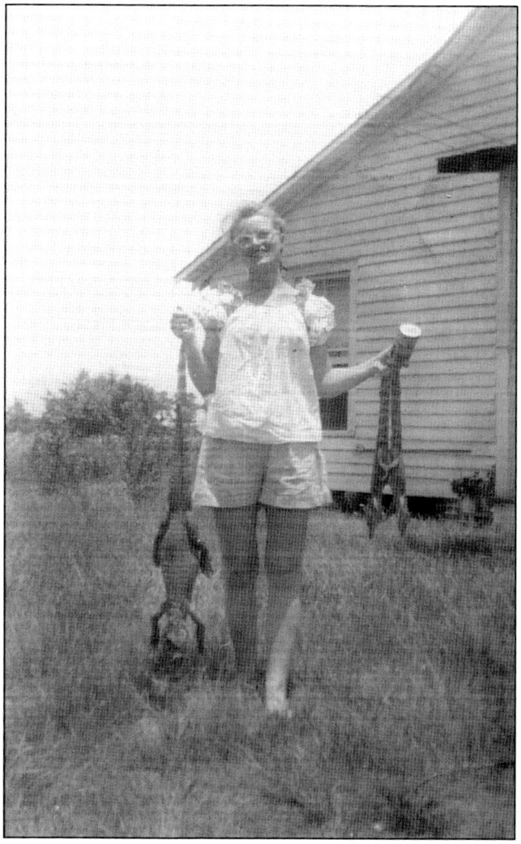

**Gators.** Ann Price holds a medium-sized alligator and two babies caught in one of the many creeks on the 600-acre Price farm. The creeks were home to alligators, which posed a threat to livestock. To help protect the farm animals, they often hunted alligators and turned them into dinner. (Courtesy of Andrea P. Clemmons.)

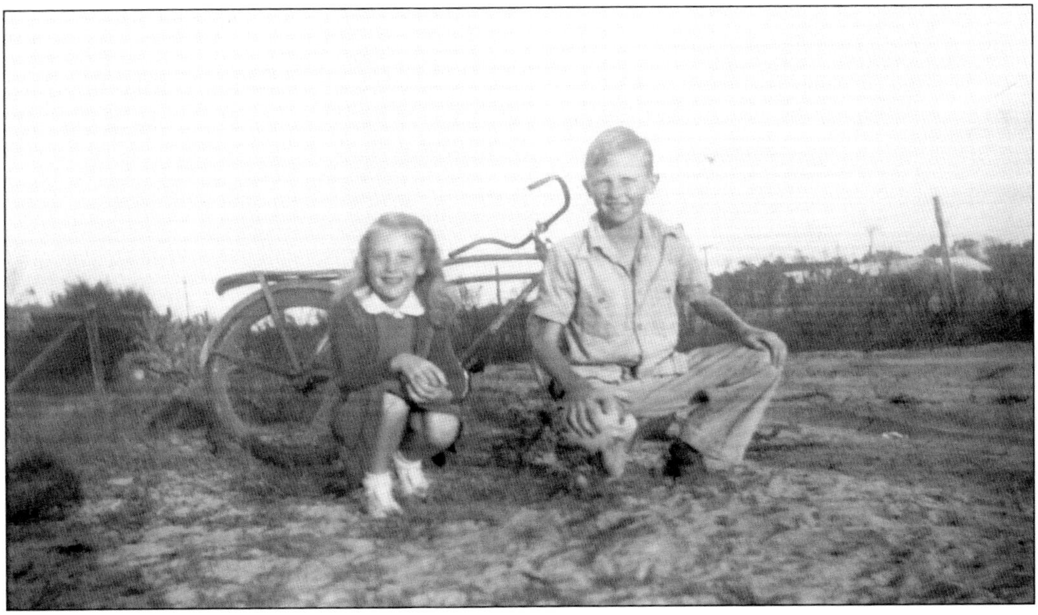

**BICYCLE ON THE FARM.** James and Patsy Price take a break from riding the bike on the Price family Farm in the 1940s. (Courtesy of Andrea P. Clemmons.)

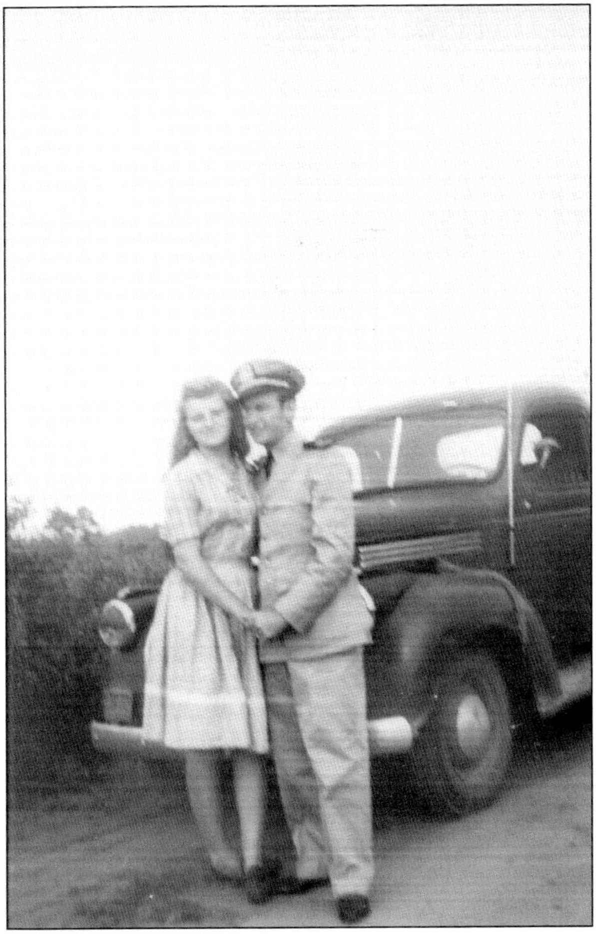

**ANN AND LEROY.** Leroy Price poses with his bride-to-be in 1942. (Courtesy of Andrea P. Clemmons.)

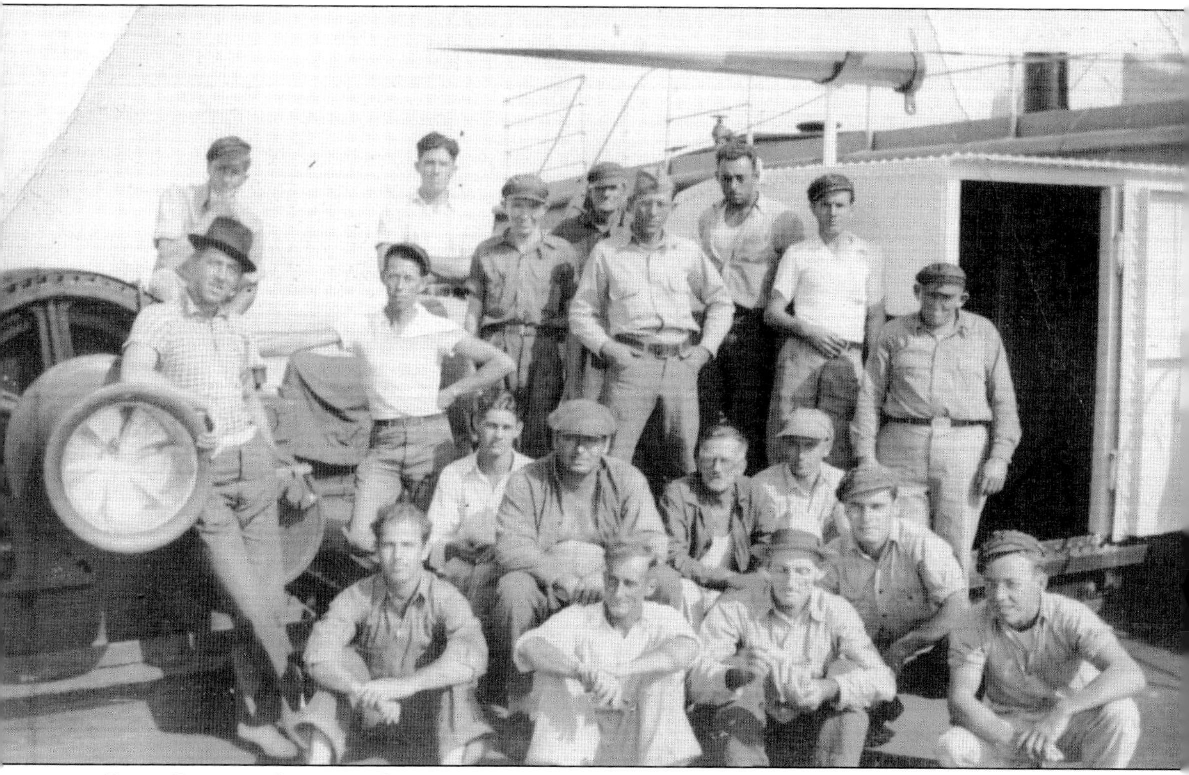

**CAMP SAPONA, CIVILIAN CONSERVATION CORPS (CCC).** A federal program created during the Great Depression as part of Pres. Franklin D. Roosevelt's New Deal, the CCC was a public-works relief program for unemployed, unmarried men between 18 and 25. The young men were paid $30 a month, $25 of which went to their parents. Camp Sapona, named after the Native American name for the upper Cape Fear River, opened in Southport in October 1934. It was situated in a pine grove on Leonard Street next to the former Southport baseball field. The living quarters, the mess hall, and the administration buildings were on the north side of the street, and the shops and storage sheds were on the south side. Several men came to the camp, married local girls, and remained citizens of Southport. The Southport camp closed in December 1937 amid loud protests. The CCC led to greater public awareness and appreciation of the outdoors. Nearly three billion trees were planted to help reforest the nation, and more than 800 parks were built in the United States as a result of the program. (Courtesy of Andrea P. Clemmons.)

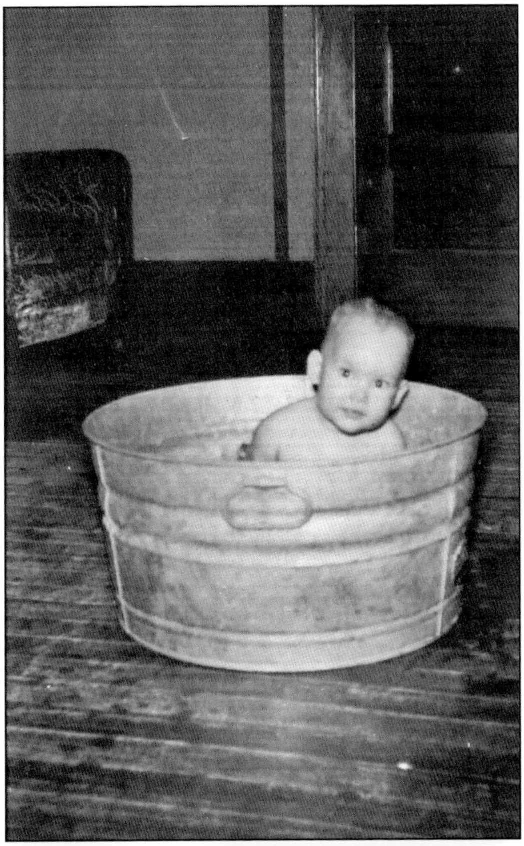

**Baby in a Tin Tub.** Baby Linda Ann Price is having some fun in a tin tub at the Price family farm in 1951. (Courtesy of Andrea P. Clemmons.)

**Andrea's First Birthday, 1956.** Andrea Price's (now Andrea P. Clemmons) extended family gathered for her first birthday. From left to right are Andrea's maternal great-grandmother Dicy Muncy; Donnie Coker, her first cousin; Evelyn Coker, her aunt; Baby Andrea; Scarlette Price, her sister; and Martha Couch, her great-grandmother. (Courtesy of Andrea P. Clemmons.)

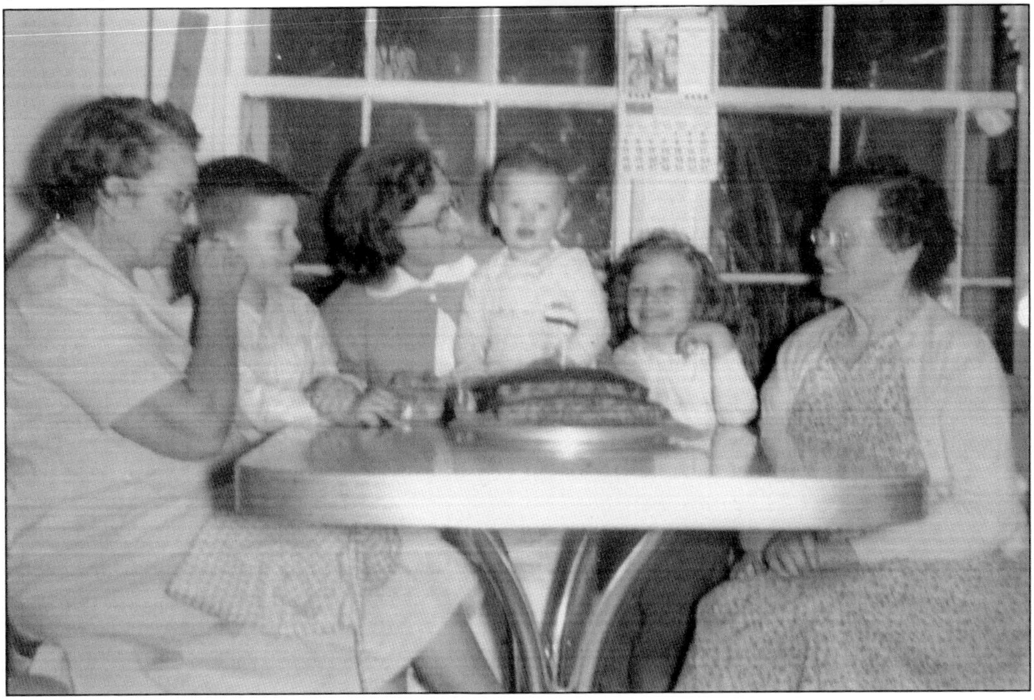

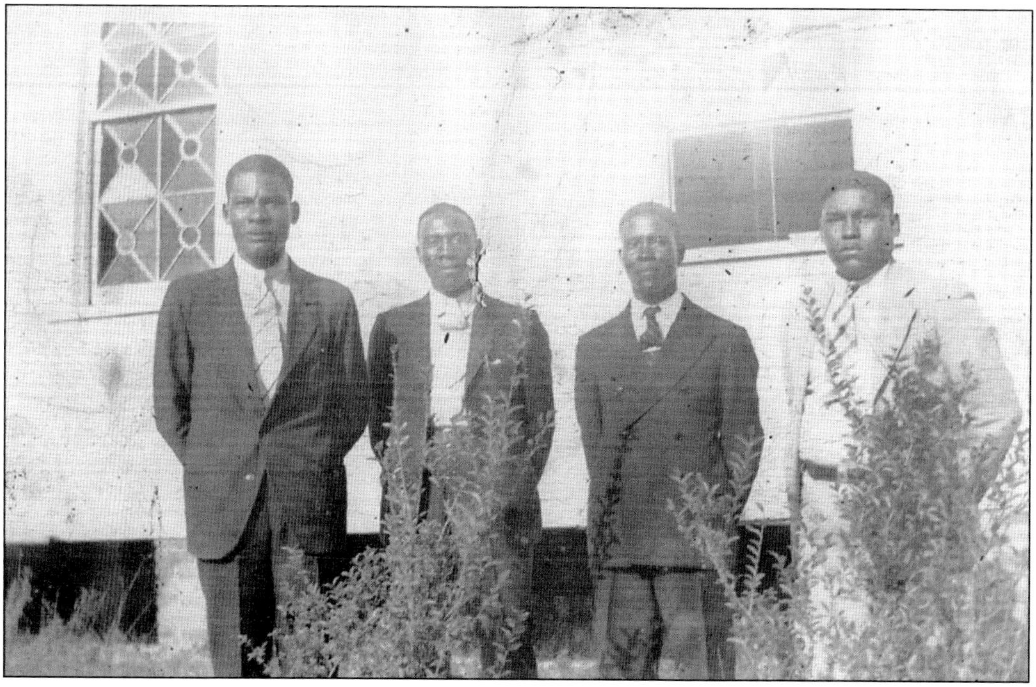

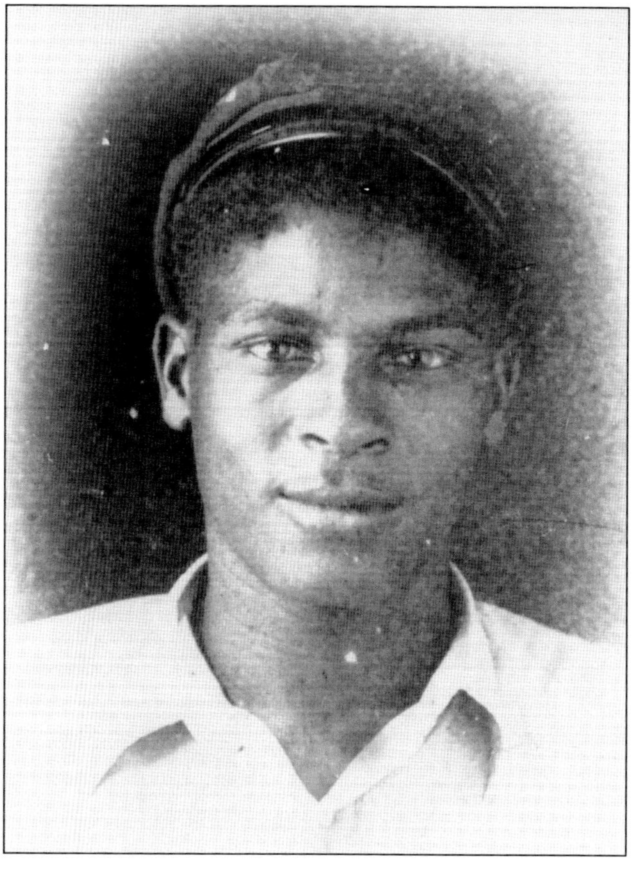

**THE GOSPEL FOUR.** A popular Christian singing group during the 1930s and 1940s, the Gospel Four traveled around and performed in churches and programs for many organizations. The Gospel Four included, from left to right, Ernest Joyner, bass; Eugene Gore, baritone; Harvis Hill, tenor; and Ervin Brown, lead singer. (Courtesy of Donnie Joyner.)

**"BIGGIE."** Southport native Cleveland "Biggie" Joyner and his brothers all earned nicknames beginning with the letter *B*. He is seen here in the 1930s. (Courtesy of Donnie Joyner.)

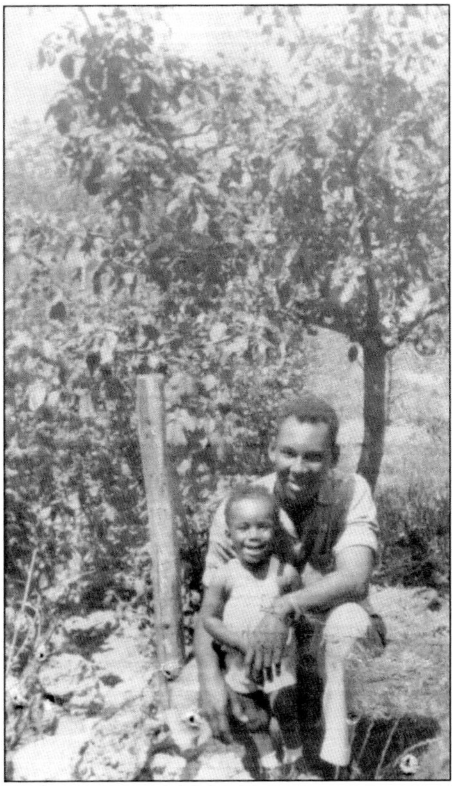

**FATHER AND SON.** Robert Earl Brown Sr. poses with his young son Robert Earl "Bobby" Brown Jr. at 737 Jabbertown Road, the home of Martha Elizabeth Joyner, Brown Sr.'s grandmother. (Courtesy of Donnie Joyner.)

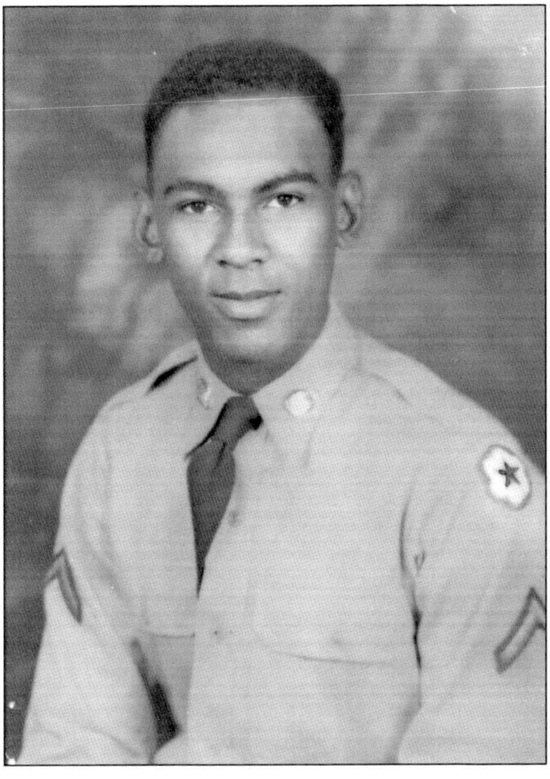

**ROBERT EARL BROWN SR.** After graduating from Brunswick County Training School in 1952 and serving in the Army, Robert Earl Brown Sr. married Gracie Foster, and they had three children. This photograph of Brown Sr. was taken during his Army days in 1955. (Courtesy of Donnie Joyner.)

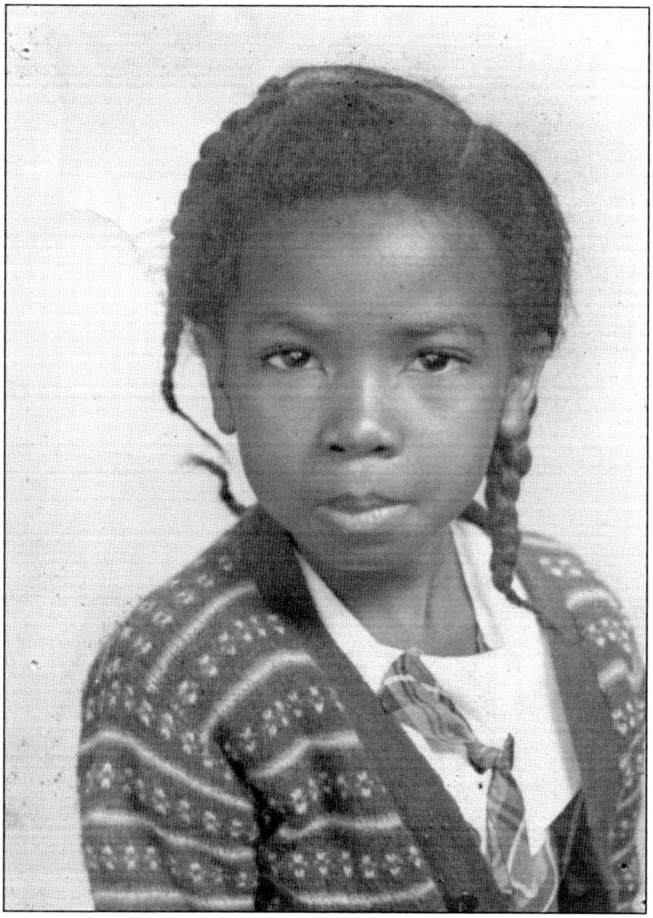

**Iris Joyner.** This photograph was taken of Iris Joyner in 1953 when she was about eight. She married Eddie Bernard and they had three children: Joann, Julia, and Anthony. (Courtesy of Donnie Joyner.)

**Boy in a Wagon.** Donnie Joyner rides around in a wagon around 1952 when he was three. Joyner was born and raised on Jabbertown Road. He married Theresa Qualls and they had one daughter, Rhonda. (Courtesy of Donnie Joyner.)

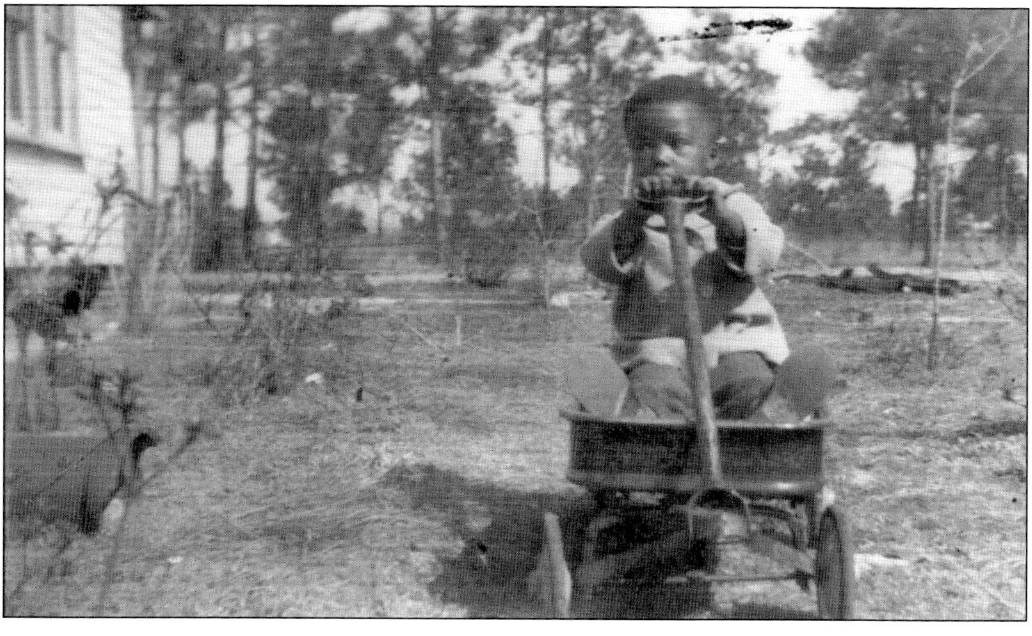

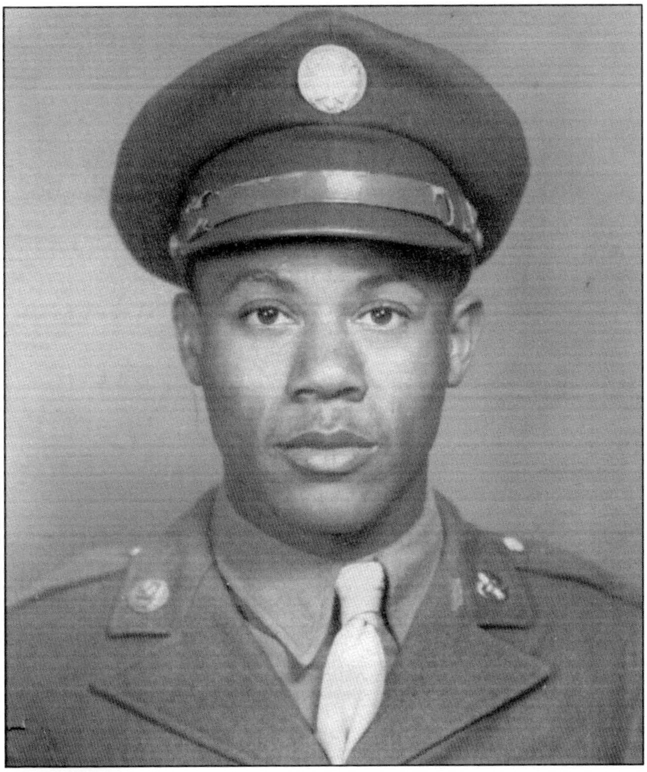

**James A. Joyner.** Joyner was a master sergeant in the Army and served in World War II and the Korean War. His last post was Camp Chaffee, Arkansas. His parents were William Joyner Sr. and Martha Hill-Joyner, and he married Cleo Sutton of Anniston, Alabama. The American Legion Joyner Bellamy Post 213 in Southport is named after him and Ellis Bellamy. (Courtesy of Donnie Joyner.)

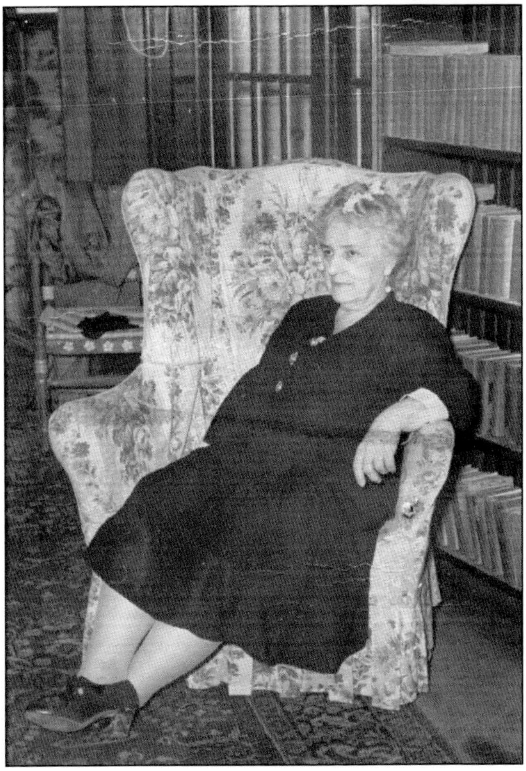

**Anna Thompson.** Emma Jane Joyner worked for Anna Thompson (seen here) for more than 10 years. (Courtesy of Donnie Joyner.)

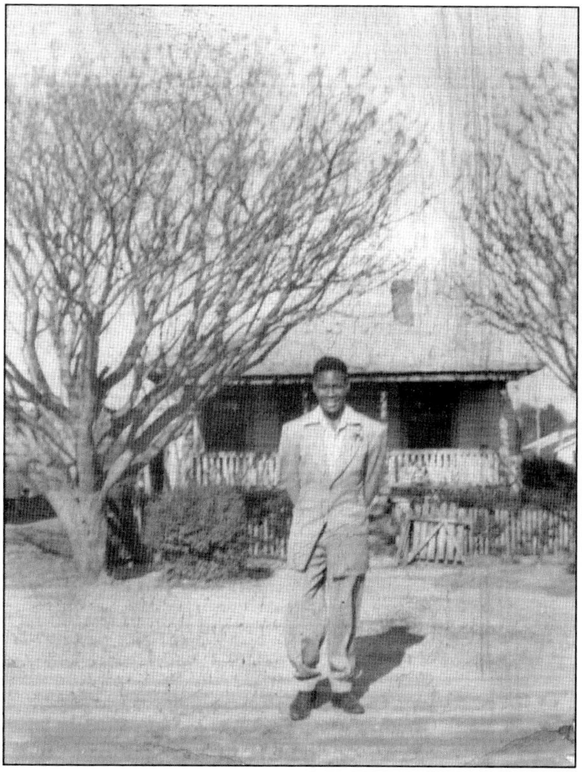

**"Pete the Tramp."** In Southport, nicknames are a tradition. Many people earned them, and Charles Joyner was no different. This 1940s image shows Charles, who received the nickname "Pete the Tramp" after a cartoon character; he is still known by it today. He married Flora Wearren and is Donnie Joyner's first cousin. (Courtesy of Donnie Joyner.)

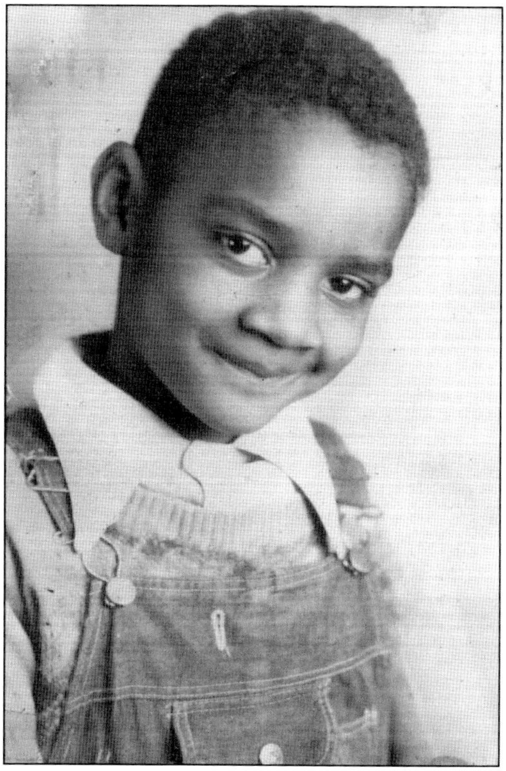

**Charles Warnette.** Charles was born and raised in Southport and actively served his community and his church. After entering the military, he became an Army medic and later married Shelley Young. He died in 2011. (Courtesy of Donnie Joyner.)

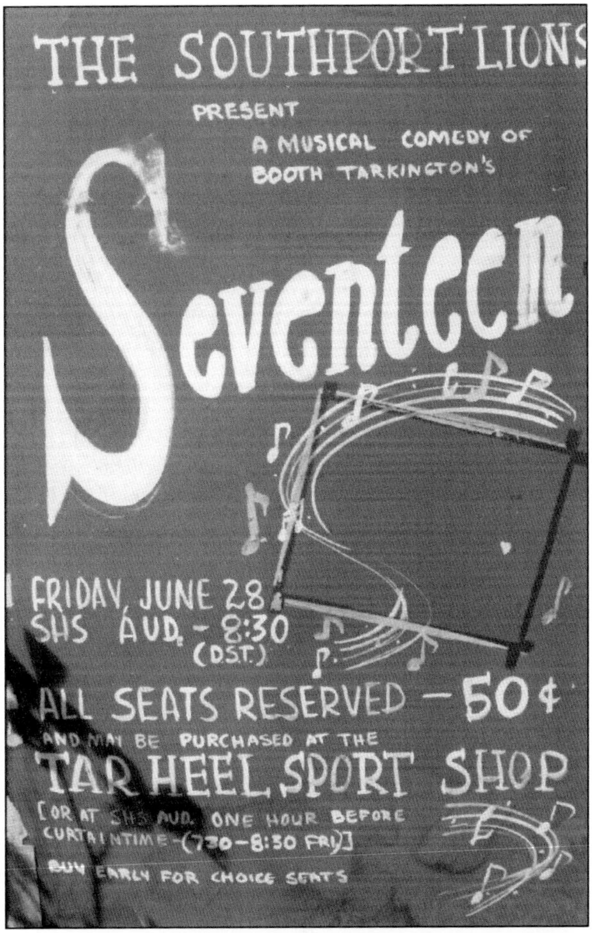


**SEVENTEEN.** A musical comedy put on at the Southport High School auditorium by the Southport Lions Club in the summer of 1957, *Seventeen* was a blast. The play featured, from left to right, Jimmy Harper, Barbara McLeod, Sharon Grant, Homer McKeithan, Barbara St. George, unidentified, Noni Rogers, and Charles Willis. (Courtesy of Lewis J. Hardee Jr.)

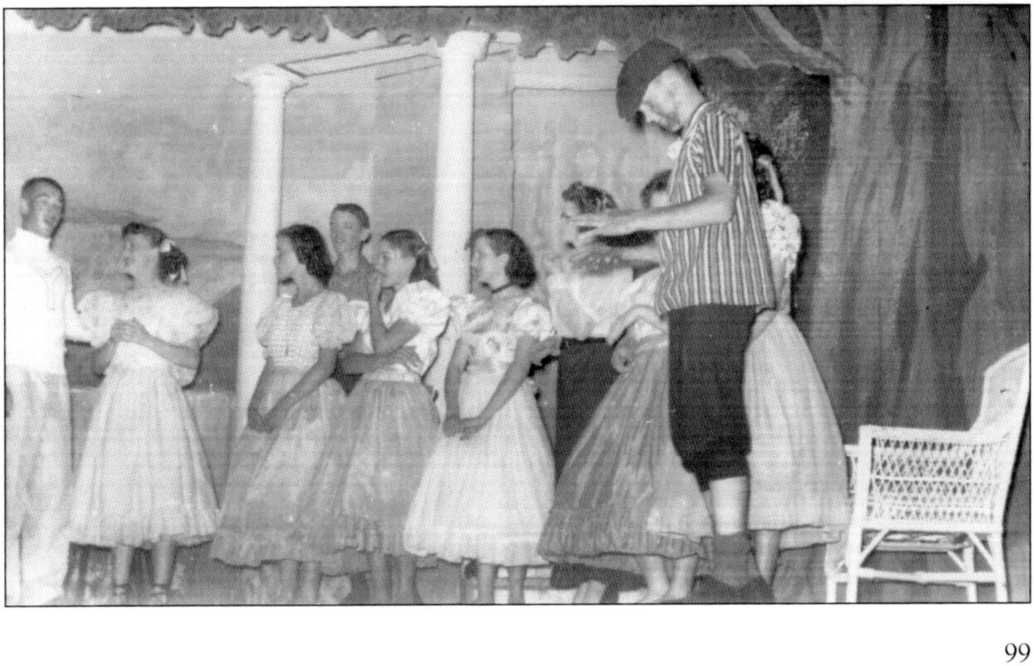

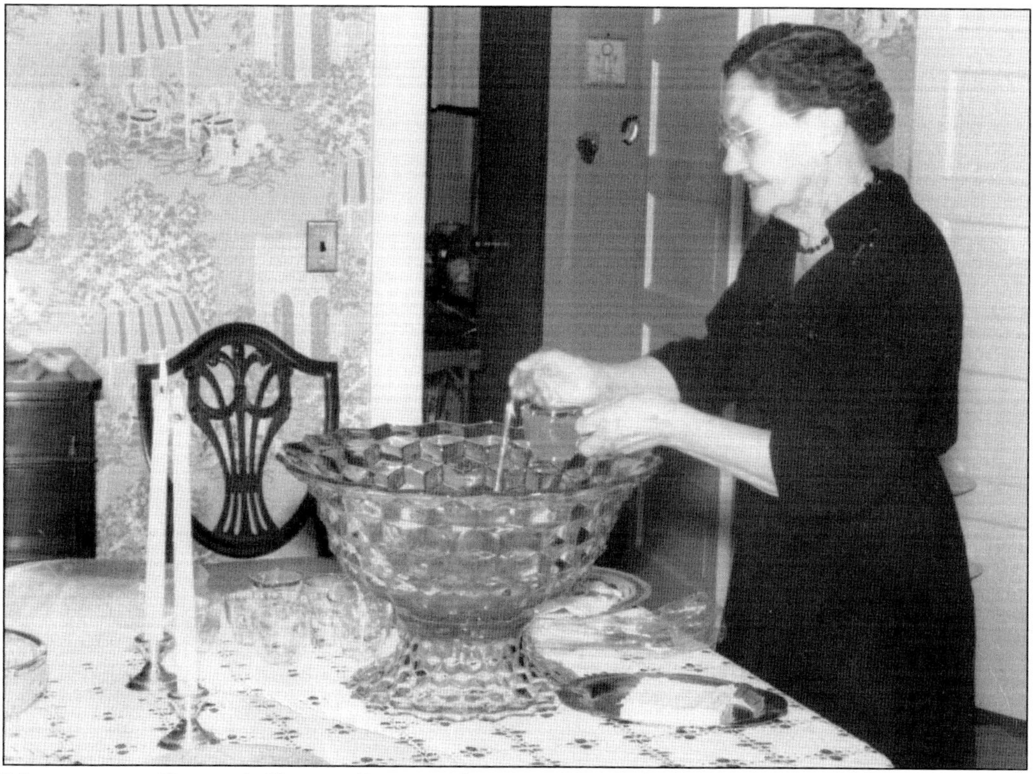

**MARGARETTE DOZIER'S PUNCH BOWL.** Alta Wescott Dosher serves punch from Margarette Dozier's pressed-glass punch bowl—one of the largest in the county—in the 1950s. (Courtesy of Lewis J. Hardee Jr.)

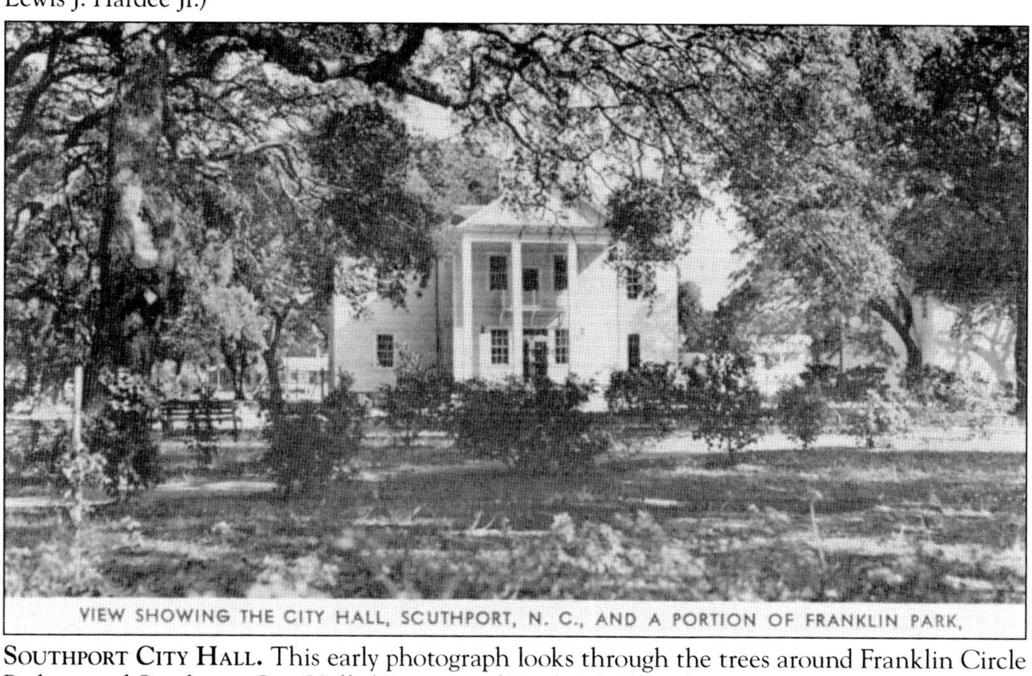

VIEW SHOWING THE CITY HALL, SOUTHPORT, N. C., AND A PORTION OF FRANKLIN PARK.

**SOUTHPORT CITY HALL.** This early photograph looks through the trees around Franklin Circle Park toward Southport City Hall. (Courtesy of Trudy M. Young.)

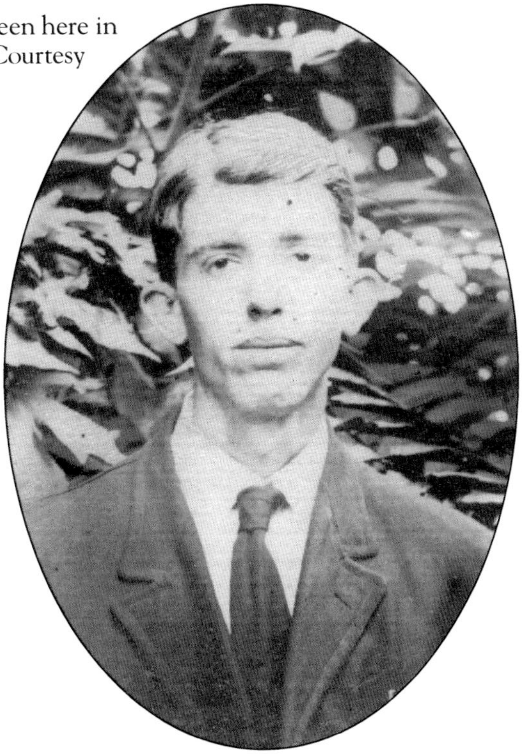

**Fred Spencer.** Early contractor Fred Spencer, seen here in the early 1900s, built Antioch Baptist Church. (Courtesy of Andrea P. Clemmons.)

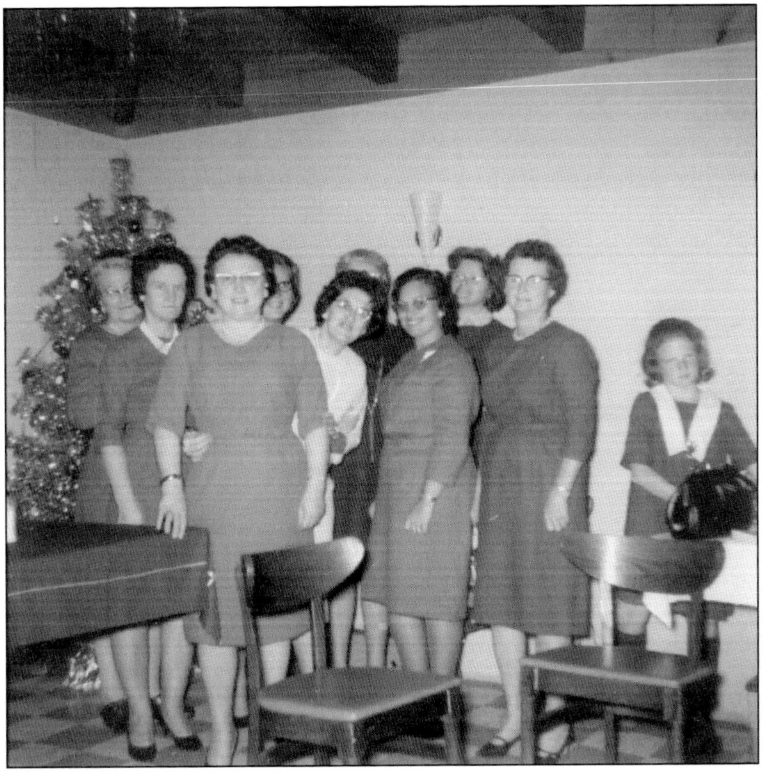

**Women's Missionary Union Christmas Party.** This Christmas party was held at Southport Baptist Church December 1963. The second lady in the front row in the white dress is Susan Carson, known as "Miss Susie." Miss Susie was a founding member and past president of the Southport Historical Society. She also served for over 20 years as a trustee for the Brunswick County Library. The child on the right looking bored is Andrea P. Clemmons. (Courtesy of Andrea P. Clemmons.)

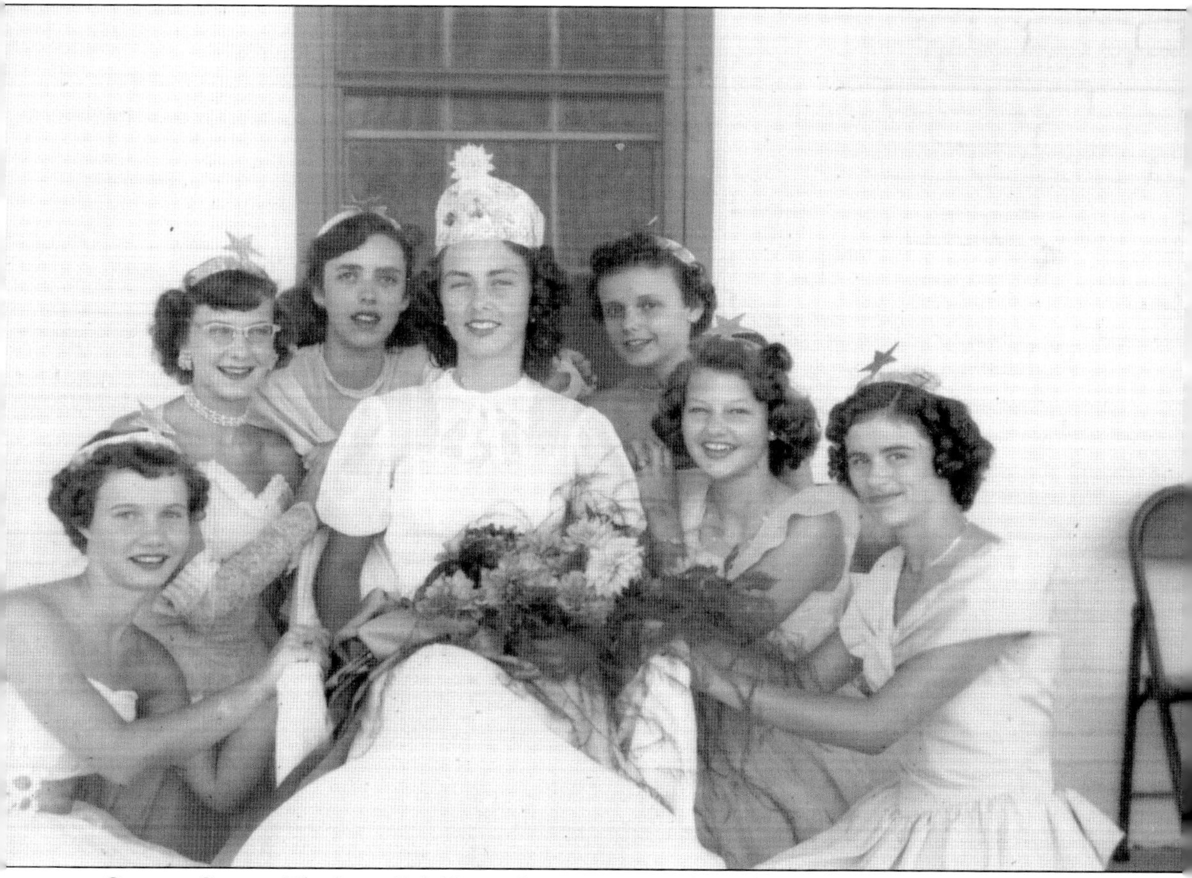

**QUEENS COURT.** The Live Oak Festival queen's court from the Fourth of July in 1951 featured, from left to right, Latitia Hickman, Stuart Arrington, Trudy McNeil (now Trudy M. Young), queen Gloria Hewett, Mary Elizabeth Lupton, Libby Caster, and Linda Hickman. (Courtesy of Trudy M. Young.)

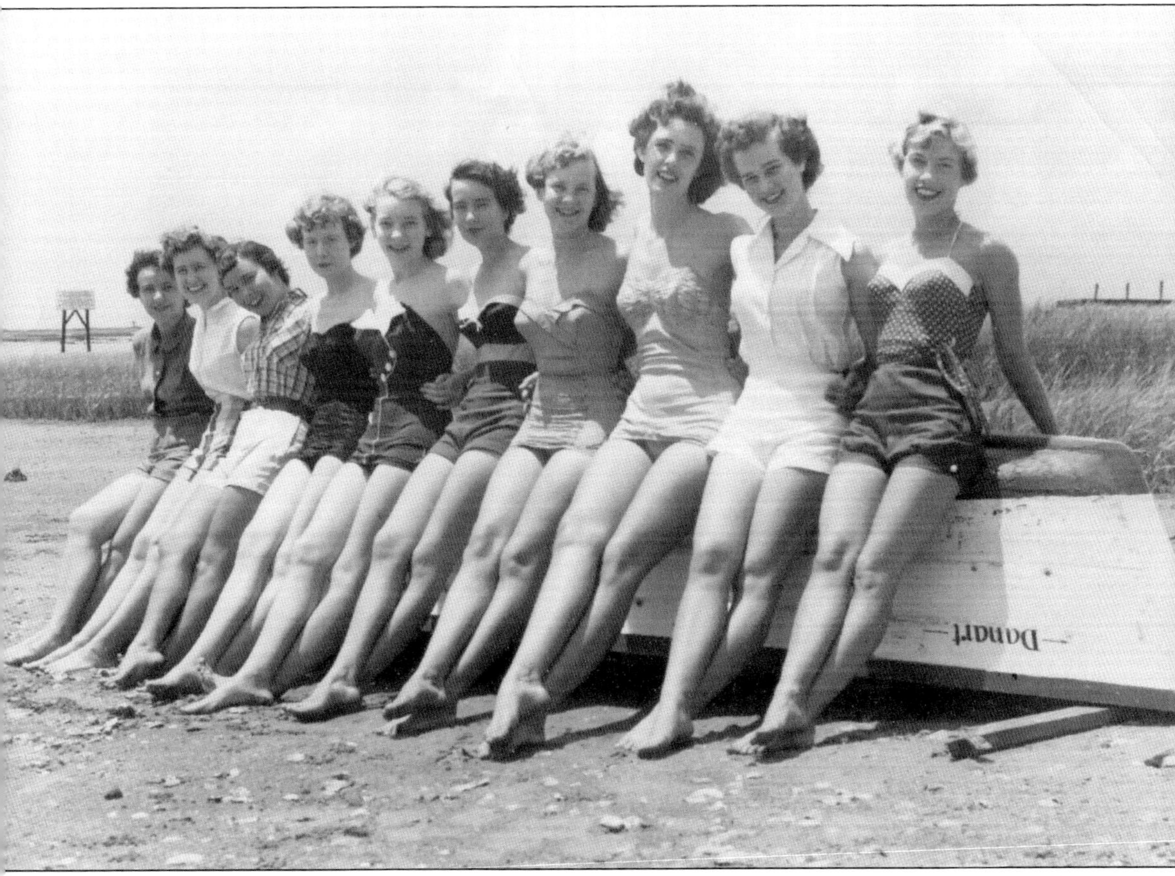

**LIVE OAK FESTIVAL.** Donning swimsuits and vying to be queen of the Live Oak Festival on the Fourth of July in 1953 were, from left to right, Marcia Dilsaver, Jacque Larsen, Patricia Adams, Iris Rabon, Arlene Kincaide, Alice Brown, Stuart Arrington, Trudy McNeil, Kathleen Edwards, and Harriett Corlette. (Courtesy of Trudy M. Young.)

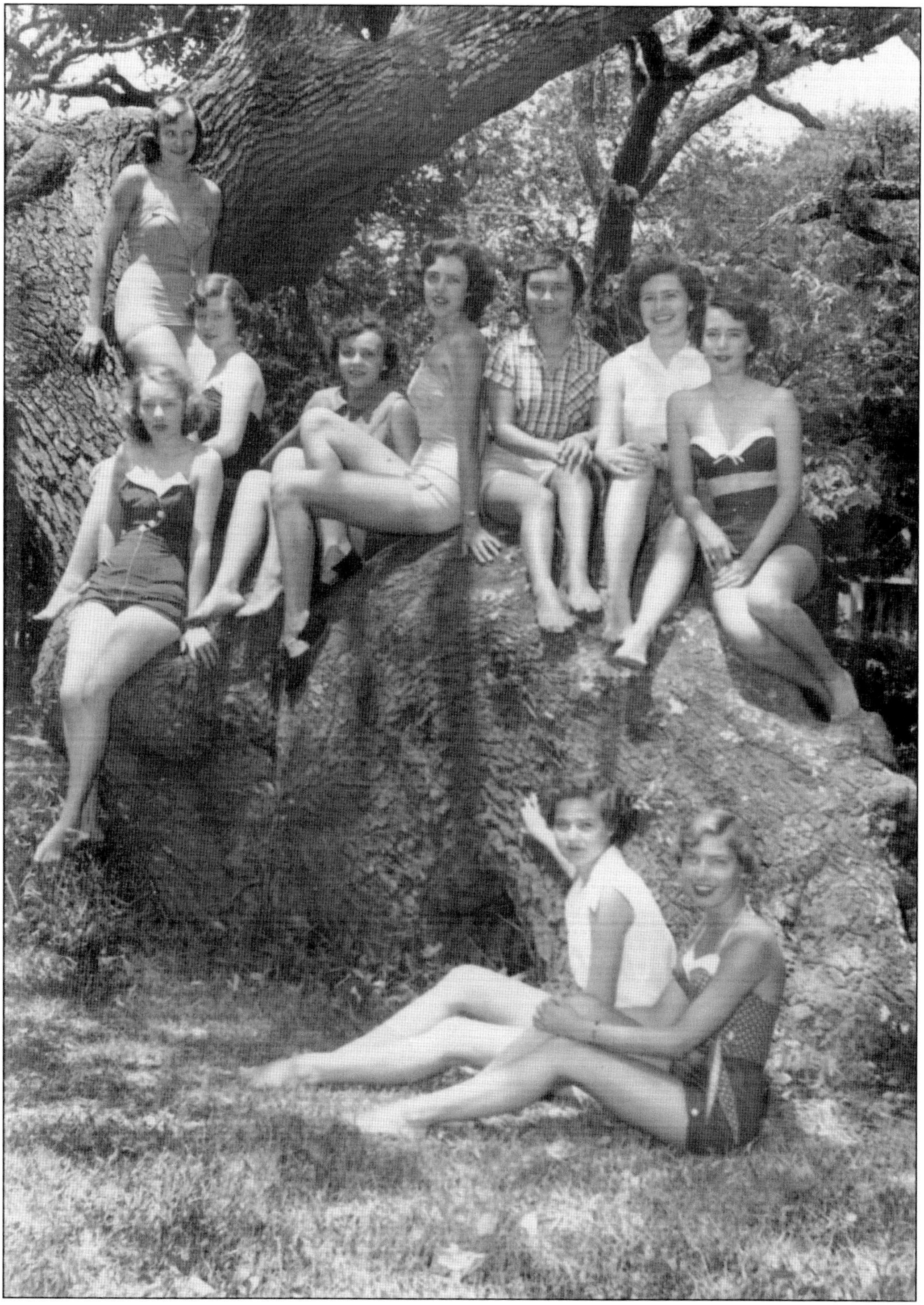

**Queen Contestants on the Indian Trail Tree.** The Live Oak Festival queen contestants pose around the Indian Trail Tree on the Fourth of July in 1953. Trudy McNeil is fifth from the left. (Courtesy of Trudy M. Young.)

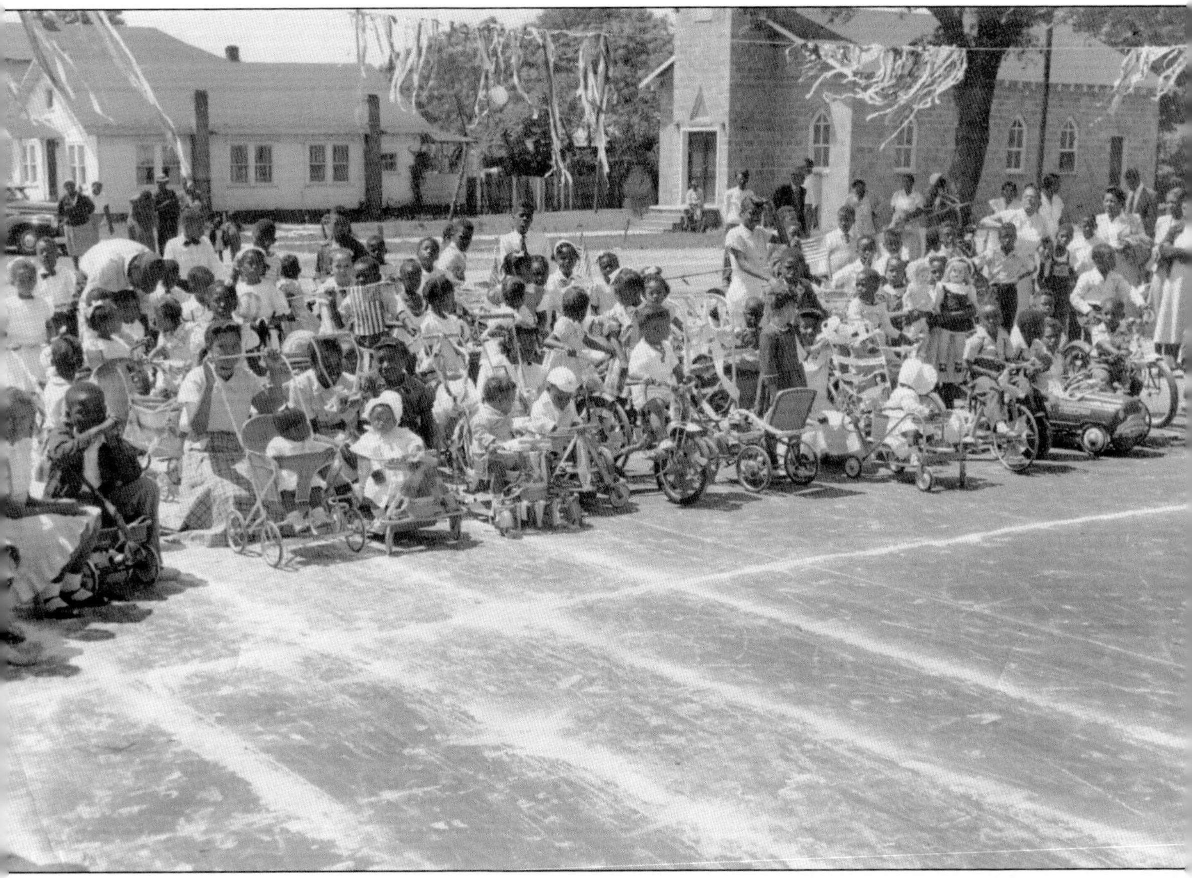

**May Day.** Members of the black community line up on Lord Street for a May Day celebration in the 1950s. May Day, celebrated on May 1, was a spring festival and public holiday. (Courtesy of Sarah P. Joyner.)

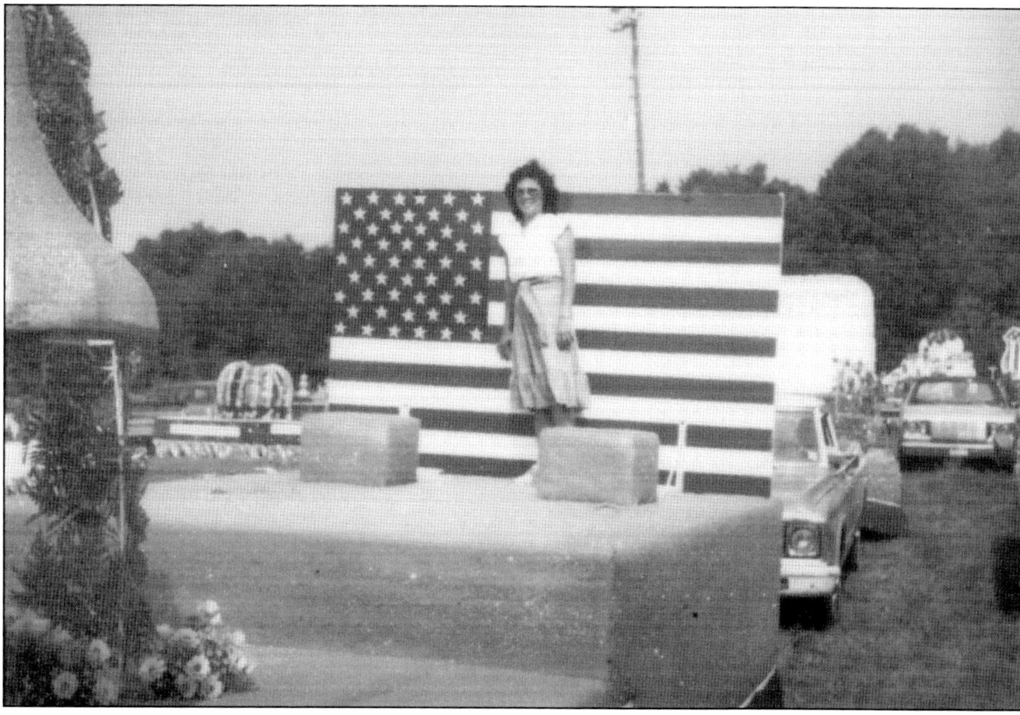

**"Y" ON A FLOAT, MID-1970S.** Hoa (pronounced "Y") Brown, the first person of Vietnamese heritage to live in Southport, rides on a float in a Fourth of July parade. (Courtesy of Joanne Kimball.)

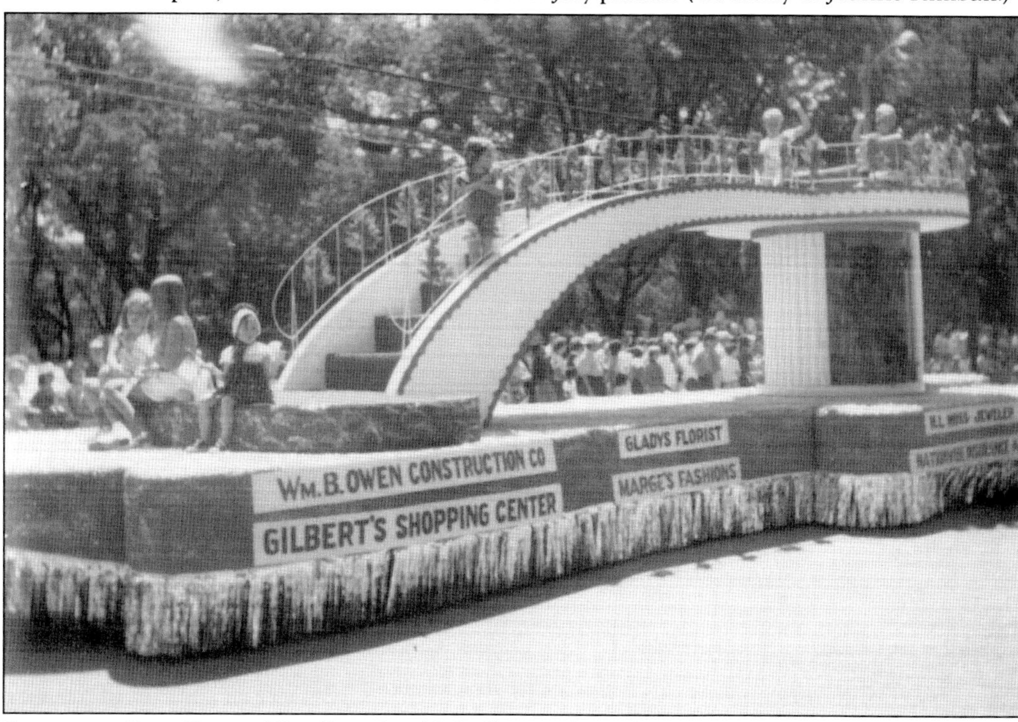


**FOURTH OF JULY FLOAT.** This Fourth of July float is from the early 1970s. (Courtesy of Andrea P. Clemmons.)

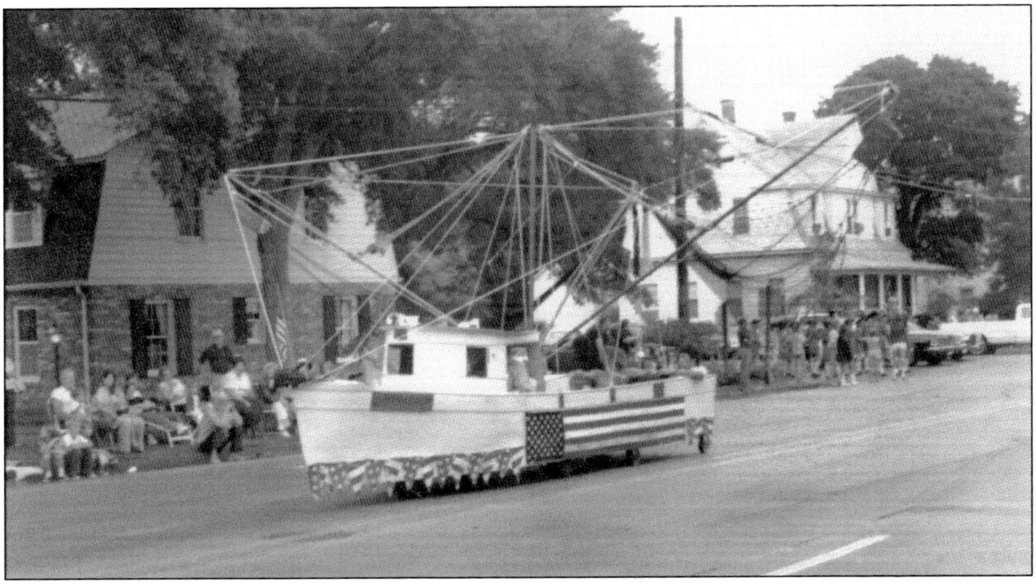

**Golf Cart Boat Float.** This float in the shape of a boat was built by Jimmy Moore for the Shrimp Boat Race in 1976. He creatively used a golf cart and built the big boat around it. (Courtesy of Jimmy Moore.)

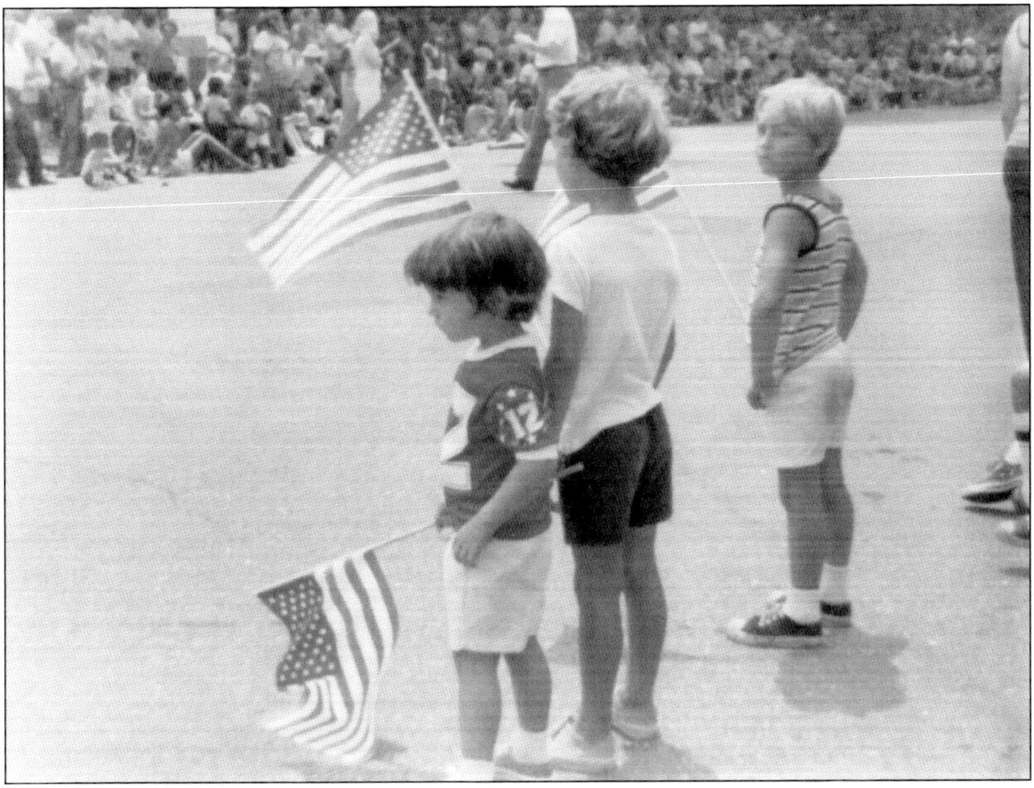

**Fourth of July Fun.** These little boys join the celebration at the Fourth of July Parade in 1975. From left to right they are John St. George, Ricky Johnstone, and Dickey Partello. (Courtesy of Andrea P. Clemmons.)

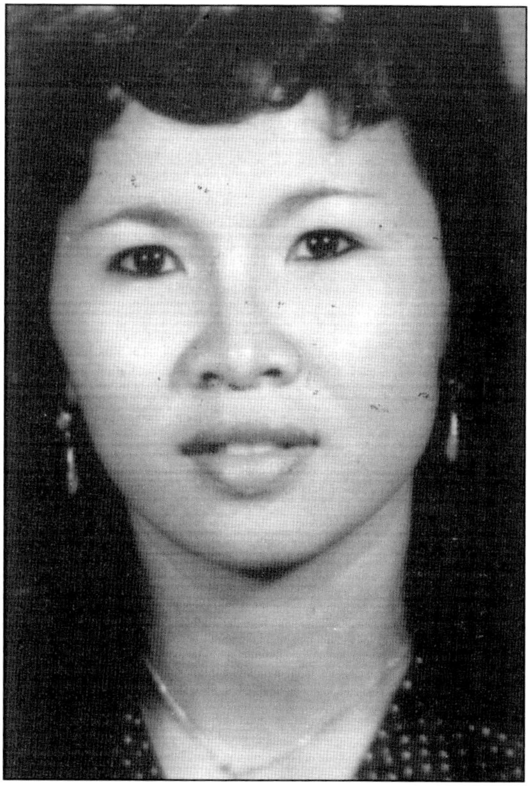

**Hoa "Y" Brown.** Brown opened Y's Restaurant in the 1980s. She had a reputation for hard work and was quite well known for her Vietnamese cuisine, especially her ribs. She passed that legacy on to her daughter Joann Kimball, who still serves those famous ribs at her restaurant, Loco Jo's, for Wednesday lunch. (Courtesy of Joann L. Kimball.)

**Merry Christmas.** "Y" takes time from her busy schedule to share a moment with her daughter Joann at Christmas time in the 1970s. (Courtesy of Joann Kimball.)

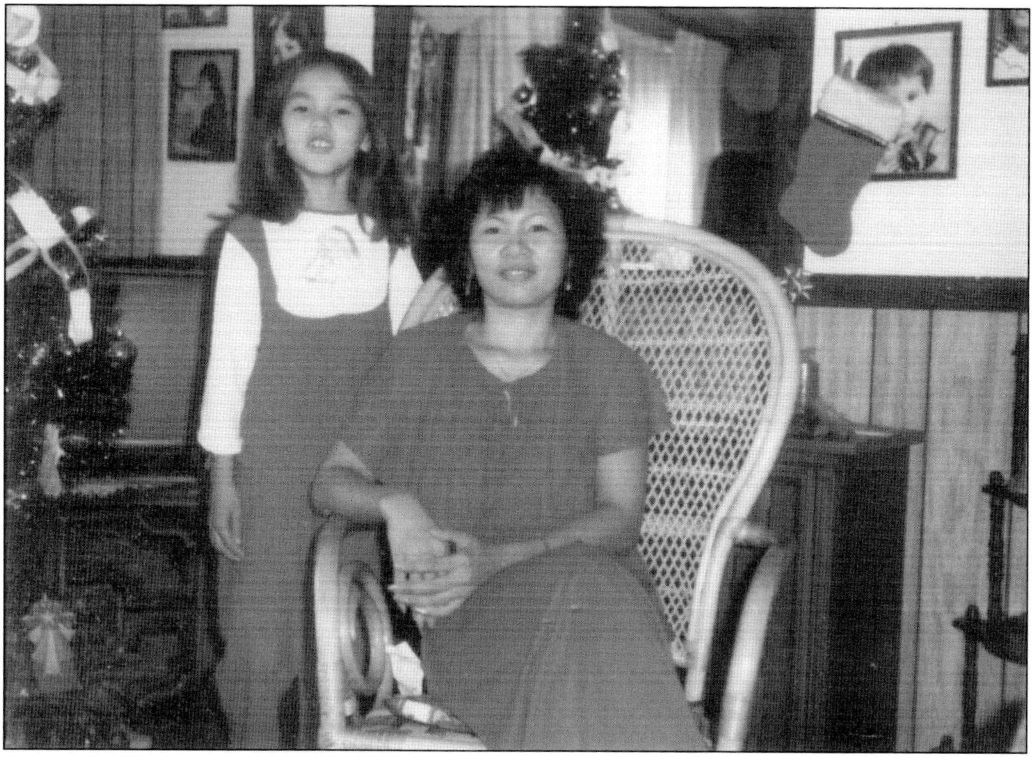

**"Y" in Hair Rollers.** "Y" was often seen around town with rollers in her hair. Her daughter Joann remembers getting picked up after school by her mother with that look and being embarrassed but recalls her mother giving a kiss and not caring what her daughter thought. (Courtesy of Joann L. Kimball.)

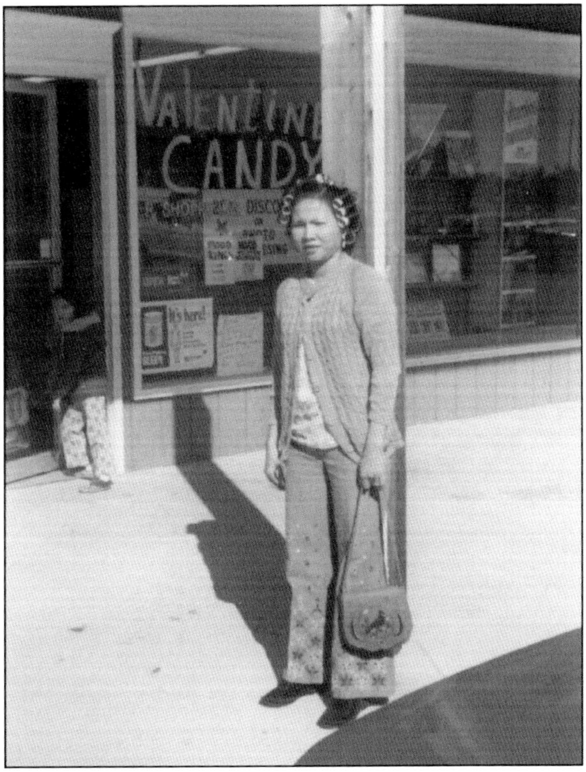


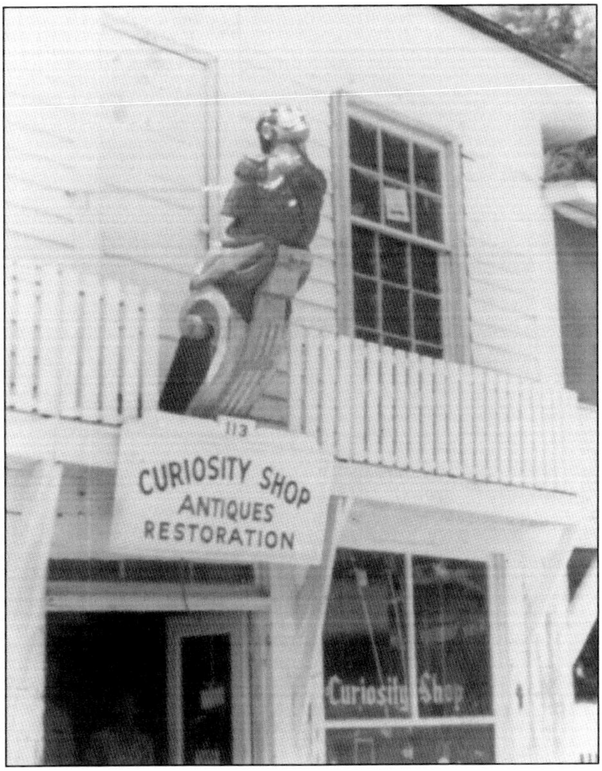


**The Curiosity Shop.** "Y" worked for Mr. Pancoast at the Curiosity Shop on North Howe Street in the early 1970s before opening her restaurant. (Courtesy of Joann L. Kimball.)

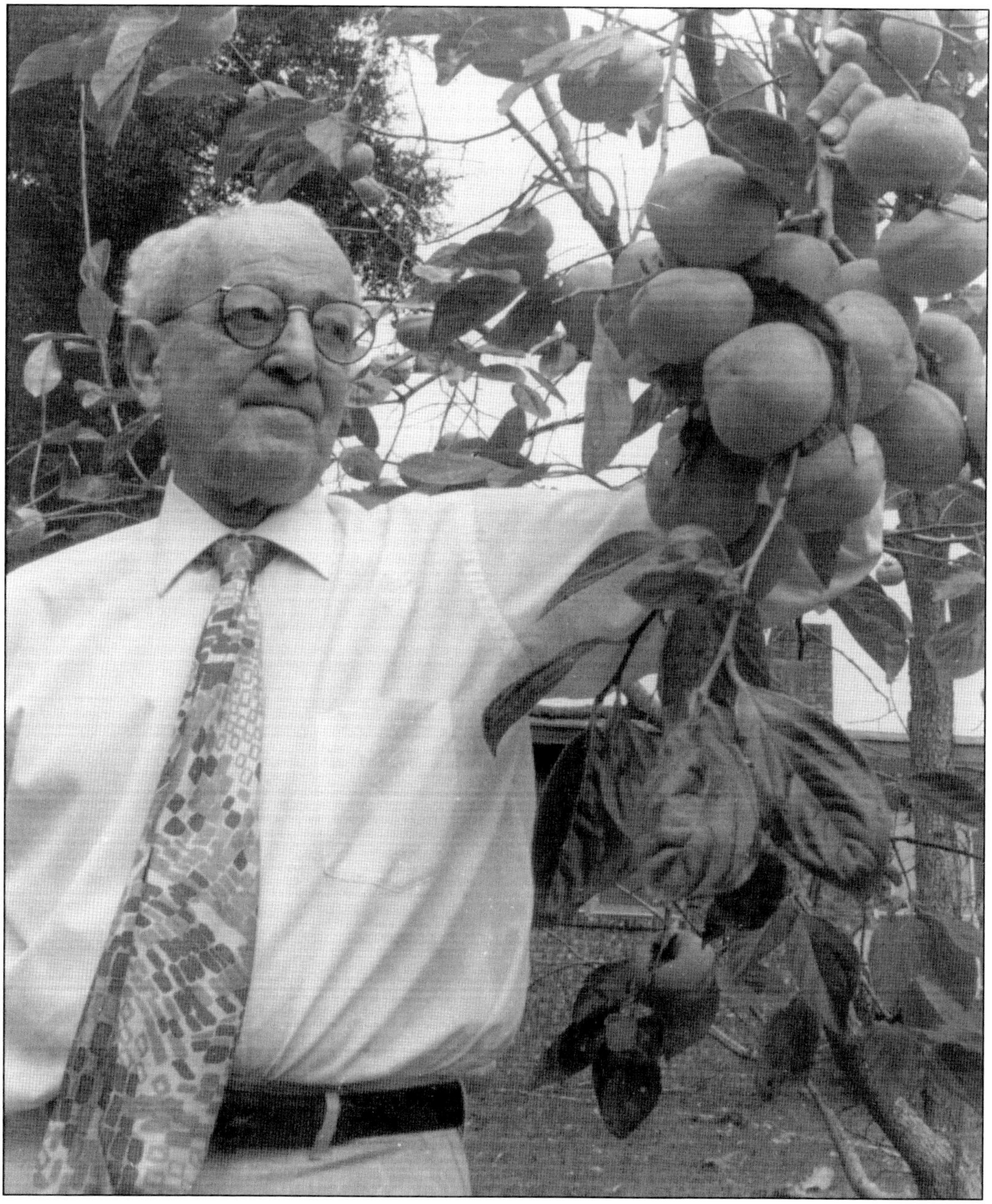

**Japanese Persimmon Trees.** Dr. Norman Hornstein moved to Southport and opened his medical practice in 1952. He was a native of New York and had worked as a surgeon in London hospitals during "The Blitz." In addition to his medical skills, he had a passion for gardening, fishing, and chess. Here he attends to his Japanese persimmon tree, a native Asian plant that requires a great deal of attention in order to produce fruit. (Courtesy of Leda Hornstein Sloat.)

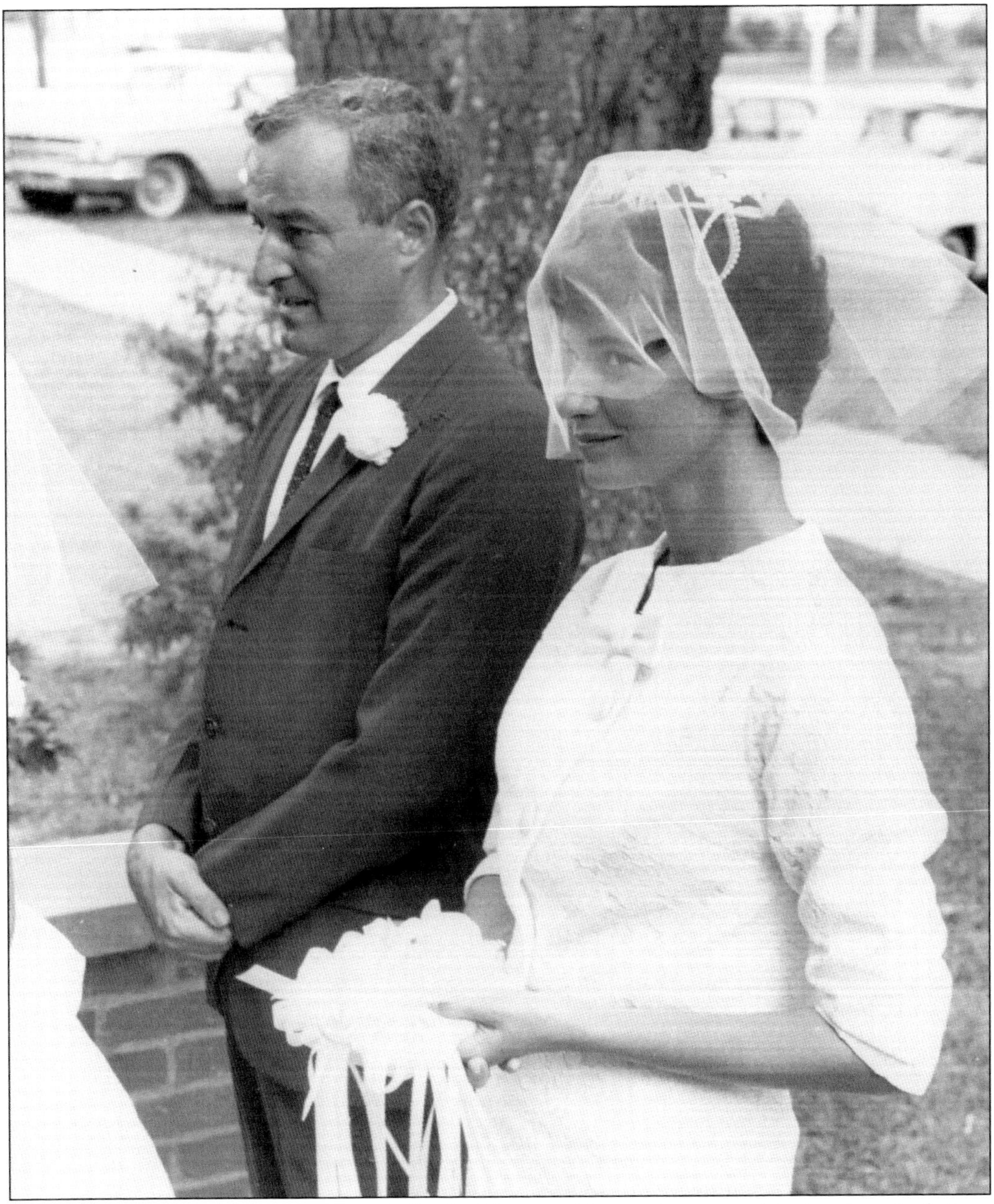

**LEDA HORNSTEIN'S WEDDING DAY, 1962.** Dr. Norman Hornstein escorts his daughter Leda into the Trinity Methodist Church on her wedding day. (Courtesy of Leda Hornstein Sloat.)

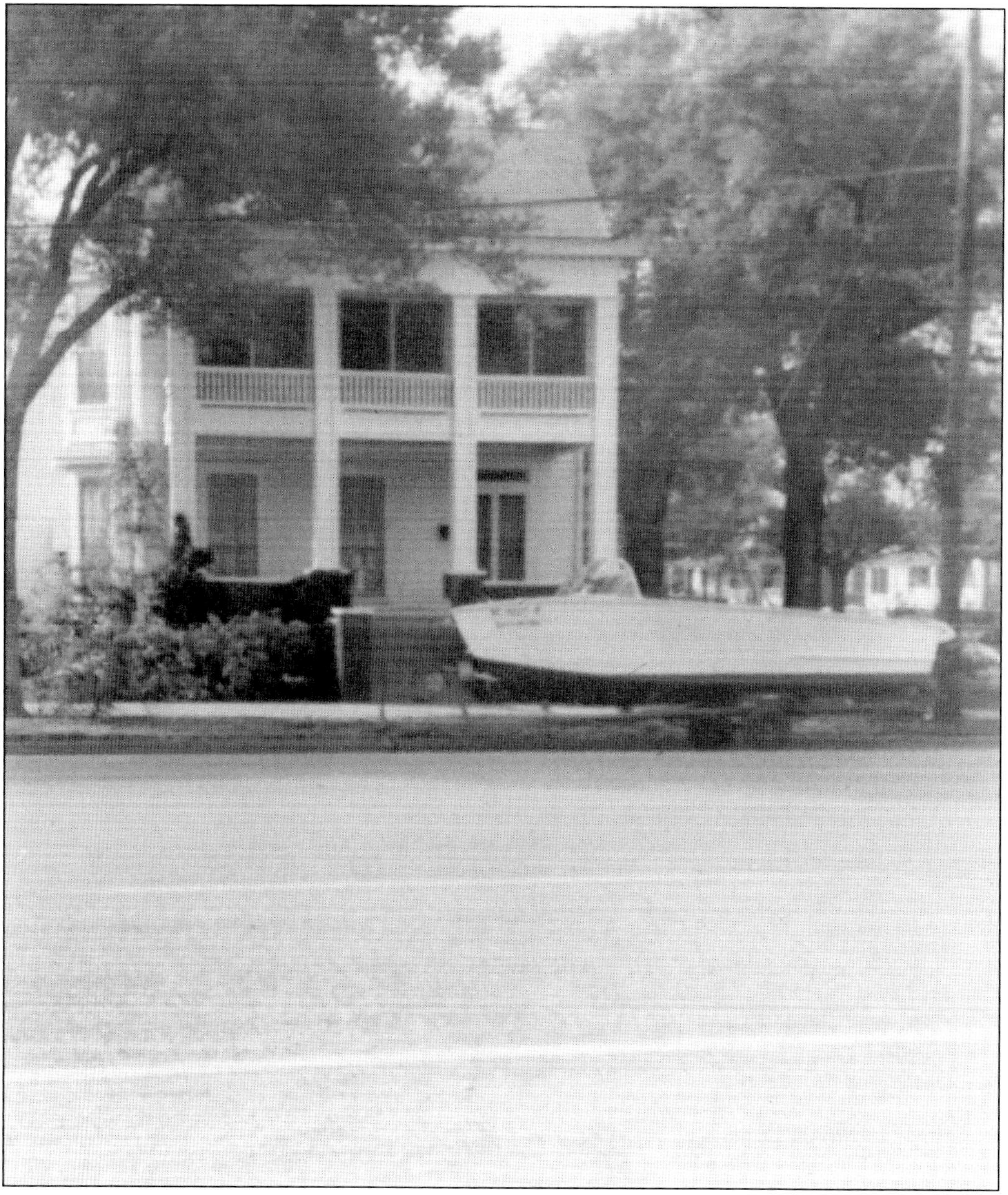

**HORNSTEIN HOME.** Dr. Norman Hornstein and his family lived in this house on Atlantic and Moore Streets until it was destroyed by fired in October 1967. An estimated $70,000 worth of art treasures was destroyed in the blaze. The art pieces consisted of 20 watercolors and drawings by the famous artist and sculptor Sir Jacob Epstein and an entire collection of paintings by his wife, Gilliam Hornstein. Dr. Hornstein was admitted to the hospital with burns and other injuries, but the rest of the family escaped unharmed. (Courtesy of Churchill Hornstein.)

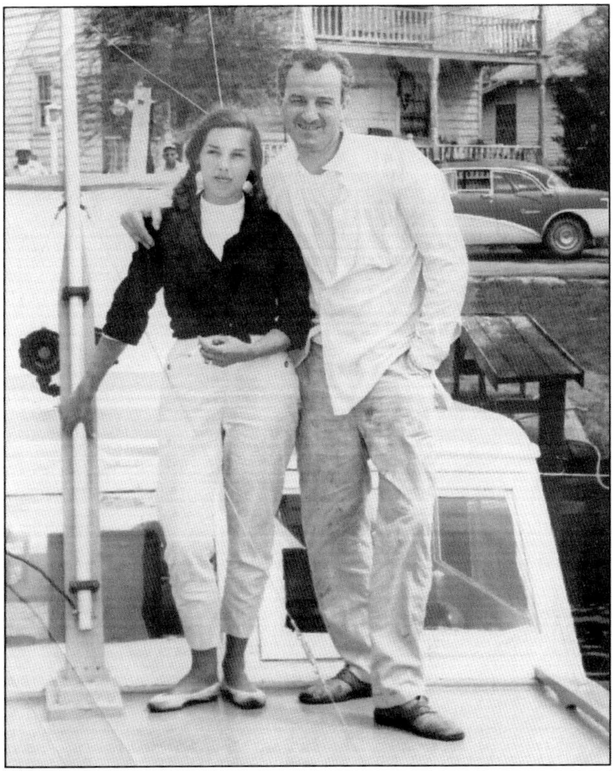

**ABOARD *ECHO*.** Dr. Hornstein and his wife, Gilliam, pose aboard *Echo* at the Southport Yacht Basin on the waterfront on April 12, 1959. (Courtesy of Churchill Hornstein.)

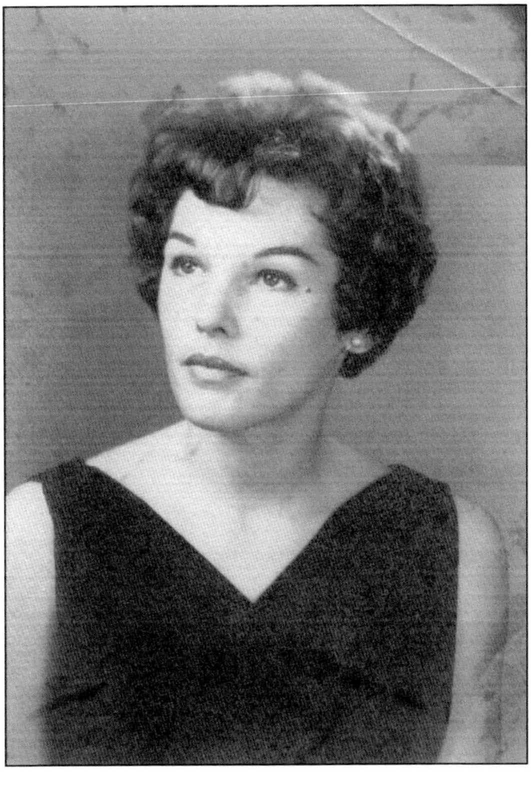

**GILLIAM HORNSTEIN.** Gilliam was actively involved in the arts and was a gifted artist herself. In the 1950s, she was one of the founders of the Southport Arts Festival. Her artwork was chosen for a traveling show in the North Carolina Artists Exhibition, as well as many other exhibitions. In August 1958, she was the chess champion in the women's division for North and South Carolina. (Courtesy of Churchill Hornstein.)

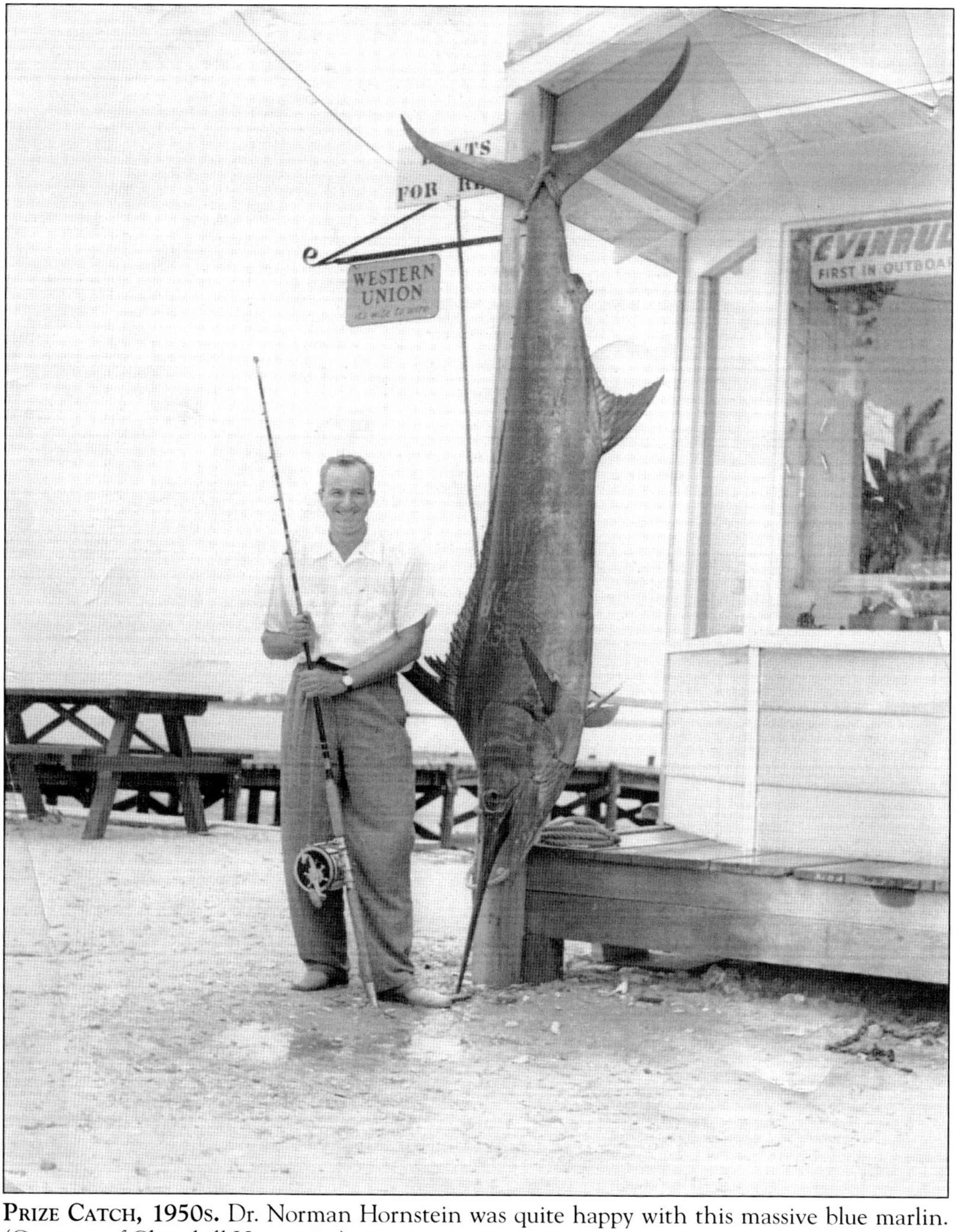


**Prize Catch, 1950s.** Dr. Norman Hornstein was quite happy with this massive blue marlin. (Courtesy of Churchill Hornstein.)

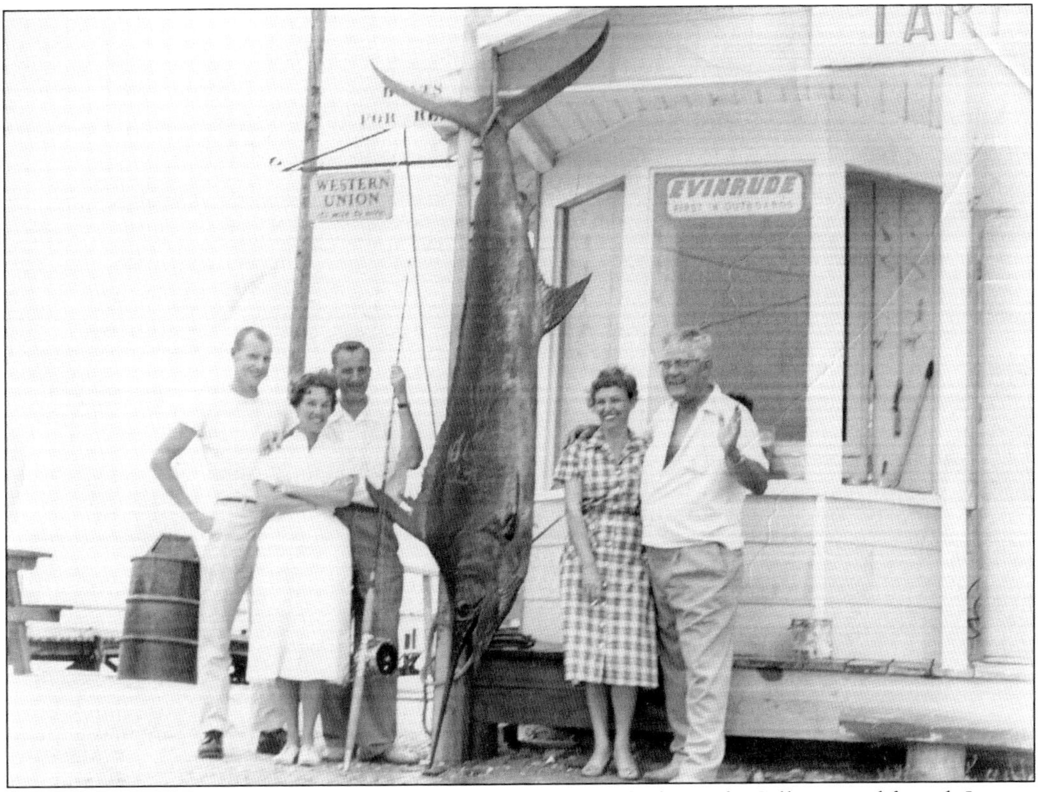


**Big Blue Marlin.** Dr. Hornstein shows off his prize catch for his wife, Gilliam, and friends Louise Bragaw Mallison Lewis and Walter Lewis. (Courtesy of Churchill Hornstein.)

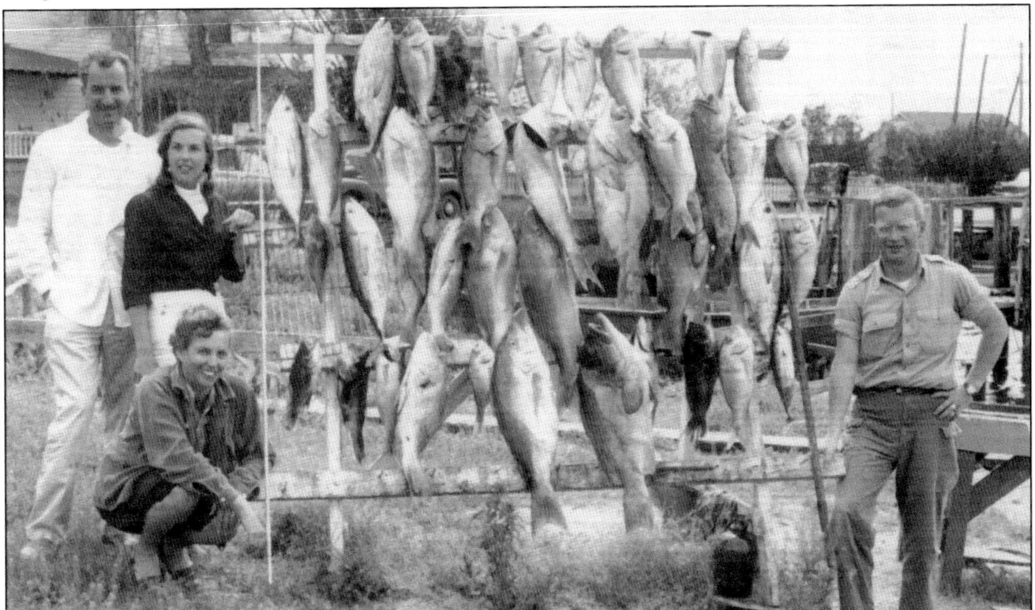

**Plenty of Fish.** In the 1950s, before overfishing became a problem, it was not uncommon to catch this many fish in the Atlantic. (Courtesy of Churchill Hornstein.)

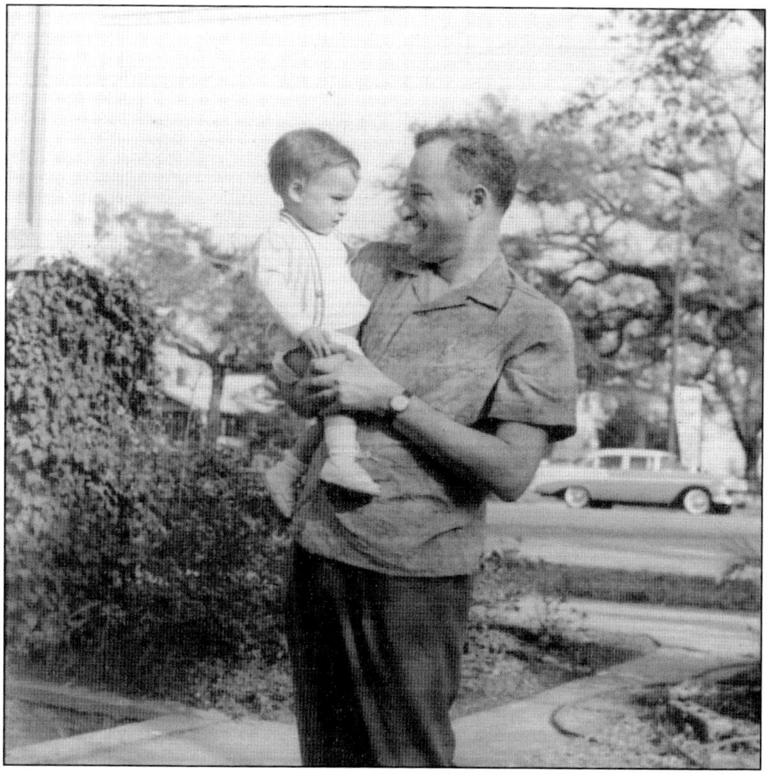

**Dr. Hornstein and Son.** Dr. Hornstein beams at his newborn son Churchill on the front walk in March 1961. (Courtesy of Churchill Hornstein.)

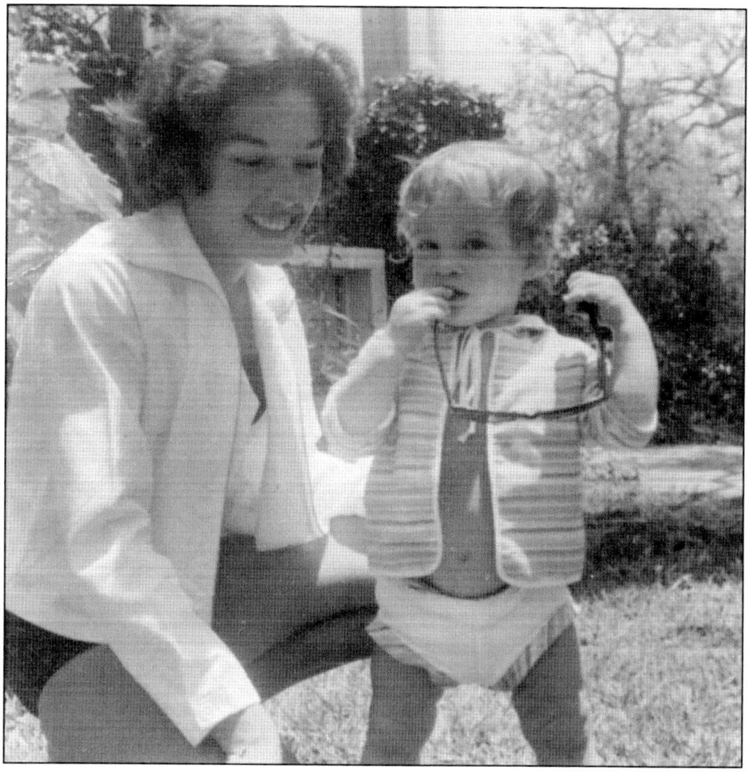

**Mother and Son.** Baby Churchill plays with his mother's sunglasses in front of their home on Atlantic and Moore Streets in October 1961. (Courtesy of Churchill Hornstein.)

**Baby Churchill.** Churchill Hornstein, born in Southport in 1960, is now the CEO of Urban e-Recyclers and is married to Sally Elizabeth Varner. They have three children and two grandchildren. (Courtesy of Churchill Hornstein.)

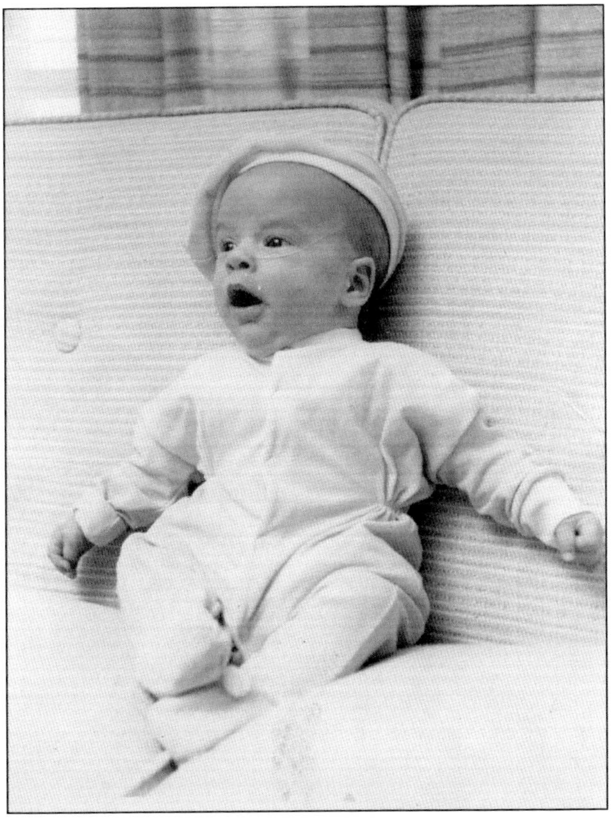

**Dr. Hornstein, 1980s.** Dr. Hornstein was a brilliant physician known for the kindness he showed to the thousands of patients he saw in Southport and other parts of North and South Carolina. He never turned anyone away who could not afford to pay, and occasionally he would receive items in exchange for his services—he once received a skunk. At age 70, he was made a fellow of the American Academy of Family Physicians. He also had a passion for chess and was a top player. (Courtesy of Churchill Hornstein.)

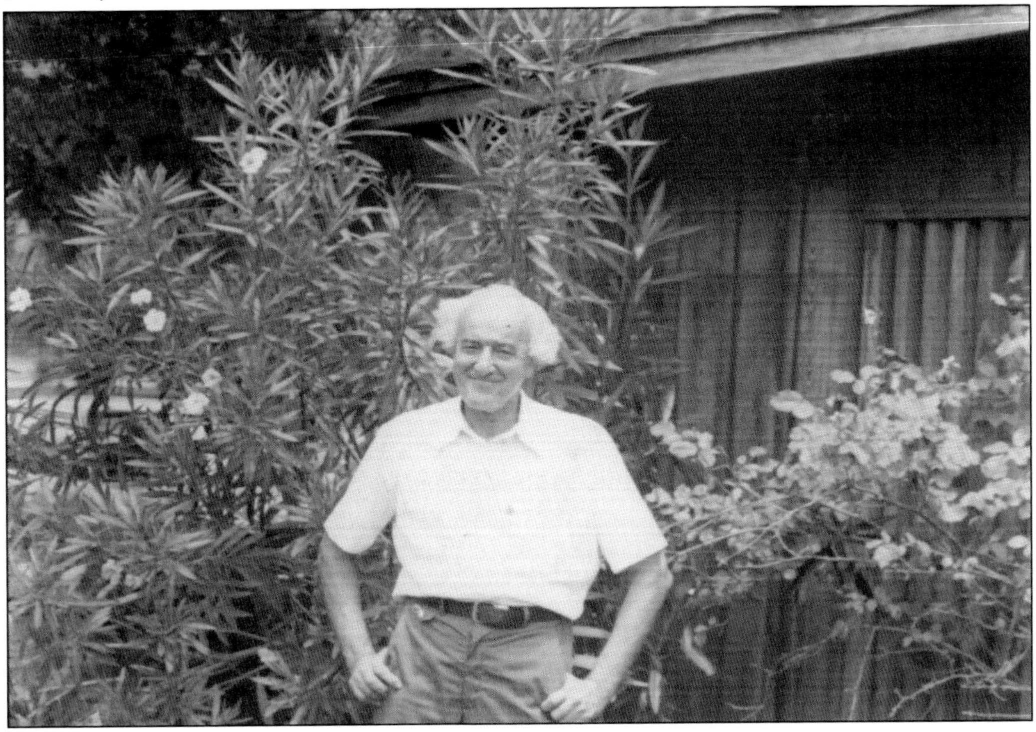

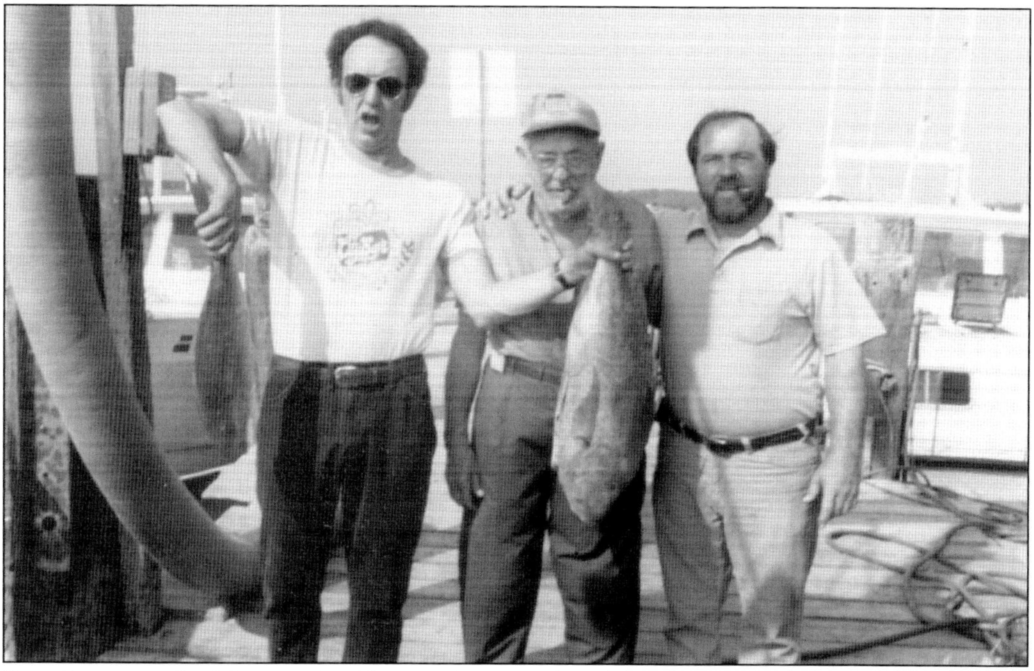

**Red Snappers.** Dr. Hornstein's older son Ian introduced Southport residents to red snapper in the 1970s. The locals had never heard of them, but once they got a taste, they could not get enough. Here, Ian (left) poses with Pappy Stubbs (center) and Charlie Perry. (Courtesy of Leda Hornstein Sloat.)

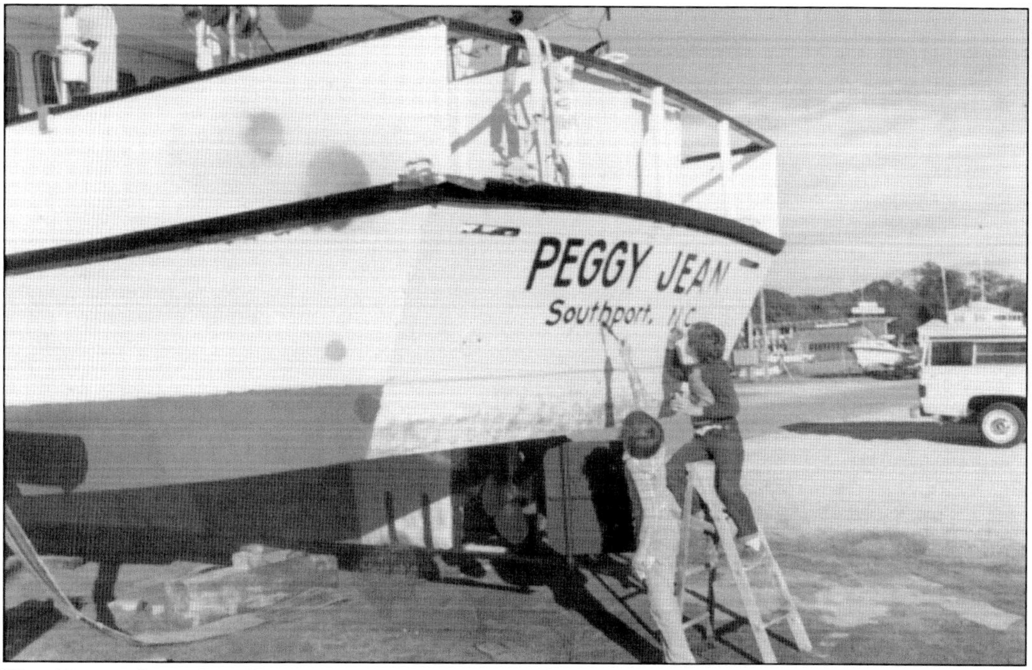


**The *Peggy Jean*.** Ian Hornstein's sons Lucian and Norman touch up the letters on the *Peggy Jean*, which Hornstein named after his mother, Peggy Jean Epstein Hornstein-Lewis. (Courtesy of Leda Hornstein Sloat.)

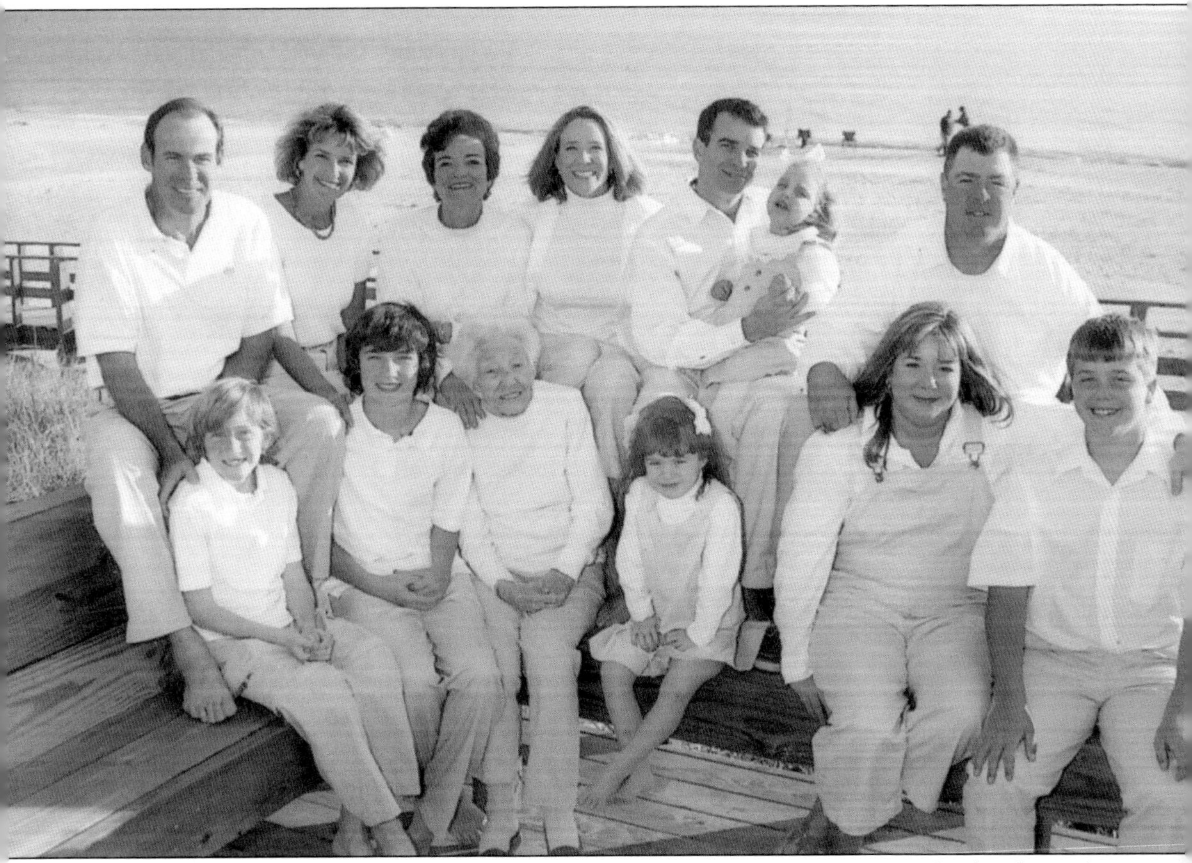

**Four Generations of Epsteins.** Family matriarch Peggy Jean Epstein Lewis is the daughter of famous sculptor Sir Jacob Epstein. This four-generation photograph includes, from left to right, (first row) Logan Wain, Justin Wain, Peggy Jean Epstein Lewis, Amelia Sloat, Devon Moore, and Carleton Holden; (second row) David Wain, Amy Wain, Leda Hornstein Sloat, Pam Sloat, Mark Sloat, Pattison "PJ" Sloat, and Mark Moore. (Courtesy of Leda Hornstein Sloat.)

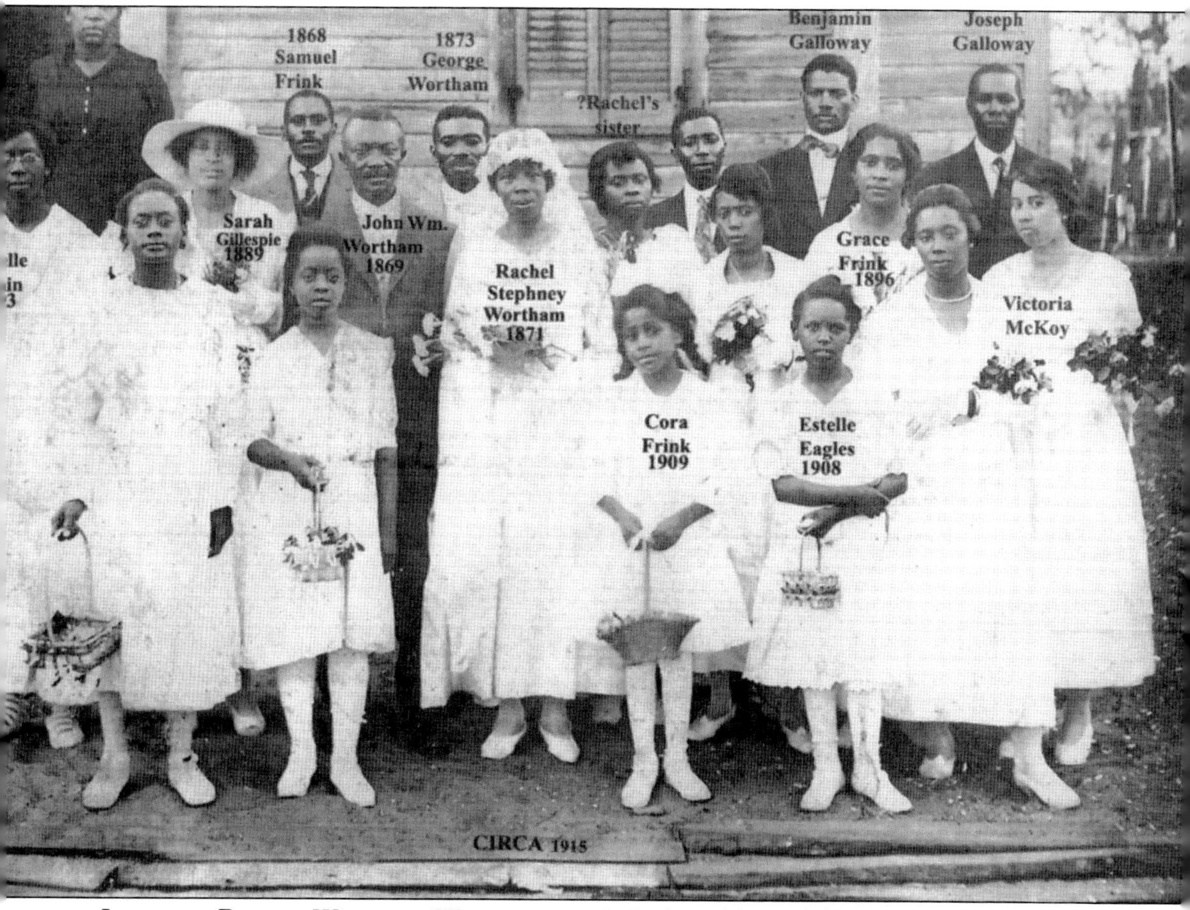


**John and Rachel Wortham Wedding, c. 1915.** A wedding of this size was very unusual in the early 1900s in the black community. John Wortham, the groom, was the brother of George Wortham, the "river legend." (Courtesy of Ennis Tobler.)

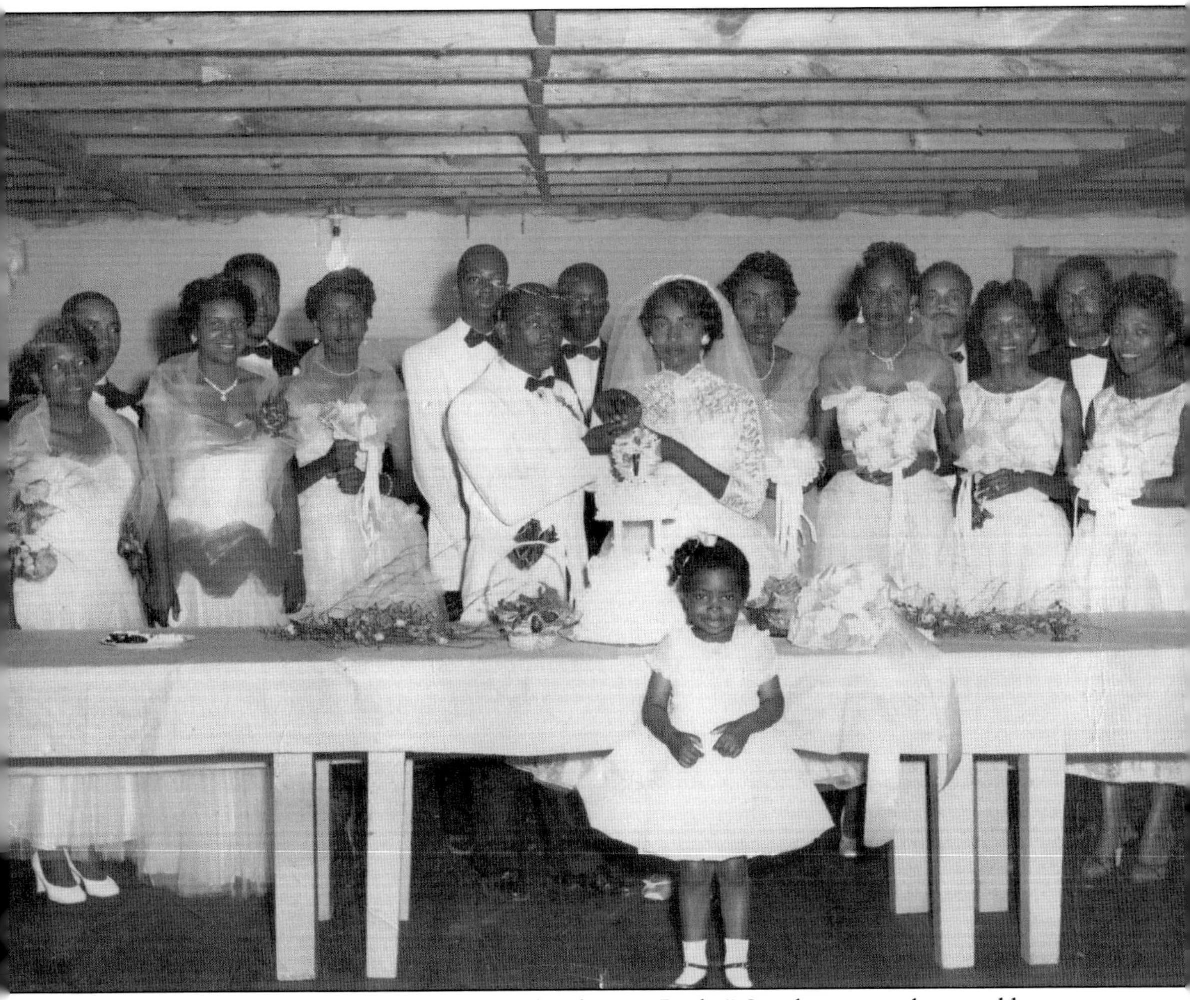

**SMITH WEDDING PARTY.** James "Bubba" and Rebecca "Becky" Smith pose at their wedding on May 5, 1956. The wedding party included flower girl Angela Gore; bridesmaids (from left to right) Orabelle Clemmons, unidentified, Anna Clemmons, Elizabeth Riggs, Elizabeth Young, Willa Mae Lawings, and Mary S. Gore; and groomsmen James Frink, Jones Bryant, Curtis Lewis, Howard Davis, Lorenzo Clemmons, and Harvey Clemmons. (Courtesy of Rebecca B. Smith.)

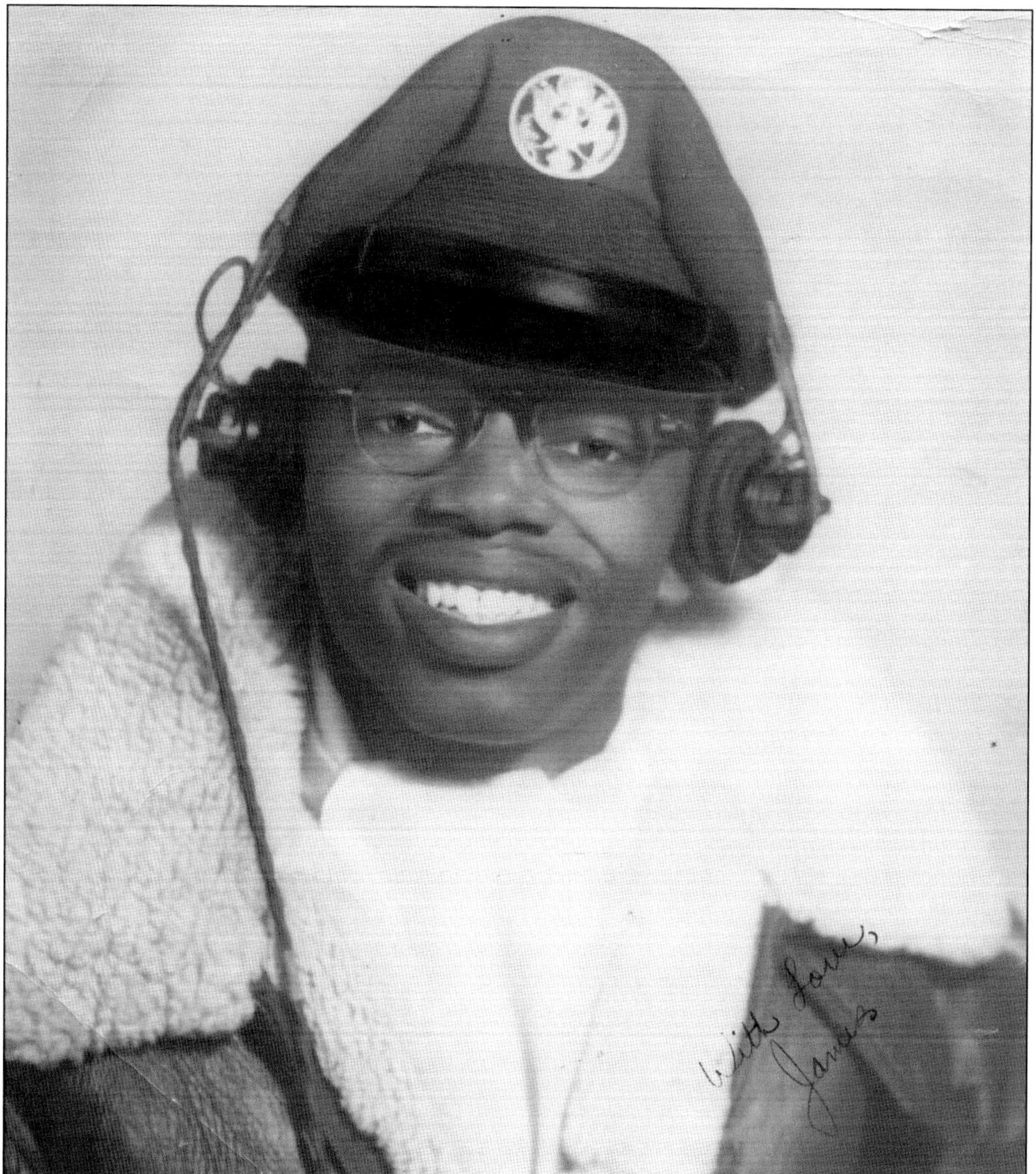


**US Air Force, 1954.** James "Bubba" Smith was born in Southport on June 4, 1932, to Romia and Mattie Smith. He married Rebecca Brown, and they had four children. He served in the Air Force from 1952 to 1956. He also excelled in various occupations, including dispatcher for the International Longshoremen's Association, real estate broker, farmer, deacon, Sunday school teacher, county commissioner, commissioner for the Employment Security Commission of North Carolina, and chairman of the Southeast Brunswick Sanitary District. He was also an authoritative scholar on the history and culture of Brunswick County and North Carolina. He showed a particular interest in Civil War artifacts, Colonial living, and the American Revolution, and was a lifetime member of the Historical Society. (Courtesy of Rebecca B. Smith.)

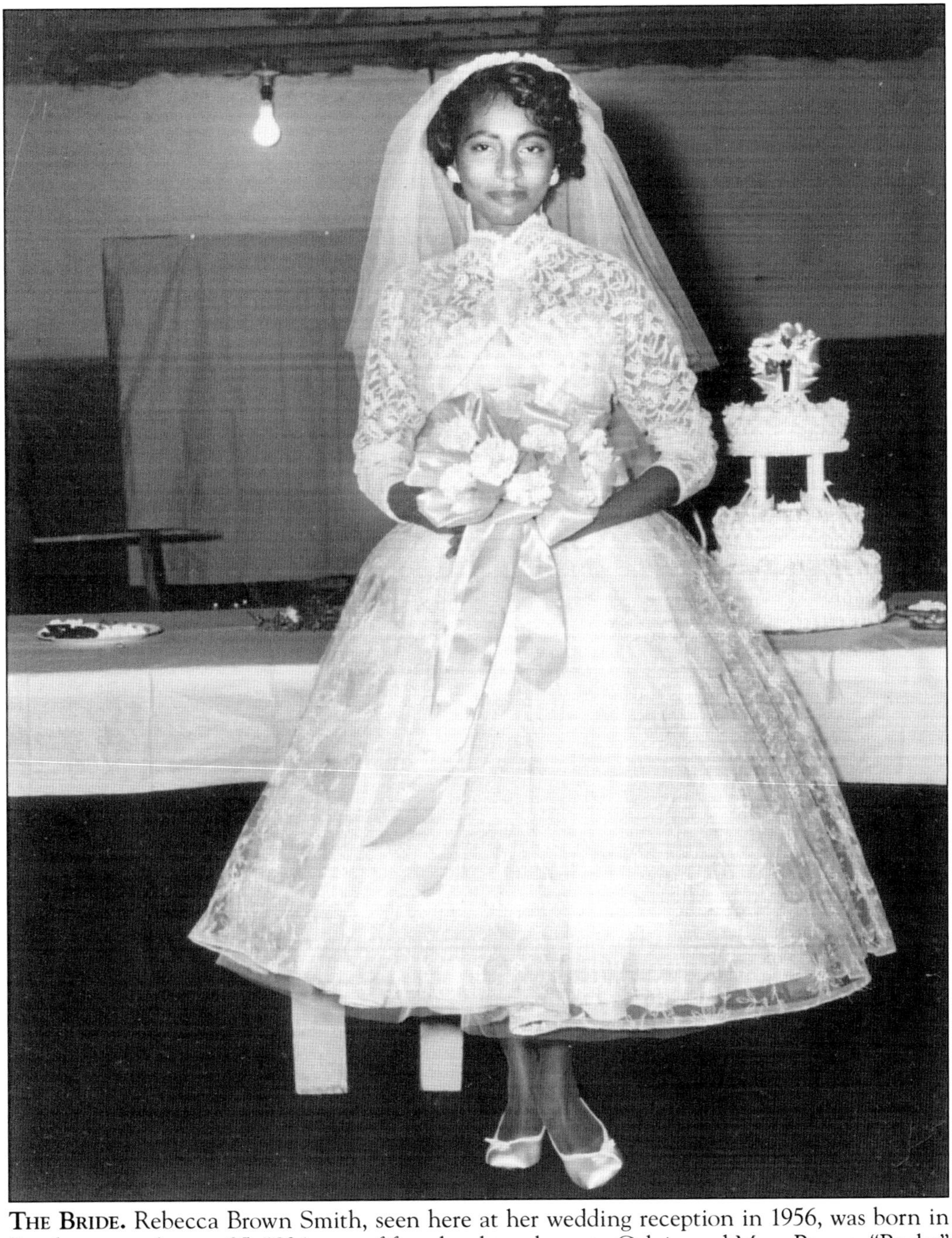

**The Bride.** Rebecca Brown Smith, seen here at her wedding reception in 1956, was born in Southport on August 25, 1934, one of five daughters born to Calvin and Mary Brown. "Becky" and "Bubba" had four children. Rebecca was the first black person hired to list taxes for Brunswick County in the late 1960s. (Courtesy of Rebecca B. Smith.)

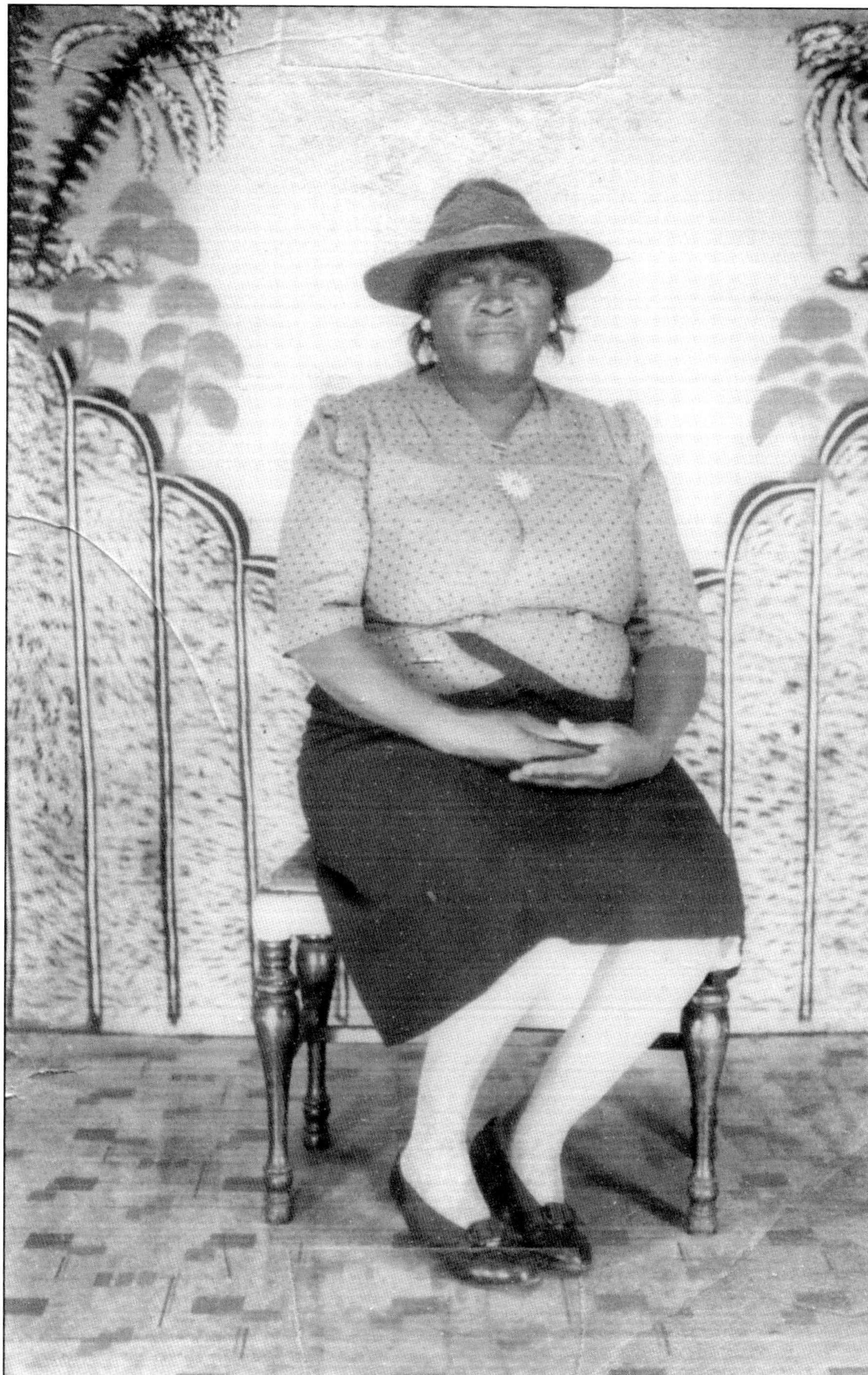

**The Midwife.** Mary Eliza Wortham was born in Smithville on May 19, 1885. She married the "river legend," George Wortham, and they had three children: Sylvester, Marie, and Mattie. Mary Eliza was a midwife and delivered many babies in Southport, working with Dr. J. Arthur Dosher. She is the great-grandmother of author Sharon Claudette Smith. (Courtesy of Rebecca B. Smith.)

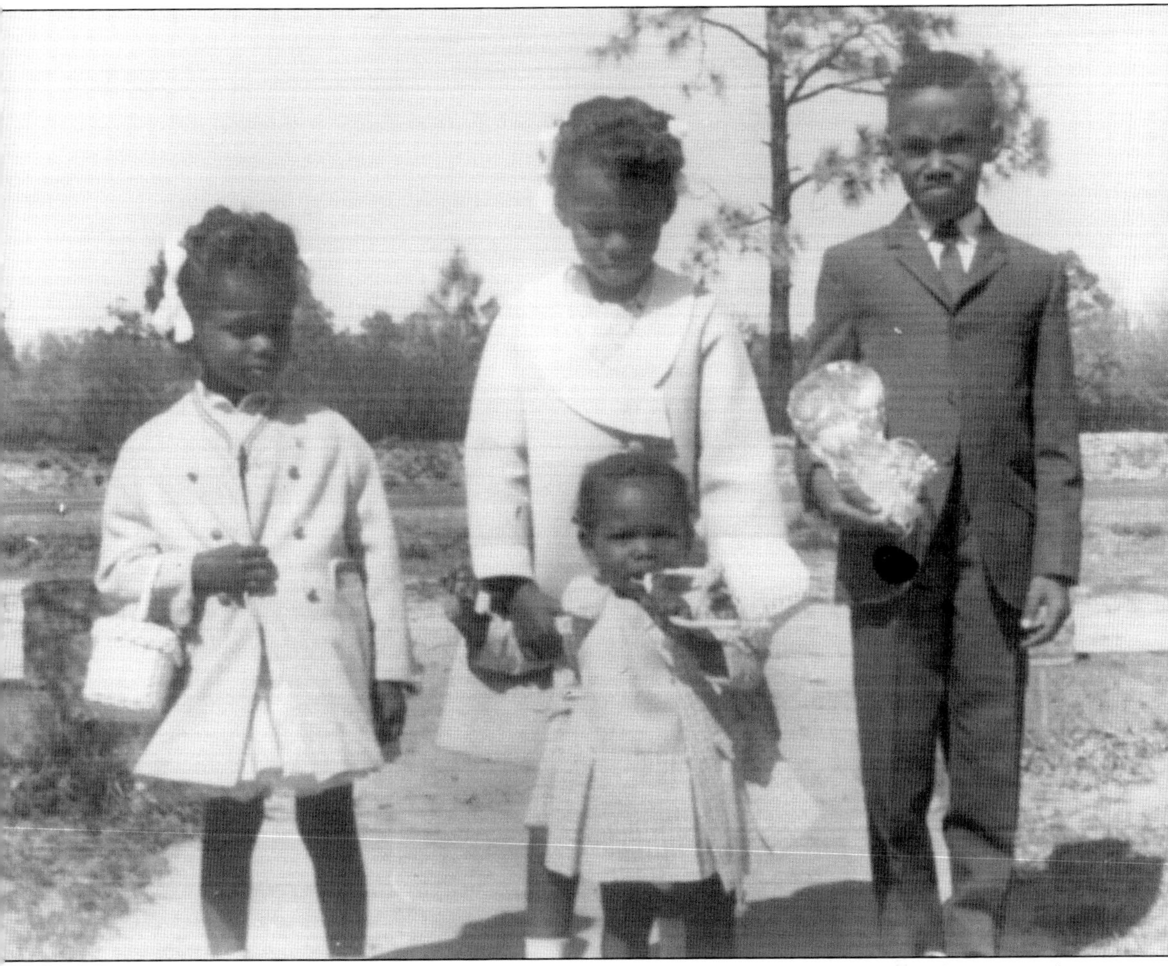

**The Smith Children, 1966.** The Smith kids are all dressed up in their Easter finery on the Smith farm. They are, from left to right, Julie, Sharon, Gina, and Maurice. The Security Savings Bank stands on this property today. (Courtesy of Rebecca B. Smith.)

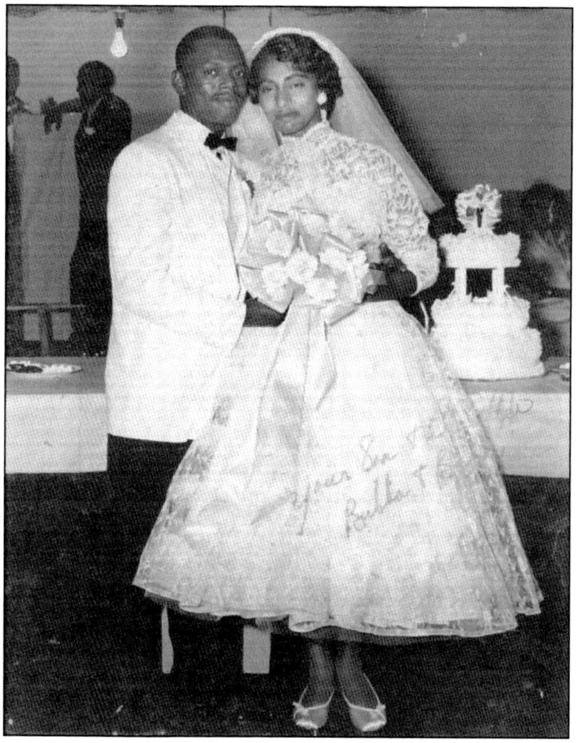

**Bride and Groom.** James "Bubba" and Rebecca "Becky" Smith pose for a portrait at their wedding, on May 5, 1956. They bought the Johnson farm in 1966 and operated Dutchman Creek Acres Vegetable Market until 1974. (Courtesy of Rebecca B. Smith.)

**Brothers-in-Law.** These men married the five daughters of Calvin and Mary Brown. From left to right, they are Raymond Gill, husband of Violet Brown; George Riggs, husband of Elizabeth Brown, Kenneth "Bubba" Bellamy, husband of Malissa Jane Brown; James "Bubba" Smith, husband of Rebecca Brown; Harvey "Bubba" Clemmons, husband of Anna Brown. Kenneth Bellamy served in the Korean War and was awarded a Purple Heart with a cluster because he was wounded twice by enemy fire. (Courtesy of Rebecca B. Smith.)

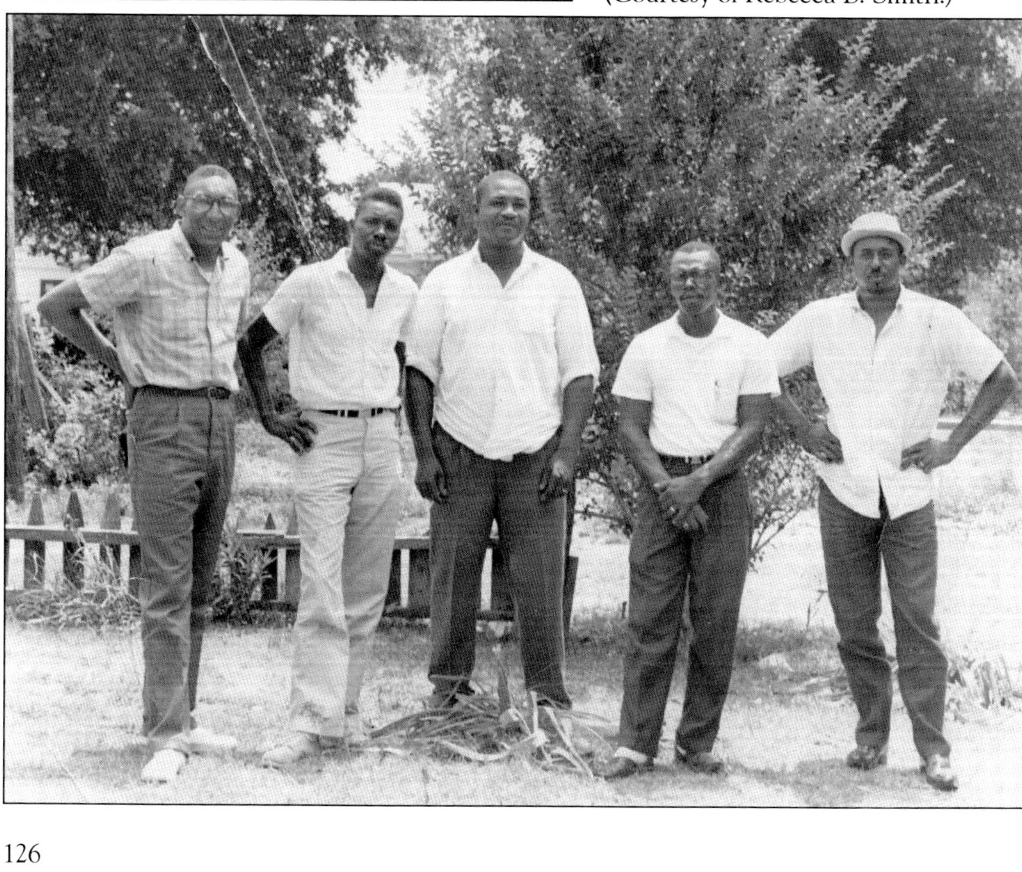

# Bibliography

Carson, Susan S. *Joshua's Dream*. Southport, NC: Carolina Power & Light Company, 1992.

——— and Lewis Carson. *Jon C. Joshua's Legacy*. Southport, NC: Southport Historical Society Inc., 2003.

Hardee, Lewis Jr. *Classic Southport Cooking*. Southport, NC: Southport Historical Society Inc., 2008.

Hardee, Lewis Jr. *Of Home and the River*. Southport, NC: Southport Historical Society Inc., 2008.

Maisel, Larry. *Before We Were Quaint*. Southport, NC: Southport Historical Society Inc., 2009.

Reaves, Bill. *Southport (Smithville): A Chronology, Volume I (1520–1887)*. Southport, NC: Southport Historical Society Inc., 1978.

———. *Southport (Smithville): A Chronology, Volume II (1887–1920)*. Southport, NC: Southport Historical Society Inc., 1990.

———. *Southport (Smithville): A Chronology, Volume III (1920–1940)*. Southport, NC: Southport Historical Society Inc., 1996.

———. *Southport (Smithville): A Chronology, Volume IV (1941–1970)*. Southport, NC: Southport Historical Society Inc., 1999.